Plumbing

Prerequisite Modules for NVQ Level 2

Robert Boyce

with Arnold Masterman

D1079525

Stanley Thornes (Publishers) Ltd

First published in 1994 by:
Stanley Thornes (Publishers) Ltd
Delta Place
27 Bath Road
CHELTENHAM
GL53 7TH
United Kingdom

  02 03 04 05 / 10 9 8 7 6 5

A catalogue record for this book is available from the British Library.

ISBN 0 7487 1816 8

Outline design by Wendi Watson
Page make-up by P&R Typesetters, Salisbury

Printed and bound in Great Britain by Athenæum Press

Contents

Acknowledgements

The author and publishers are grateful to the following for permission to reproduce textual material and illustrations:

British Plumbing Employers Council (BPEC) Ltd; City and Guilds of London Institute; Electrical Electronic Telecommunication and Plumbing Union; George Fisher Sales Ltd; Hillmoor Ltd; Institute of Pumbing; IMI Yorkshire Fittings Ltd; John Guest (J.G. Speedfit); Monument Tools Ltd; Rothenberger; The Council for Registered Gas Installers; The Worshipful Company of Plumbers; and the Telegraph Colour Library for the cover photograph.

Figures 3.10, 3.17, 3.19, 3.20, 3.21, 3.22, 4.12, 4.73, 4.74, 4.77 and 4.78(b) are reproduced from *Hot and Cold Water Supply* with the kind permission of BSI. Complete copies can be obtained by post from

BSI Sales,
Linford Wood,
Milton Keynes MK14 6LE.

Every effort has been made to reach copyright holders but the publishers would be grateful to hear from any source whose copyright they may have unwittingly infringed.

Introduction

The work of a skilled person in the plumbing and mechanical services industry can be divided into various tasks, e.g. fixing a radiator, weathering a chimney stack, installing a wash basin, servicing a boiler, etc. These tasks, along with many others, are called **units of competence**.

This book has been written with three main aims in mind:

- to provide you with information relating to plumbing and mechanical engineering services qualifications
- to provide you with support materials for gathering evidence of your knowledge and competence
- to provide you with evidence of competence that may be included in your assessment portfolio and used to provide evidence of the underpinning knowledge specified in the various units.

The learning package that you are about to start is made up of modules, and forms a foundation of common information that is essential knowledge and must be completed before progression to the 'system' modules. The modules group together to form units of competence and once successfully completed will form part of an NVQ qualification.

Figure 0.1 shows an outline of the **training scheme** for plumbing NVQ Level 2, and Table 0 provides a list of the units of competence at this level. The training scheme is divided into 'systems' or groupings of technology, e.g. cold water, hot water, heating, above ground drainage, etc., which is the way these topics are usually taught and learnt, whereas the units of competence are put together as 'functions', which a skilled person would have to complete as a plumber working in the mechanical services industry.

This book deals with the content of the four prerequisite modules shown in Figure 0.1, i.e. Induction, Safety, Basic Principles including Electrical and Basic Processes.

Table 0

Level 2 units	Units of competence
P2/1	Install and test the components of the system
P2/2	Commission and decommission systems
P2/3	Maintain the effective operation of systems
P2/4	Maintain the safe working environment
P2/5	Maintain effective working relationships
P2/6	Contribute to quality development and improvement of products and services
P2/7	Fabricate, install and check sheet weathering system components
P2/8	Maintain sheet weathering systems

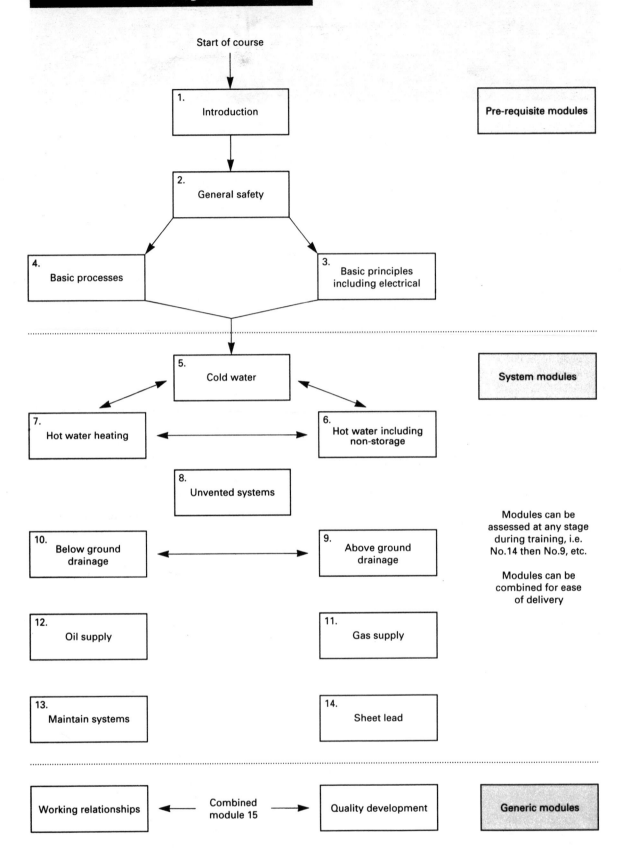

Figure 0.1 Outline of the MES Plumbing Training Scheme at Level 2

How to use this book

This book is a self-study package designed to be used by persons wishing to gain knowledge and competence in plumbing and mechanical services and should be supported by:

- tutor reinforcement and guidance
- group discussion
- additional reading
- slides, videos and films.

You should read and work your way through each section of a module, discuss its content with your tutor or study group and then attempt to answer the questions in that section.

This process is intended to support learning and to enable you to evaluate your understanding of the particular section and to monitor your progress through each module and the entire package. Where you find a question difficult or are unable to answer it, then further reading and discussion of the section is required.

The questions for you to answer in this book are either multiple choice answer questions, or short written or sketch answer questions. In certain cases it may be preferable for the question and answer to be dealt with verbally between you and your tutor.

Multiple choice questions consist of a question or statement followed by four possible answers. Only *one* answer is correct, the others are distracters. Your choice of answer should be recorded by drawing a line under the appropriate letter.

Example 1

1. Patent spring toggle bolts would be most suitable for securing pipe brackets to

   (a) wooden floors
   (b) hollow partition walls
   (c) solid walls
   (d) concrete.

Short-answer questions consist of a statement or question to which a short written answer is required. The length of the answer will vary depending on what is required by the question or statement. *List* or *Name* normally require only one or two words for each answer, whereas *Explain*, *Describe*, *State* or *Define* will require a short sentence.

Example 2

2. Name a metallic material used for weathering chimneys.

Answer: Lead.

Example 3

3. Explain why the cover fixed to a feed cistern of a gravity-fed open-vent hot water system is required to be close fitting but not air tight.

Answer: The natural (ambient) air pressure must be allowed to act on the free surface of the stored water and yet the cover must prevent contamination of the stored water by dust or debris.

Induction

In the pages that follow you will gain an understanding of:

- What are NVQs and SVQs?
- Quality assurance: roles and responsibilities
- Assessment
- Certificates in plumbing
- Assessment documentation
- Organizations within the plumbing industry

What are NVQs and SVQs?

National Vocational Qualifications (NVQs) and their equivalent Scottish Vocational Qualifications (SVQs) are a new system of qualifications that replace the traditional examinations and certificates that have in the past been used by industry to recognise the attainment of industry standards. The new NVQs and SVQs reflect standards agreed by the plumbing industry bodies.

The standards for the award of the plumbing mechanical engineering services NVQs have been developed by the British Plumbing Employers' Council (training). The qualification is awarded jointly by the City and Guilds of London Institute (CGLI), the Joint Industry Board for Plumbing Mechanical Engineering Services in England and Wales (JIB) and the National Association of Plumbing, Heating and Mechanical Services Contractors (NAPH & MSC).

How are NVQs applied to the plumbing industry?

For the plumbing industry, the standards within the new qualifications have been developed by the British Plumbing Employers Council (BPEC), which is called the Lead Body and has worked together with the employer and trade union organizations and the Joint Industry Boards. Figure 1.1 provides an overview of NVQ activities nationally.

What NVQs mean to the individual

Unlike traditional assessment and qualification systems (with their written and practical tests and examinations), the NVQ system permits candidates to offer a variety of evidence as proof of their competence (although formal assessment of practical activities and the underpinning knowledge necessary to prove competence may still take place). Under the NVQ provisions, candidates have a greater personal responsibility for organizing and submitting their portfolio (or collection) of evidence for consideration by approved assessors. The basic principle of the NVQ system is that any appropriate previous learning and/or experience can be offered as evidence counting towards a qualification. The system also permits a person to carry forward from one qualification any appropriate competence that has common applications to more than one occupation.

The structure of NVQs

The overall aim of NVQs is to prepare individuals more fully for the real needs of employment. Unlike traditional education and training, which often relies on knowledge-based testing, NVQs are awarded through a process of assessment in the workplace or in educational centres that have been approved as providing a realistic work environment (RWE). The whole system relies on assessors, who are also technically competent in the subject area, being available in the working environment and working with the effective quality control processes to ensure that the awards have national validity.

All NVQs have the same basic components: units of competence (which incorporate elements of competence), performance criteria, range statements and underpinning knowledge requirements. The performance criteria contain the standards to be assessed. Figure 1.2 illustrates the NVQ structure.

Units of competence

These represent free-standing, logical groupings of activities carried out in the workplace or RWE. A qualification is achieved by the accumulation of a specified cluster of units at a particular level. A unit is made up of one or more **elements**.

Elements

These describe actions, behaviour or outcomes

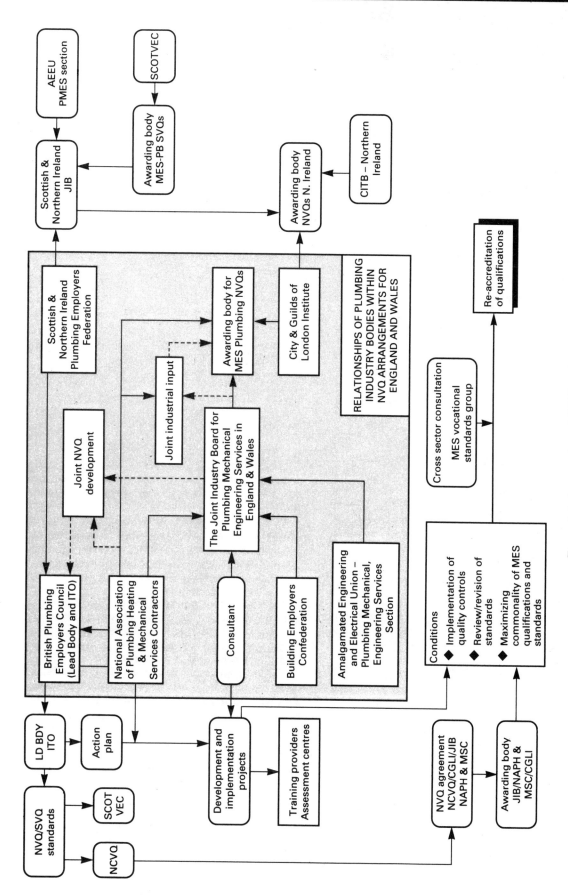

Figure 1.1 An overview of NVQ activities

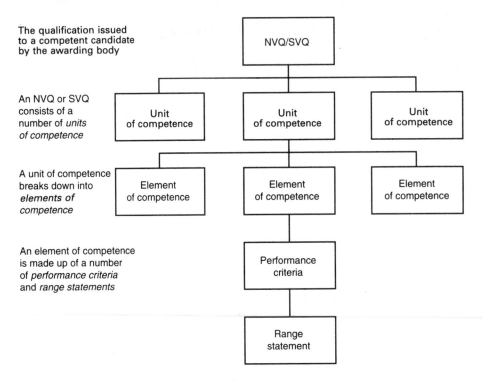

The qualification issued to a competent candidate by the awarding body

An NVQ or SVQ consists of a number of *units of competence*

A unit of competence breaks down into *elements of competence*

An element of competence is made up of a number of *performance criteria* and *range statements*

Figure 1.2   The NVQ/SVQ structure

that the candidate should be able to demonstrate to prove their competence. Each element is made up of a set of **performance criteria**, a number of **range statements** and the **underpinning knowledge** required.

Performance criteria

These specify the standard that a candidate must reach when carrying out an activity.

Range statements

These describe exactly the context in which a candidate needs to be assessed against the performance criteria and specify the breadth of competence required.

Underpinning knowledge

This specifies the areas of knowledge a candidate needs to have in order to be deemed competent in their work. Knowledge may be difficult to assess purely by observation of the candidate's performance and is usually assessed by verbal questioning or the use of multiple choice questions, or short written or sketch answer questions.

Levels of competence

The qualification structure is at present made up of *five* different levels of competence. Definitions of

these levels are as follows:

Level 1: competence in the performance of a range of varied work activities, most of which are routine and predictable.

Level 2: competence in a significant range of varied work activities, performed in a variety of contexts. Some of the activities are complex or non-routine, with some individual responsibility. Collaboration with others (perhaps a work group or team) may often be required.

Level 3: competence in a broad range of (mostly) complex and non-routine work activities, performed in a wide variety of contexts. There is considerable responsibility and autonomy, and control or guidance of others is often required.

Level 4: competence in a broad range of complex, technical or professional work activities, performed in a wide variety of contexts and with considerable personal responsibility and autonomy. Responsibility for the work of others and the allocation of resources is often a requirement.

Level 5: competence that involves the application of a significant range of fundamental principles and complex techniques across a wide and often unpredictable variety of contexts. Very substantial personal autonomy and often significant responsibility for the work of others and for the allocation of substantial resources feature strongly, as do personal accountabilities for analysis and diagnosis, design, planning, execution and evaluation.

Quality assurance: roles and responsibilities

The assessor

The assessor is most likely to be the candidate's immediate supervisor in the workplace or RWE. In some cases, however, he/she may be another appropriate person within the organization who has regular contact with the candidate. In the case of small businesses, the assessor may be a locally based individual appointed to cover organizations within the particular area.

It is the assessor's duty to judge the evidence presented by the candidate and to decide whether or not he/she has attained competence. Competence must always be measured against the performance criteria and underpinning knowledge statements specified in each element. No other benchmarks can be used.

The assessor will be required to be technically competent in the units being assessed and be able to carry out the assessment to the standards laid down by the Training and Development Lead Body (TDLB).

The internal verifier

The internal verifier provides the first check point for quality control of the assessment. It is the duty of the internal verifier to check that the assessor is judging the evidence gathered by the candidates against the performance criteria, range statements and underpinning knowledge statements in accordance with the guidelines laid down by City and Guilds.

The external verifier

This person is appointed by the awarding body and their job is to oversee the verification process within an approved assessment centre. He/she provides an important link between the assessment centre and the awarding bodies and will visit the centre according to the criteria laid down by City and Guilds.

Figure 1.3 illustrates the quality control system for NVQs.

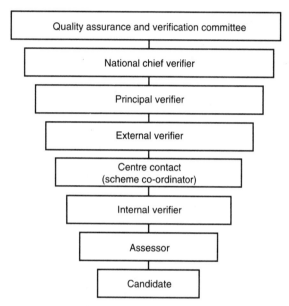

Figure 1.3   The quality control system for NVQs

Assessment

In NVQ terms, assessment is thought of as the gathering and judging of evidence of competent performance. The national standards provide a framework on which assessors can base their judgements of a candidate's performance.

The process of assessment involves

- the candidate, in producing evidence of their ability to perform the activities and achieve the outcomes described by the elements of competence, and
- the assessor, in judging whether or not the evidence meets the standards described, and therefore proves competence, and also deciding what additional evidence may be required to cover the range specified.

The assessment must also include observation of candidates, to take into account general perfor-

mance in everyday situations. This will demonstrate a candidate's depth of underpinning knowledge and understanding and therefore their ability to transfer performance over a range of situations.

For some basic levels of competence, little knowledge may be required. For most higher levels of competence however, the knowledge required to ensure transferability will be considerably greater.

By combining assessment of performance with assessment of knowledge (including the required underpinning knowledge), the assessor is in a good position to judge whether candidates can transfer their skills to any situations they may meet in the future.

Accurate assessment is essential to the success of the process. This allows for the effective use of the national standards established by the TDLB, and assists in the quality control surrounding the awarding of NVQs.

As the gathering of evidence takes place over a period of time, it may be necessary to use more than one assessment method to assess a candidate's competence. There are no graded assessments; the candidate is judged to be either competent or not yet competent. Candidates who are considered to be not yet competent will need to provide more evidence of their ability to perform to the specified standards.

The range statements within the units will give you an understanding of the variety of situations (the scope) in which you must demonstrate competence. In assessment terms, all of the performance criteria must be met in all of the areas in the specified range. The assessor is seeking confirmation that the candidate can perform to the required standards, repeatedly and under normal working conditions.

The assessor is also, by crediting their competence, inferring that the candidate is likely to be able to sustain that level of performance in the future, hence the need for evidence to be gathered over a period of time and in a range of situations.

Figure 1.4 illustrates the assessment pyramid.

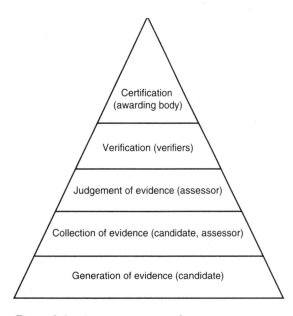

Figure 1.4   Assessment pyramid

Collection of evidence and assessment

There are several different sources of evidence that you can use to establish that you can perform the activities described in a unit. Each source has its strengths and weaknesses, which is why it may be necessary for you to collect evidence in a number of different ways.

Observation

Workplace assessment, i.e. observing the candidate carrying out their job, is the method of assessment recommended in the vast majority of the units and elements. This is the preferred way of collecting evidence about workplace performance and is often the most cost-effective and straightforward method of assessment.

Candidates usually prefer this method of assessment as they should feel relaxed and assured working in a familiar environment, completing a task or job that they have performed before.

Performance of specially set tasks

In certain instances, it may be necessary to assess how the candidate is most likely to behave in a real work situation by setting up a simulation. This method is for situations that occur infrequently and for those where it is not practical to assess by direct observation, such as putting out a fire.

Evidence from prior achievements

As well as making competence judgements about current performance, it may be possible to make decisions about your performance based on historical evidence. This might consist of documents, portfolios of work or testimonials collected by yourself and presented to the assessor in order to help them make an assessment decision.

Verbal questioning

This is one of the most appropriate ways of assessing evidence that you may have collected and is used to assess your understanding and level of underpinning knowledge. Candidates will generally be familiar with this question and answer technique and this will help develop a rapport with the assessor and provide an opportunity for you to demonstrate your knowledge. The questioning can be carried out whilst you are completing a particular task (but allowing you time to think and to make sure that you understand what you are doing) or immediately after you have finished the task. It may be possible, if you wish, to record the question session on tape, otherwise you are encouraged to keep records of the questions and answers in your evidence diary.

Pictorial questioning

This may be more appropriate for some units than others, e.g. to test whether you are aware of potential dangers when working on a scaffold or in a trench. You may be asked to identify hazards depicted on a drawing or photograph and to explain the dangers they represent. Pictorial questioning will always be supplemented by verbal questioning.

The use of verbal and pictorial questioning will be of great assistance to candidates with learning difficulties or special needs.

Short written answer questions

These will generally be used by an assessor to establish your level of understanding of the under-pinning knowledge necessary to prove competence. The questions used throughout this book are examples and are typical of the questions used.

Certificates in plumbing

The certificates in Mechanical Engineering Services – Plumbing are offered in collaboration with the British Plumbing Employers Council (BPEC). The certificates offered are

- the NVQ Certificate in Mechanical Engineering Services – Plumbing Level 2
- the NVQ Certificate in Mechanical Engineering Services – Plumbing Level 3.

The competence statements, associated performance criteria and range statements dictate what is to be assessed, and the assessment programme for each element of competence comprises

- practical observations (evidence required)
- verbal questions
- written questions.

The certificates provide formal recognition of success in units of competence, which are made up of a number of elements of competence. Each element can be separately assessed. To gain formal recognition of success in a unit of competence, the candidate must demonstrate the ability to meet *all* the criteria

for *every* element of competence in the unit as a consistent pattern of work, i.e. the candidate must

- successfully meet all the criteria for an element
- satisfy the knowledge requirements for the element during the course of assessment.

There is no requirement for one unit of competence to be completed before going on to a different unit. Candidates may, therefore, gain success in elements from a variety of units and so build partial success in a number of units, before completing any one of them.

To gain the NVQ certificate at each level, the candidate must succeed in *all* the units of competence at the level concerned.

Candidates wishing to join the scheme and gain certification must register at an approved centre. The scheme co-ordinator at the centre arranges for the payment of fees, registers the candidates for assessments and corresponds with the awarding body. The scheme co-ordinator also receives all certificates and correspondence on behalf of the centre's candidates.

Assessment documentation

Once a candidate has registered at an approved centre, they will receive the following documentation

- candidate portfolio
- candidate record of assessment
- candidate activity log book.

The portfolio

In the most general sense, a **portfolio** is a folder or file within which is kept all the evidence of assessments taken towards a qualification. *It is the candidate's responsibility to safeguard this document at all times and to complete and submit it as required.*

The portfolio will include a completed record of assessment containing an activity record, assessment record and the relevant supplementary evidence. It could also contain authenticated photographs, job cards, time sheets, appraisals from line managers, supervisors, forepersons, charge hands and customer's assessments – anything that can be considered as evidence to illustrate competence. Examples of forms of evidence include testimonials, audio and video tapes, and computer disks.

The portfolio should be viewed as a portable document that is both a statement of what has been achieved and a plan of personal progression. It should be organized and managed in such a way that it is readily accessible to the reader, e.g. divided into sections to reflect the units and elements of the qualification. The candidate will be expected to present evidence in a way that is clear and coherent and includes: a contents page, dates on all entries, titles and headings on all entries describing their purpose and content, and cross-references to related entries including the relevant units and elements of the standards.

Record of assessment

The **record of assessment** provides a way of recording achievements in specific tasks and the knowledge required to carry them out. It contains the performance criteria that need to be assessed and the evidence that must be provided to show how each performance criterion has been satisfied. Sources of evidence are included to help you complete the record. The sources of evidence listed are not exhaustive but are presented as a guide to what an assessor might expect to see in the portfolio of evidence that candidates are expected to complete.

As well as assessing performance, the assessor will also determine whether the candidate possesses the required knowledge that underpins competent performance. The record of assessment indicates the range and depth of knowledge to be assessed (i.e. the supplementary assessment). Where appropriate, the awarding body will supply the supplementary assessment material.

When the candidate has completed all the activities undertaken for assessment purposes and is confident that he/she has met the standards in each element, he/she should tick the appropriate boxes in the record of assessment. This 'self-assessment' should then be confirmed by the candidate's employer/employer representative (or other person, as approved by the awarding body) and presented to the centre assessor. When the assessor is satisfied that competent performance has been achieved and that the required knowledge has been demonstrated, both the assessor and candidate should sign the relevant sections which appear at the end of each element of the assessment record. An entry is only valid when it has been signed by the assessor.

The record of assessment provides part of the documentary evidence of achievement. The awarding body reserves the right to collect and examine this document at any stage before certification.

Activity log book

The **activity log book** provides a self-assessment record of practical installation activities and supporting knowledge in which you achieved competence or understanding through work with your employer, work provider or through training activities at a college or other centre.

The log book is divided into units and elements of competence, and each element is then sub-divided into two sections called:
- performance evidence – this relates to practical work activities, and
- supplementary knowledge evidence – this is the underpinning job knowledge specific to the work activities in each element.

Boxes are provided against performance and supplementary knowledge evidence and should be ticked only when you feel competent to carry out the activities listed and fully understand the requirements of the supplementary knowledge.

The log book should be completed neatly and accurately, and be countersigned by your employer, work provider or college trainer as appropriate. You will also be provided with **activity record sheets**, which you should complete to provide details of the entries in your log book.

When you have completed all the self-assessment entries for a particular element, you should show your log book and activity record sheets to your assessor, together with any other evidence of competence that you may have gathered (e.g. statements from customers, dated photographs, etc.).

Your assessor will then decide whether or not you will have to provide further evidence to prove your competence, and if required, what that evidence should be. During your induction sessions at your college or centre, you will have been given details of the NVQ assessment requirements, but if you have any doubts, you should consult your trainer or assessor.

The log book and activity record sheets contain important evidence of competence and should be kept in your candidate portfolio in a safe place at all times, other than when required for signing by your employer or trainer, or for inspection by the assessor or verifier.

Organizations within the plumbing industry

There are several organizations and institutions associated with the plumbing industry. They are:

- The Worshipful Company of Plumbers
- The Institute of Plumbing
- The Joint Industry Board for Plumbing Mechanical Engineering Services in England and Wales
- The Electrical, Electronic, Telecommunications and Plumbing Union
- The Council for Registered Gas Installers
- The National Association of Plumbing Teachers
- The National Association of Plumbing, Heating and Mechanical Services Contractors
- The Scottish and Northern Ireland Plumbing Employers Federation
- British Plumbing Employers Council.

On the following pages, the history and functions of these various organizations are described.

The Worshipful Company of Plumbers

There are 94 Livery Companies. The oldest, the Mercers' Company, received its charter in 1394. The Plumbers' Company ranks 31st in the order of precedent having received its first Royal Charter in 1611. The charter was withdrawn by James II and subsequently restored in the reign of William and Mary. The ordinances governing how the company should operate are much older, the first being laid down in 1365 and subsequent ordinances in 1488.

Figure 1.5

The company was the instigator of the concept of a Register of Plumbers, a logical successor to the medieval role of the company. The Register of Plumbers was inaugurated in 1886 and efforts to get 'The Plumbers' Registration Act' through Parliament occupied the activities of the Company in the 1890s. In 1893 the company equipped a laboratory in King's College, London, during the Mayoralty of Alderman Sir Stuart Knill, who was Master of the Company. Today the Institute of Plumbing carries on the tradition. The company maintains close links with the Institute of Plumbing, Copper and Lead Development Associations, and all branches of industry.

In addition, the company has sponsored and equipped a museum which is housed at the Weald and Downland Open Air Museum, Singleton, near Chichester, West Sussex. Every summer, plumbing students and staff from colleges and training centres demonstrate their skills in the Court Barn by working with lead and other traditional materials.

The company exists to:

- foster, maintain and develop links with the plumbing craft and allied disciplines in the construction and other industries
- promote as appropriate youth activities in the craft by financial and technical contributions to educational and vocational ventures
- contribute to the City of London Charities
- support the 'pursuit of excellence' so that through contact with other organisations the company is able to call on past experience for the benefit of future enterprises
- provide a pleasant social ambience for those in the company.

The Institute of Plumbing

The institute is an independent organization embracing all interests in the plumbing industry.

The institute sees its prime role as the identification and promotion of competence, skill, good quality and standards for the public benefit.

Whereas most other professional institutions are somewhat élitist in outlook and cater only for those above craft level, the institute's requirements for entry are broad in scope, reflecting the largely practical nature of the UK plumbing industry.

Figure 1.6

The institute encourages young people to progress up the ladder of qualification it offers from apprentice to technician engineer.

The institute was founded as the Institute of Plumbers in 1906 by the National Association of Master Plumbers with the objective of developing both the industrial and technical aspects of the plumbing trade. Membership was limited to Master Plumber members of the Association.

In 1925 that Association became the National Federation of Plumbers and Domestic Engineers (now the National Association of Plumbing, Heating and Mechanical Services Contractors – NAPH & MSC). The institute withdrew from the industrial field and concentrated on developing the science and practice of plumbing. Membership was, however, still restricted to Master Plumbers.

The constitution of the Institute of Plumbers was revised in 1957 and the Institute of Plumbing then came into existence under the name which it still proudly enjoys. In that year, for the first time, membership extended to plumbers holding technical qualifications irrespective of their position in the industry.

In the late 1960s discussions began between the institute and the Registered Plumbers' Association with the object of effecting a merger of the two bodies. The main role of the RPA was to manage a voluntary register on behalf of the Worshipful Company of Plumbers.

After considerable negotiation, the IOP/RPA merger was completed in 1970, when it was realised there was a pressing need for a single organization to establish the technical authority of the plumbing industry in the wider field of building services and to manage the Register of Plumbers.

Today, the institute is an independent, non-political organization pursuing its major objectives of raising the science and practice of plumbing in the public interest and managing the Register of Plumbers, with compulsory registration in mind.

In 1979 the institute became a Registered Charity, thereby acknowledging that its aims and objectives are primarily in the public interest.

The institute's activities reflect its role as both a qualifying body and learned society. A wealth of information and expertise exists within the membership and this is used to great effect when the institute is called upon by government departments, technical and educational institutions to give its views on a wide range of topics.

At national level the institute is represented on a number of organizations and committees associated with its work. For example, the institute is represented on the DoE Standing Technical Committee on Water Regulations which prepares technical requirements for new water bye-laws.

The institute plays an active role in the drafting of standards and codes of practice affecting plumbing work, subsequently published by the British Standards Institution.

It supports the work of other organizations which promote high installation standards, namely the Council for Registered Gas Installers (CORGI), of which it is a founder constituent organisation, and the National Inspection Council for Electrical Installation Contracting (NICEIC).

There is an excellent relationship between the institute and the manufacturing and distributing sectors of the plumbing industry. Communication is through the Industrial Associate category of membership and its Liaison Committee of representatives nominated by Industrial Associate members.

The institute's historical close links with the Worshipful Company of Plumbers continue today. There is contact through regular meetings and the institute is an active supporter of the Company's Plumbers' Workshop and Museum, established in the Weald and Downland Open Air Museum at Singleton, near Chichester, Sussex.

In the education and training field the institute gives help and guidance to the Plumbing Examinations Committee of the City and Guilds and the relevant committees of the Technician Education Council and the Scottish Technical Education Council. It is also represented on the Mechanical Engineering Services Committee of the Construction Industry Training Board, as well as several regional and local committees dealing with construction training. Many lecturers of plumbing at colleges are members of the institute.

At local level, the institute's District Councils arrange lectures, visits and other events to increase the knowledge and expertise of members and Registered Plumbers, updating their appreciation of new materials and methods, etc. and broadening their interests. They also arrange events that enable like-minded people to meet socially.

The institute regularly stages exhibitions in major towns and cities throughout the country and these often attract large attendances, not only of plumbers, but also of architects, engineers, merchants and others with an interest in plumbing. There is also an annual conference, when significant papers are presented and important topics discussed.

The Register of Plumbers

As part of its policy to achieve better plumbing standards, the institute condemns the present system in the UK which permits incompetent persons to practise as plumbers. The institute considers this presents a constant threat to the health, safety and well being of the community. There is ample evidence to support this belief and the dangers are increasing as plumbing services become more sophisticated and complex. With the advent of fully pressurised hot and cold plumbing systems the risks will multiply and become even more serious in nature.

The institute believes that all those who install plumbing work for gain should be registered and required to perform to the highest standards of workmanship.

Applicants for admission to the Fellow, Member, Associate and Affiliate categories who can produce adequate evidence of practical competence in plumbing are automatically enrolled to a class of the Register of Plumbers appropriate to their training, qualifications and experience.

Application forms can be obtained from:
The Institute of Plumbing, 64 Station Lane, Hornchurch, Essex RM12 6NB.

Electrical Electronic Telecommunications and Plumbing Union (EETPU)

The EETPU is a powerful organization of over 420,000 members in every industry and area of the country. It was founded in the last century and has a great deal of experience in representing members. But the organisation and service is right up-to-date, using modern techniques and employing highly qualified staff.

In addition to the recruitment of skilled and apprentice electricians and plumbers, the union also has in membership both male and female production workers, storemen, etc. and is at present rapidly

Figure 1.7

expanding into those areas of technical and administrative employment where for many years it has represented the interests of skilled manual employees.

The members are serviced by a structure of officials headed by the union's General Secretary and Executive Council. National Officers cover nationwide those members employed in specific industries whilst Area Officials and full-time Branch Officials represent the members within their own geographical area. District shop floor liaison between members and the union is made via the shop steward or convenor and the various officials.

The union provides a number of financial benefits to its members, including accident benefit, funeral benefit, disablement grants and strike benefit. In addition the union provides convalescence facilities to members at it's convalescent home at Torquay and makes a grant towards holidays for long service members. Training for shop stewards and members is provided by one-week residential courses at the union's college in Surrey. The union has its own Legal Department and provides legal aid to all members in respect of cases ranging from unfair dismissal to injury through accident at work.

The services provided by the union, both from its officials and by way of the benefits and facilities, have firmly established the EETPU as one of the most progressive unions in the country.

For more details write to: EETPU, Hayes Court, West Common Road, Bromley, Kent.

The Joint Industry Board for Plumbing Mechanical Engineering Services in England and Wales (JIB)

The JIB's main function is to establish national conditions of service for the Plumbing Mechanical Engineering Service Industry in England and Wales. After negotiations between the organizations representing the employers of plumbing and labour operative plumbers, the JIB lays down rates of pay, hours of work, holidays, etc. The JIB is also a registered body for the plumbing industry craft apprenticeship scheme and is involved in the design and operation of courses of further education and specialised training courses for the plumbing industry. The JIB's constituent bodies are:

The National Association of Plumbing, Heating and Mechanical Services Contractors
The Electrical, Electronic, Telecommunication and Plumbing Union
The Building Employers' Federation

Plumbing is no longer concerned just with working in lead as the name would suggest, but has developed into an important component of both environmental and mechanical engineering, embracing a wide variety of systems, services and complex equipment. This is reflected in the scope of training and further education and has led to the change of title from Plumber Craftsman to Plumbing Mechanical Engineering Services Craftsperson.

The skills and related knowledge of such craftspersons are in demand for many industries beyond the construction industry and the limited requirements of domestic housing installations. The board's grading system provides sections of the industry with the opportunity of management status for those undertaking the available courses of further study.

The apprenticeship scheme

In order to provide and maintain the skilled workforce required by the industry the JIB has laid down an apprenticeship scheme which encourages apprentices to study for qualifications which will permit them to progress through the industry's career structure and qualify for additional allowances.

It is essential to those young people entering the industry that their apprenticeship is registered under a Training Service Agreement with the JIB. This ensures that the apprentice will be employed under the correct terms and conditions and that the employers will support college attendance. Apprenticeships served under a JIB Training Service Agreement are recognised by all industrial bodies and are insisted upon by some countries for immigration purposes.

The grading scheme

This scheme is designed to ensure that entrants to the industry have the opportunity to progress within the industry as their qualifications and experience increase. The industry pay structure is linked to the grading scheme so that progression through the grading scheme leads to increased rates of pay. Figure 1.8 shows a typical career pattern.

Pay allowances and benefits

1) All operatives and apprentices enrolled in the industry's Benefit Scheme are entitled to Sick Pay additional to that provided by the State Scheme. They are also covered for accidental loss of limbs and permanent disability.
2) A weekly Tool Allowance is paid by employers to all apprentices and operatives who possess the full range of tools as stipulated by the JIB.
3) Operative plumbers in possession of JIB Certificates of Competency in Welding are entitled to an hourly pay supplement.
4) Travelling time and expenses are paid by employers to apprentices and operatives when and where appropriate.
5) All operatives and apprentices employed in the industry are entitled to be enrolled in the Plumbing Industry Pension Scheme operated by Plumbing Pension (UK) Ltd.

Additional information on the plumbing mechanical services industry can be obtained from the regional offices of the JIB as shown in Figure 1.9.

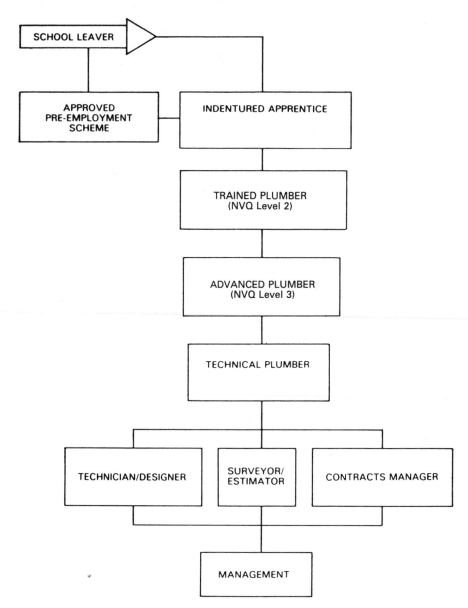

Figure 1.8   Typical career pattern

The Council for Registered Gas Installers (CORGI)

During the 1960s, there was a major gas explosion in a tower block, which claimed several lives. Since then there has been a progressive tightening of the law relating to gas safety, allied to attempts to improve safety performance through voluntary trade bodies.

Despite the Gas Safety regulations of 1972 and 1984, which require gas work to be undertaken by 'competent' persons, continuing incidents in the 1980s led to public concern over gas safety.

In April 1990, the Gas Safety (Installation and Use) (amendment) Regulations 1990 were laid before Parliament. They require the compulsory registration of those engaged in the installation and servicing of gas equipment.

The Health and Safety Executive decided that CORGI should operate such a registration scheme. To comply with the law, which came into force on 30 March 1991, all gas installers must be registered with CORGI.

Who has to be registered?

All businesses – employers or self-employed people – who undertake work on gas fittings using piped gas must be registered.

'Piped gas' includes not only mains supply, but also the supply of liquefied petroleum gas (LPG)

REGIONAL OFFICE

The Joint Industry Board for Plumbing
Mechanical Engineering Services in
England and Wales,
North West/West Midlands Region,
Egerton House,
Wardle Road,
Rochdale,
Lancs   OL12 9EN
Telephone Number: 01706–522849

REGIONAL OFFICE

The Joint Industry Board for Plumbing
Mechanical Engineering Services in
England and Wales,
North East/East Midlands Region,
4 Greenwood Mount,
Meanwood,
Leeds   LS6 4LQ
Telephone Number: 01532–786172

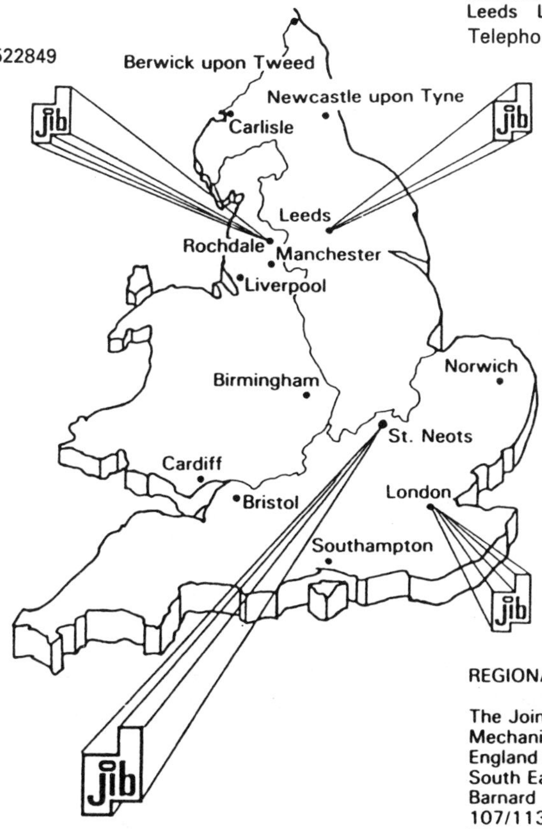

Berwick upon Tweed
Newcastle upon Tyne
Carlisle
Leeds
Rochdale
Manchester
Liverpool
Birmingham
Norwich
St. Neots
Cardiff
London
Bristol
Southampton

NATIONAL OFFICE

The Joint Industry Board for Plumbing Mechanical
Engineering Services in England and Wales,
Brook House,
Brook Street,
St. Neots,
Huntingdon
Cambridgeshire,
PE19 2HW
Telephone Number: 01480–76925

REGIONAL OFFICE

The Joint Industry Board for Plumbing
Mechanical Engineering Services in
England and Wales,
South East/South West Region,
Barnard Close,
107/113 Powis Street,
Woolwich,
London   SE18 6JB
Telephone Number: 0181–855–7438

Figure 1.9

Figure 1.10

through pipes, e.g. metered supplies to an estate. It
does not include LPG stored on the consumer's own
premises in bulk tanks or bottled supplies, unless
that gas is subsequently metered or 'sold'.

'Work on gas fittings' covers service, maintenance
and repair as well as the actual installation of gas
appliances, pipework, equipment and flues.

'Employers or self-employed people' includes not
only those businesses which deal primarily with gas,
but also, for example, the direct work departments
of local authorities and health authorities: the
operatives, kitchen installers or builders who may
only work on gas fittings occasionally.

Those engaged in DIY do not have to register, though they may be liable to prosecution if they are not competent. Payrolled employees of installation and servicing businesses are also excluded from the need to register in their own right, though their employer must be registered. Those whose work is restricted exclusively to factories or mines do not need to register.

What is CORGI?

CORGI was originally the 'Confederation for the Registration of Gas Installers', a voluntary body set up to improve gas safety standards, funded by British Gas. In December 1990 a new CORGI, the 'Council for Registered Gas Installers', was set up to operate the compulsory registration scheme. The new body is built on the experience and activities of the old CORGI, but is an independent, self-financing organization. It is controlled by a Board and Council, which are representative of the industry, and include gas suppliers, manufacturers, consumer groups, training organizations, trade associations, professional bodies and trade unions.

CORGI's costs are met from registration fees and British Gas is subject to the same registration standards as any other installer. Both the structure and the operational practices of CORGI have been set up to satisfy the Health and Safety Executive's demanding criteria for openness and fairness in the enforcement of gas safety. CORGI's objective is to help the industry towards better safety practices through practical and constructive advice.

CORGI is the only registration body approved under the regulations. Installers who remain outside CORGI and continue with piped gas work are not complying with the law.

How does the CORGI registration scheme work?

The rules for registration are set out in detail in a booklet that is supplied to each applicant.

First-time applicants must give some basic details about their business and its operational branches, sign a declaration undertaking to observe safety requirements, and pay a fee. Prior to enrolment on the CORGI register, new applicants will also need to demonstrate competence. Inspections are carried out to assess this.

If the inspections are satisfactory, registration will be processed and a certificate of registration will be issued to the business as a whole. This will expire at the end of the registration year, which is 31 March.

If the inspections are not satisfactory, remedial action and/or operative training will normally be requested, based on practical guidance. CORGI's aim is to bring about improved safety practices, not to catch people out over honest error. When CORGI is satisfied that competence has been achieved, a certificate will be issued.

If the application is not successful, there is a hearing and appeals procedure that can be invoked to ensure absolute fairness in the refusal of registration. Registration hearings and appeals are held at locations around the country as appropriate.

In subsequent years, CORGI will ask registered installers to make a renewal application. This renewal will normally be processed on the basis of the declaration and fee alone, but there will also be ongoing monitoring inspections and investigation of safety complaints, should they arise. Should any later inspection lead to a decision to deregister a business, a full hearing and appeals procedure is available to protect the installer's interest.

Administration operates from a national headquarters but each installer will be assigned to an inspector who will be part of a locally led team.

To further the main objective of practical and constructive support for better safety practice, CORGI also operates a technical 'hot line' and offers a publications service on gas safety matters.

Applications forms and information packs etc. can be obtained from: CORGI – Council for Registered Gas Installers, 4 Elmwood, Chineham Business Park, Crockford Lane, Basingstoke, Hampshire RG24 0WG, Telephone: (0256) 708133, Fax: (0256) 708144.

The National Association of Plumbing Teachers

The National Association of Plumbing Teachers (NAPT) is a voluntary professional body and was founded by an eminent plumbing teacher, J. Wright Clarke. Its first meeting at The Polytechnic, Regent Street, London, on the 31 August 1907, makes it one of the oldest bodies in the plumbing industry and indeed one of the first associations for teachers in this country. Subsequently, other professional groups have followed this lead, and construction education owes a considerable debt of gratitude to Wright Clarke's vision and foresight.

The purpose of the National Association of Plumbing Teachers as defined in its constitution

Figure 1.11

can be summarized as follows:

- to consider educational and training aspects for the benefit of the industry
- to preserve quality and standard of work
- to keep its members informed of technical developments and educational trends.

To serve its members, spread widely across the United Kingdom, Ireland and overseas, the NAPT works through its regional councils which are linked to the national council with the president, elected annually, as its head. Although an independent association, the NAPT has established working relationships with other important bodies in the industry. It also has representation, at national level, on committees that formulate the implementation of educational and training policy.

The National Association of Plumbing, Heating and Mechanical Services Contractors (NAPH & MSC)

There were local associations of master plumbers in existence in a number of centres by the middle of the nineteenth century. They combined in 1885 to form the National Association of Master Plumbers of Great Britain and Ireland, which was the forerunner of the NAPH & MSC. The association as we know it today started life in 1925 as the National Federation of Plumbing and Domestic Engineers. The name was changed in 1965 to the National Federation of Plumbing and Domestic Heating Engineers. Finally, in 1972, the federation gave way to a unified structure and adopted its present title, The National Association of Plumbing, Heating and Mechanical Services Contractors, to reflect the increased amount of mechanical services work (e.g. ventilation, air conditioning and sprinkler systems) being carried out by members.

Figure 1.12

The change of name and structure also took account of the growing need of members for services that could best be provided from a central source rather than under the original federated form. The advent of the NAPH & MSC meant that issues and problems with policy implications could be dealt with more effectively and facilitated representations to, and relations with, Government and other organisations involved. However, the knowledge, experience and enthusiasm provided at local level under the federated structure has been retained with a network of local associations and a regional structure, channelling information, views and concerns between members at the grass roots and the head office of the association.

One particularly important task carried out at local level is the vetting of applicants for membership, who are required to provide evidence of technical competence and commercial soundness. The local association has the final say as to whether a prospective member should be admitted to full membership.

Today the association has approximately 2600 members in England and Wales who carry out work varying from the installation and maintenance of household plumbing and heating to complex heating, ventilation, air conditioning and pipework systems in large-scale developments.

To cater for the needs of the members, the association provides services which include, amongst others, information about legislative and other changes affecting the industry and business in general, help and advice with legal and contractual problems, employers' liability and public liability insurance at favourable rates, and warranty schemes for domestic central heating systems for use by members and their customers.

In the field of industrial relations and training, the association maintains harmonious and effective relations with the Electrical, Electronic, Telecommunications and Plumbing Union through the Joint Industry Board.

NAPH & MSC member firms are bound by the industry's Code of Fair Trading for domestic work, agreed with the Office of Fair Trading, so that customer satisfaction is assured. Householders and specifiers are increasingly coming to realise that the best way to locate a competent and reliable plumbing and heating firm is to ask the NAPH & MSC for a free list of firms in their area on its register of members.

Application forms and information can be obtained from: The National Association of Plumbing, Heating and Mechanical Services Contractors, 14 and 15 Ensign Business Centre, Westwood Business Park, Westwood Way, Coventry CV4 8JA, Telephone: (0203) 470626.

The Scottish and Northern Ireland Plumbing Employers' Federation (SNIPEF)

Long before the federation was formed, there were active local associations of master plumbers in various parts of the country. The oldest of these

Figure 1.13

seems to have been the Glasgow and West of Scotland Association, founded in 1856, with the Dundee Association being formed in 1874, Aberdeen in 1892, Edinburgh and Leith in 1911, Moray and Banff in 1912, and others following later.

The local associations were formed to protect the interests of their members and the plumbing trade generally, and they dealt with a wide range of problems. Slaters and joiners doing plumbers' work was an early matter of concern, as was the continual upward spiral of wages. Gradually, local associations began to realise that many of the matters with which they were dealing were of national and not just local interest, and the idea slowly emerged that there should be some kind of formal liaison between associations. Thus the idea of a federation was born.

The inaugural meeting was held on 3 May 1923 in Dowell's Rooms, 18 George Street, Edinburgh. After discussion, the resolution that a federation be formed was unanimously approved. It was agreed that the title should be 'The Scottish Federation of Plumbers and Domestic Engineers (Employers) Associations'. The present title was adopted in 1975 when the Northern Ireland Association joined the federation.

During the 1920s the federation did much stalwart work in the formation of new local associations and in gaining new members. Indeed, by the end of that decade, the total membership stood at over 1100. Much effort was also expended in devising working rules and in attempting to conclude an agreement with merchants whereby only member firms would be supplied with plumbing materials. As did every other trade, plumbing suffered from the depression in the 1930s. Work was scarce, and wages were lowered on a number of occasions. The outbreak of war brought many problems to the trade. Even though plumbing was made a reserved occupation, many young men and apprentices were called up, and much of the federation's excellent work in the institution of a sound apprenticeship scheme came to naught. Indeed there was such a shortage of plumbers during the severe winters of 1940 and 1941 that the federation made successful appeals to temporarily release a number of plumbers from the forces to cope with the amount of work.

In 1950 the federation took a major step forward

in the acquisition of its own offices in Edinburgh and in the appointment of its first full-time employee, Mr W. Todd Soutar who was originally appointed as Assistant Secretary and subsequently became Director and Secretary of the federation. Under his guidance the federation grew from strength to strength, has instituted many new services to member firms and today has a staff of 24. Todd Soutar retired in 1988 after thirty-eight years' service to the industry and Mr Robert D. Burgon was appointed in his place as Director and Secretary. The federation took over the publication of the monthly journal through its own publishing company, S.P. Technical Publications Ltd, and also instituted the Sickness and Holidays with Pay Schemes, and the federation's own finance company, S.P. Finance Ltd., through which members may obtain loans to purchase business premises and essential equipment for their business. A venture of major importance in 1970 was the part the federation played in the constitution of the Joint Industry Board, and in the introduction of a grading scheme. In 1973, the federation took the initial steps to set up an industry-wide pension scheme for employees in the industry, which was then joined by the industry in England and Wales.

The 1980s was a period of significant development for the federation and saw the establishment of a managing agency for the operation of the Youth Training Scheme in the plumbing and mechanical engineering services industry in Scotland. The managing agency was awarded Approved Training Organisation status and the YTS operation was supplemented in 1989 by the introduction of an Adult Entrant Scheme using the Government's Employment Training Scheme as the first year of a three-year training programme. Also of major significance was the introduction in 1977 of the federation's Code of Fair Trading, which outlines general principles of good and fair trading between member firms and their customers and which provides a complaints procedure offering conciliation and arbitration in the event of disputes between customers and member firms. These provisions were strengthened in 1989 with the introduction of a Guarantee of Work Scheme.

In response to changes in technology, the federation has taken a lead in the provision of training courses for the industry. One particular area of success was the introduction of unvented hot water heating systems in the UK and the federation took the lead in arranging training and a registration system as agents of the British Board of Agrément. This was achieved through the establishment of a subsidiary association, the Association of Installers of Unvented Hot Water Systems (Scotland and Northern Ireland). This was followed by the establishment of the Water Byelaws Certification Scheme under which suitably qualified firms become eligible to self-certify that their work complies with the Water Byelaws and other regulations.

Another important development during the 1980s was a policy decision that the federation should undertake an annual advertising and marketing campaign aimed at promoting the benefits of using a member of a recognized trade association to members of the general public. These campaigns, which have included television, radio, bus and newspaper advertisements, have been run on an annual basis and there are many indications that the SNIPEF name and distinctive membership logo are now recognised widely.

British Plumbing Employers Council (BPEC)

The British Plumbing Employers' Council was reconstituted in April 1991 in response to the decision of the plumbing sector to withdraw from the scope of the statutory levy and grant system operated by the Construction Industry Training Board in October 1990. BPEC comprises representatives of the NAPH & MSC and SNIPEF.

Figure 1.14

BPEC has been recognized by the Employment Department as the Industry Training Organisation (ITO) and the Industry Lead Body for plumbing in Great Britain. Both founding organizations are Trade Associations, the NAPH & MSC covering England and Wales having a membership in the region of 3000 firms and SNIPEF covering Scotland and Northern Ireland with a membership of approximately 1100 firms. The scope of the membership of both associations varies usually depending upon the size of the company. In the main the companies will design, install, repair, maintain, commission and test a range of mechanical engineering services installations including plumbing, heating and gas services in domestic, industrial and commercial environments. The size of companies in membership again varies from sole traders up to companies employing in excess of 200 people.

The mechanical engineering services industry has seen major changes in skills and technology over the last 20 years. There has been a trend away from some of the traditional skills, such as lead joint wiping, and an increase in the use of increasingly sophisticated technological products, including combination and highly efficient condensing boilers, 'intelligent' building control systems and a demand for the use of water purification systems and more efficient soil waste appliances. Many of these changes have resulted from an ever-increasing awareness of the need for energy conservation and the protection of the total environment. Dramatic changes in material technology have resulted in pipework systems being both easier to join and install. Consequently this has lead to an increase, on the smaller domestic installations, in DIY, which has accounted for a reduction in the range of work available to skilled sole traders.

As a result of these changes in working practices and the continuing pace of technological advances, BPEC believes that the industry faces an enormous challenge in training terms in order that all firms operating in the plumbing industry are adequately geared to meet the demands imposed by these changes. This implies a consolidation of the considerable effort that has already been put into the training of new entrants to the industry and the continuing development and promotion of training in new technology and skills at all levels of employment, including management.

As an ITO, BPEC has a responsibility for training at all levels of the plumbing company and this 'whole firm' approach is seen as an important role for the organisation.

As the industry Lead Body for plumbing, BPEC has a commitment to develop standards. It is treading new ground but has experience in training derived from the officers and staff of the two organisations, NAPH & MSC and SNIPEF. The standards work has already progressed and continues to be a priority, in order that appropriate National and Scottish Vocational Qualifications are developed for the industry.

Questions for you

1. Name the *three* constituent organizations that form the awarding body for plumbing mechanical engineering services NVQs.

   (a) _____

   (b) _____

   (c) _____

2. Name the Lead Body for plumbing NVQs.

   _____

3. List the *three* items of documentation that a candidate will receive when they have registered at an approved centre.

   (a) _____

   (b) _____

   (c) _____

4. State the title of the person whose job it is to carry out the verification process within an approved assessment centre.

   _____

5. State the titles of *three* persons employed within an approved assessment centre who are involved with the organisation and quality control system for NVQs.

   (a) _____

   (b) _____

   (c) _____

6. Describe what is meant by the term 'supplementary knowledge'.

   _____

   _____

7. Who is responsible for the security and safety of a candidate's course documentation?

   _____

8. Name *three* types of 'evidence of competence' that may be submitted for assessment.

   (a) _____

   (b) _____

   (c) _____

9. Name the organization that administers the registration of those engaged in the installation and servicing of gas equipment.

   _____

10. Name *three* organizations that provide representatives for the Joint Industry Board for Plumbing Mechanical Engineering Services in England and Wales.

    (a) _____

    (b) _____

    (c) _____

Safety

In the pages that follow you will gain an understanding of:
- Personal safety and the safety of others
- Health and Safety at Work Act 1974
- Construction regulations
- Safety signs
- General safety
- In the event of an emergency
- Hazardous substances, materials and processes
- Fire prevention and control

Personal safety and the safety of others

Accidents are generally caused by people disregarding recommended procedures. They may feel that accidents only happen to other people and that, in any case, they have completed a particular work operation several times before without any problem.

Regardless of how much health and safety legislation is available, it will only succeed if all participants, both employers and workers, are aware of their obligations and respond accordingly. The two basic principles of accident prevention are:

- implement safe methods of working to reduce the chance of a mistake
- implement precautions to reduce the chance of injury even if someone does make a mistake.

It should be the aim of everyone to prevent accidents. Remember, you are required by law to be aware of and to fulfil your duties under the Health and Safety at Work Act. The main contribution you as an operative can make towards the prevention of accidents is to work in the safest possible manner at all times, thus ensuring that your actions do not put at risk yourself, your colleagues or the general public.

This chapter deals with matters of general safety and highlights many of the causes of accidents in the construction industry. It also deals with health and safety legislation and the responsibilities of those working in the construction industry with particular reference to mechanical engineering services operatives.

Health and Safety at Work Act 1974

The Health and Safety at Work Act 1974 (HASAWA) has wide implications. Its purpose is to provide the legislative framework to promote, stimulate and encourage high standards of health and safety and to ensure the welfare of all personnel at work, as well as the health and safety of the public as affected by work activities. It concentrates on the promotion of safety awareness and effective safety organization and performance channelled through schemes designed to suit the particular industry or organisation. The Act is an enabling measure superimposed over existing health and safety legislation and consists of four main parts: Part I relates to health, safety and welfare at work, Part II relates to the Employment Medical Advisory Service, Part III relates to building regulations, and Part IV relates to a number of miscellaneous and general provisions.

The scope of the Act includes all 'persons at work', whether employers, employees or self-employed persons. It also covers the keeping and use of dangerous substances and their unlawful acquisition, possession and use. Requirements can be made imposing controls over dangerous substances in all circumstances, including all airborne emissions of obnoxious or offensive substances that are not a danger to health but would cause a nuisance or damage the environment.

All of the existing health and safety requirements operate in parallel with the HASAWA until they are gradually replaced by new regulations and codes of practice etc. made under the Act. The main health and safety legislation applicable to building sites and workshops is indicated in Table 1.

Table 1 Health and safety legislation

Acts of Parliament	Regulations
Control Of Pollution Act 1974	
Explosives Act 1875 and 1923	
Factories Act 1961	Abrasive Wheels Regulations 1970 Asbestos Regulations 1969 Construction (General Provision) Regulations 1961 Construction (Lifting Operations) Regulations 1961 Construction (Health and Welfare) Regulations 1966 Construction (Working Places) Regulations 1966 Construction (Head Protection) Regulations 1989 Diving Operations Special Regulations 1960 Electricity (Factories Act) Special Regulations 1908 and 1944 Highly Flammable Liquids and Liquefied Petroleum Gases Regulations 1972 Lead Paint Regulations 1927 Protection of Eyes Regulations 1974 Woodworking Machines Regulations 1974 Work in Compressed Air Special Regulations 1958 and 1960
Fire Precautions Act 1971	Fire Certificates (Special Premises) Regulations 1976
Food and Drugs Act 1955	Food Hygiene (General) Regulations 1970

Health and Safety at Work Act 1974	Hazardous Substances (Labelling of Road Tankers)
	   Regulations 1978
	Control of Lead at Work Regulations 1980
	Safety Signs Regulations 1980
	Health and Safety (First Aid) Regulations 1981
	Control of Asbestos at Work Regulations 1987
	Control of Substances Hazardous to Health Regulations
	   1988 (COSHH)
	Reporting of Injuries, Diseases and Dangerous Occurences
	   Regulations 1985 (RIDDOR)

Mines and Quarries Act 1954	
Offices, Shops and Railway Premises Act 1963	

HASAWA objectives

The four main objectives of the HASAWA are as follows:

1) To secure the health, safety and welfare of all persons at work.
2) To protect the general public from risks to health and safety arising out of work activities.
3) To control the use, handling, storage and transportation of explosives and highly flammable substances.
4) To control the release of noxious or offensive substances into the atmosphere.

These objectives can be achieved only by involving everyone in health and safety matters. This includes:

- employers and management
- employees (and those undergoing training)
- self-employed persons
- designers, manufacturers and suppliers of equipment and materials.

Employers' and management duties

Employers have a general duty to ensure the health and safety of their employees, visitors and the general public. This means that the employer must:

1) Provide and maintain a safe working environment.
2) Ensure safe access to and from the workplace.
3) Provide and maintain safe machinery, equipment and methods of work.
4) Ensure the safe handling, transport and storage of all machinery, equipment and materials.
5) Provide their employees with the necessary information, instruction, training and supervision to ensure safe working.
6) Prepare, issue to employees and update as required a written statement of the firm's safety policy.
7) Involve trade union safety representatives (where appointed) with all matters concerning the development, promotion and maintenance of health and safety requirements.

Note: An employer is not allowed to charge an employee for any work done, or any equipment provided, to comply with any health and safety requirement.

Employees' duties

An employee is an individual who offers his or her skill and experience etc. to his or her employer in return for a monetary payment. It is the duty of all employees while at work to comply with the following:

1) Take care at all times and ensure that their actions do not put at risk themselves, their colleagues or any other person.
2) Co-operate with their employers to enable them to fulfil the employers' health and safety duties.
3) Use the equipment and safeguards provided by the employers.
4) Never misuse or interfere with anything provided for health and safety.

SAFETY BEGINS WITH YOU

Self-employed duties

The self-employed person can be thought of as both the employer and employee; therefore their duties under the Act are a combination of those of the employer and the employee.

Designers', manufacturers' and suppliers' duties

Under the Act, designers, manufacturers and suppliers as well as importers and hirers of equipment, machinery and materials for use at work have a duty to:

1) Ensure that the equipment, machinery or material is designed, manufactured and tested so that when it is used correctly no hazard to health and safety is created.
2) Provide information or operating instructions as to the correct use, without risk, of their equipment, machinery or material.
   Note: Employers should ensure this information is passed on to their employees.
3) Carry out research so that any risk to health and safety is eliminated or minimised as far as possible.

Enforcement

Under the HASAWA a system of control was established, aimed at reducing death, injury and ill-health. This system of control consists of the Health and Safety Executive (HSE). The Executive is divided into a number of specialist inspectorates or sections which operate from local offices situated throughout the country. From the local office, inspectors visit individual workplaces.

Note: The section with the main responsibility for the building industry is the Factory Inspectorate.

The Health and Safety Executive inspectors have been given wide powers of entry, examination and investigation in order to assist them in the enforcement of the HASAWA and earlier safety legislation. In addition to giving employers advice and information on health and safety matters, an inspector can do the following:

1) *Enter premises* in order to carry out investigations, including the taking of measurements, photographs, recordings and samples. The inspector may require the premises to be left undisturbed while the investigations are taking place.
2) *Take statements* An inspector can ask anyone questions relevant to the investigation and also require them to sign a declaration as to the truth of the answers.
3) *Check records* All books, records and documents required by legislation must be made available for inspection and copying.
4) *Give information* An inspector has a duty to give employees or their safety representative information about the safety of their workplace and details of any action he/she proposes to take. This information must also be given to the employer.
5) *Demand* The inspector can demand the seizure, dismantling, neutralising or destruction of any machinery, equipment, material or substance that is likely to cause immediate serious personal injury.
6) *Issue an improvement notice* This requires the responsible person (employer or manufacturer etc.) to put right within a specified period of time any minor hazard or infringement of legislation.
7) *Issue a prohibition notice* This requires the responsible person to stop immediately any activities that are likely to result in serious personal injury. This ban on activities continues until the situation is corrected. An appeal against an improvement or prohibition notice may be made to an industrial tribunal.
8) *Prosecute* All persons, including employers, employees, self-employed persons, designers, manufacturers and suppliers who fail to comply with their safety duty may be prosecuted in a magistrates' court or in certain circumstances in the higher court system. Conviction can lead to unlimited fines, or a prison sentence, or both.

Construction regulations

These are the regulations made under the Factories Act 1961 which are specific to construction operations. They are divided into five parts, each dealing with a different aspect of work.

- *Construction (General Provisions) Regulations 1961* set out minimum standards to promote a good level of general safety.
- *Construction (Lifting Operations) Regulations 1961* lay down requirements regarding the manufacture, maintenance and inspection of lifting appliances used on site (gin wheels, cranes and hoists, etc.).
- *Construction (Health and Welfare) Regulations 1966* set out minimum provisions for site accommodation, washing facilities, sanitary conveniences and protective clothing. See Table 2 'Safety, health and welfare on site'.
- *Construction (Working Places) Regulations 1966* control the erection, use and inspection of scaffolds and other similar temporary structures.

- *Construction (Head Protection) Regulations 1989* place a duty on employers to provide and ensure that suitable head protection is worn on site. Employees and the self-employed are obliged to wear it when instructed to do so.

Safety documentation

In order to comply with the safety legislation, an employer is required to:

- display notices and certificates
- notify relevant authorities
- keep relevant records.

Notices and certificates

An employer must prominently display on site, in the workshop, or in an office where the employees attend, a number of notices and certificates, the main ones being (where applicable):

1) Copy of the certificate of insurance; this is

Table 2 Safety, health and welfare on site

Type of site/number of people on site	What must be provided
Every site	A clean and orderly place in which to shelter during bad weather A means of keeping warm A place to sit when eating A means of boiling water A supply of drinking water A place to store and dry work clothing A place to store personal clothing Washing facilities Toilets and urinals, clean, under cover with lockable door and lighting to be provided. Separate facilities are required for men and women, a minimum of one for every 25 persons Protective clothing to be provided if expected to work in poor weather conditions An appointed person responsible for the first aid box and summoning medical attention* A first aid box. Travelling first aid kits should be provided for those on the move or when working alone or in small groups in isolated locations*
When using lead or poisonous substances	Nail brushes, soap, towel or dryer, hot and cold or warm water, wash basin or bucket for every 5 or part of 5 persons
More than 5	Heating and drying arrangements must be adequate and suitable
More than 10	Hot food available or a means of heating one's own
20 or more	A wash basin, soap, towel or dryer, hot and cold or warm water to be provided where work is expected to last more than 6 weeks
More than 50	A person properly trained and recently certificated in first aid procedures*
More than 100	A minimum of 4 wash basins and an additional one for every 35 or part of 35 persons above 100 and an adequate supply of soap, towels or dryer, hot and cold or warm water to be provided where the work is unlikely to be completed within 12 months Additional toilet facilities, one for every 35 or part of 35 persons above 100

Note: Where the site has fewer than 5 personnel the heating and drying arrangements must be provided where reasonably practicable. Items* are required by the Health and Safety (First Aid) Regulations 1981

required under the Employers' Liability (Compulsory Insurance) Act 1969.

2) Copy of fire certificate.
3) Abstract of the Factories Act 1961 for building operations and works of engineering constructions.
4) Details of the area Health and Safety Executive Inspectorate; the employment medical adviser and the site safety supervisor should be indicated on this form.
5) Abstract of the Offices, Shops and Railway Premises Act 1963.
6) The Woodworking Machines Regulations 1974.
7) The Abrasive Wheels Regulations 1970 and cautionary notice.
8) The Electricity (Factories Act) Special Regulations 1908 and 1944. Electric shock (first aid) placard.
9) The, Asbestos Regulations 1969.
10) The Highly Flammable Liquids and Liquefied Petroleum Gases Regulations 1972.

Notifications

The following are the main notifications required. They are usually submitted on standard forms obtainable from the relevant authority.

1) The commencement of building operations or works of engineering constructions that are likely to last more than six weeks.
2) The employment of persons in an office or shop for more than 21 hours a week.
3) The employment or transfer of young persons (under 18 years of age) must be notified to the local careers office.
4) Accidents resulting in death or major injuries or notifiable dangerous occurrences, or more than three days absence from work. Major injuries can be defined as most fractures, amputations, loss of sight or any other injury involving a stay in hospital. Many incidents can be defined as notifiable dangerous occurrences but in general they include the collapse of a crane, hoist, scaffolding or building, an explosion or fire, or the escape of any substance that is liable to cause a health hazard or major injury to any person.
5) A poisoning or suffocation incident resulting in acute ill-health requiring medical treatment.
6) Application for a fire certificate, if required under the Fire Certificates (Special Premises) Regulations 1976.

Records

Employers are required to keep various records. These should be kept ready for inspection on site or at the place of work and should include the following:

1) The general register for building operations and works of engineering constructions. This is used to record details of the site or workshop and the nature of work taking place, any cases of poisoning or disease and the employment or transfer of young persons.
2) An accident book in which details of all accidents are recorded.
3) A record of accidents, dangerous occurrences and ill-health enquiries. Entries in the record must be made whenever the Health and Safety Executive is notified of an accident resulting in death, major injury or a notifiable dangerous occurrence.
4) Register for the purposes of the Abrasive Wheels Regulations 1970. A register used to record details of persons appointed to mount abrasive wheels.
5) Records of inspections, examinations and special tests. This is a booklet of forms on which details of inspections etc. on scaffolding, excavations, earthworks and lifting appliances must be recorded.
6) Record of reports. This provides forms for recording the thorough examination of lifting appliances, hoists, chains, ropes and other lifting gear and also the heat treatment of chains and lifting gear.
7) Register and certificate of shared welfare arrangements. To be completed where an employer, normally the main contractor, provides the welfare facilities for another employer (sub-contractor).
8) Certificates of tests and examinations of various lifting appliances. These are records of the weekly, monthly or other periodic tests and examinations required by the construction regulations as follows:

cranes
hoists
other lifting appliances
wire and ropes
chains, slings and lifting gear.

Safety signs

Formerly there were many vastly different safety signs in use. British Standard BS 5378 Part 1, 1980: 'Safety Signs and Colours' introduced a standard system of giving health and safety information with a minimum use of words. Its purpose is to establish an internationally understood system of safety signs and safety colours which draws attention to objects and situations that do, or could, affect health and safety. Details of these signs and typical examples of use are given in Figures 2.1 to 2.5.

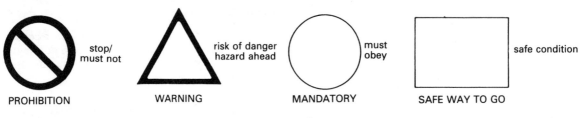

Figure 2.1   Safety signs

Prohibition signs

These are circular signs with a red border and white interior. Examples are shown in Figure 2.2. They are signs prohibiting certain behaviour.

Figure 2.2   Prohibition signs

Warning signs

These are triangular yellow signs with a black border and symbol, and are given in Figure 2.3. They *give warning* of a hazard or danger.

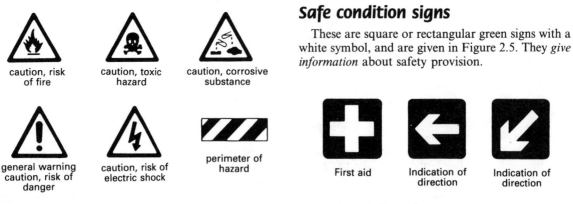

Figure 2.3   Warning signs

Mandatory signs

These are circular blue signs with a white symbol, and are given in Figure 2.4. They *give instructions* which must be obeyed.

Figure 2.4   Mandatory signs

Safe condition signs

These are square or rectangular green signs with a white symbol, and are given in Figure 2.5. They *give information* about safety provision.

First aid   Indication of direction   Indication of direction

Figure 2.5   Safe condition signs

General safety

It should be the aim of everyone to prevent accidents. Remember, you are required by law to be aware of and fulfil your duties under the Health and Safety at Work Act.

The main contribution you as an operative can make towards the prevention of accidents is to work in the safest possible manner at all times, thus ensuring that your actions do not put at risk yourself, other operatives or the general public.

Safety: on site and in the workshop

A safe working area is a tidy working area. All unnecessary obstructions which may create a hazard should be removed, e.g. offcuts of material, unwanted materials, disused items of plant, and nails in discarded pieces of timber should be extracted or flattened.

Clean up your workbench/work area periodically as tools offcuts and cleaning rags are potential tripping and fire hazards.

Learn how to identify the different types of fire extinguishers and what type of fire they can safely be used on. Staff in each work area should be trained in the use of fire extinguishers (see pp. 42–44).

Careful disposal of materials from heights is essential. They should always be lowered safely and not thrown or dropped from scaffolds and window openings etc. Even a small bolt or fitting dropped from a height can penetrate a person's skull and almost certainly lead to brain damage or death.

Ensure your tools are in good condition. Blunt cutting tools, loose hammer heads, broken or missing handles and mushroom heads must be repaired immediately or the use of the tool discontinued. Figure 2.6 shows a selection of unsafe tools.

Lifting

When moving materials and equipment always look at the job first; if it is too big for you then get help. Look out for splinters, nails and sharp or jagged edges on the items to be moved. Always lift with your back straight, elbows tucked in, knees bent and feet slightly apart, as shown in Figure 2.7. When putting an item down ensure that your hands and fingers will not be trapped.

The same basic principles apply when two or more people are lifting the same object. In addition, remember the following:

- lifting gangs must work as a team
- everyone in a lifting team should be roughly the same height
- the operation should be planned from 'lifting' to 'setting down' – route to be taken, signals etc.
- make sure everyone in the team knows precisely what to do
- appoint one person as team leader.

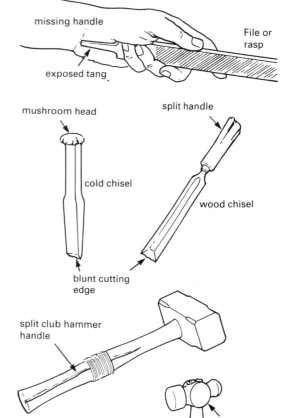

Figure 2.6   Unsafe tools

The six major points to remember when lifting are:

1) Back straight.
2) Chin in.
3) Arms close to body.
4) Feet slightly apart.
5) Bend knees and lift by straightening the legs.
6) Grip with palm of hands, not just fingers.

Lifting gas cylinders

Special care should be taken when moving gas cylinders. Use a trolley wherever possible. To lift a cylinder on to a trolley, first lift to the vertical position with a straight back and bent knees and then use your thighs as shown in Figure 2.8.

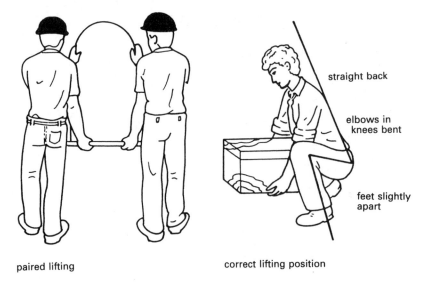

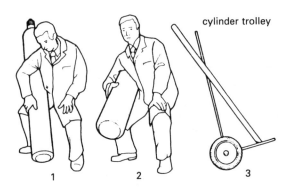

Figure 2.7   Correct positions for lifting

cylinder trolley

Figure 2.8   Lifting a cylinder

Stacking materials

Location

Materials should be readily accessible and as close as possible to the point of use, but:

- not in quantities so great as to limit working space unnecessarily
- not where they will cause obstruction
- not close to edges of excavations
- not close to moving machinery or overhead lines
- not where they will interfere with new deliveries.

Foundations and supports

A firm, even base is essential. The foundation – for example, the floor – must be strong enough to support the total weight, which may be considerable. Stacking materials against a wall may be dangerous, as the wall may not be designed to take the sideways thrust.

Size

Stacks should not normally be higher than 1.6 m to permit easy withdrawal. The shorter base should be about one-third of the height.

Structure

Batter (i.e. step back) every few tiers. Chock or stake rolling objects (for example, drums, pipes) with sound material. Bond to prevent the stack collapsing (see Figure 2.9). Avoid unnecessary protrusions – protrusions which cannot be avoided should have a distinctive marker tied to them. Oxygen cylinders may be stacked horizontally. Acetylene cylinders *must* be stored and used vertically.

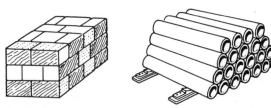

bonded material storage   chocked material storage

Figure 2.9   Types of safe storage

Use

Withdraw materials from the top of the stack – never from the bottom or sides. Do not climb on to stacks – use a ladder.

Excavations

Excavations and inspection chambers should be either protected by a barrier or covered over completely to prevent people carelessly falling into them (see Figure 2.10).

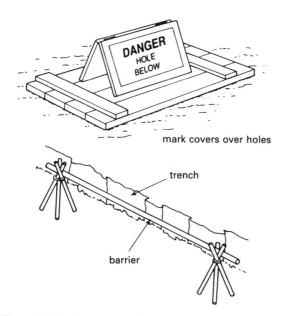

mark covers over holes

trench

barrier

Figure 2.10   Protection of excavations

Figure 2.11   Never support a ladder on its rungs

Accidents can arise when people slip into trenches, sometimes while trying to jump across them or while climbing out of them or when supports give way. The following precautions should be taken:

- warn people to look where they are going
- provide proper walkways across trenches
- erect barriers round excavations where necessary
- do not leave holes uncovered or unfenced
- take care when doing below-ground work
- fence openings or cover them with heavy material appropriately marked.

Ladders

When used incorrectly or in bad condition a ladder becomes a hazard. Working from a ladder is inherently dangerous. Where possible always provide a working platform. Most falls from ladders are the result of a person simply slipping or falling from the ladder, but movement of the ladder also causes a considerable number of accidents – the ladder either slips outwards at the bottom or sideways at the top. Accidents are also caused by missing or broken rungs or by the ladder itself breaking. Always observe the following points:

- stand the ladder on a firm, even base with the trussed side underneath if reinforced
- never wedge one side up if the ground is uneven – either level the ground or bury the foot of ladder
- beware of wet, icy or greasy rungs. Clean any mud or grease from boots before climbing
- watch out for live overhead cables, particularly when using metal ladders.
- never support a ladder on its rungs (Figure 2.11)
- never work on a ladder set at an incorrect angle (75° is recommended)

Figure 2.12   Asking for trouble

- never overload a ladder (use a hoist)
- never use a ladder which is too short or stand it on something, for example a drum or dustbin, to get extra height (Figure 2.12).
- Do not over-reach sideways from a ladder – move it (Figure 2.13).

The correct method of climbing and descending a ladder is:

1) Be aware of your limitations.
2) Check the ladder for security
3) Clean mud etc. from your footwear.
4) Face the ladder squarely. Using both hands either grasp the stiles, or grasp the rungs (fireman fashion).
5) Keep feet placed well into the rungs.
6) Eyes should be directed at working level above – do not look down.

Figure 2.13   Never over-reach

7) Don't carry anything in your hands. Tools and materials may fall when carried up ladders, even if carried in pockets. Where possible provide a hoist line. Alternatively, use a shoulder bag.

Securing ladders

Too much importance cannot be placed on this part of your work. In addition to the obvious lashing of the top of the ladder, the foot of the ladder should also be suitably anchored. When it is not possible to tie the top then side guys should be used. These should be secured to the stiles (never the rungs) and should form an angle with the horizontal of approximately 45° (see Figure 2.14).

Platforms

A hook-on foot platform is useful to provide something more comfortable than a rung to stand on (see Figure 2.15). Foot platforms should be capable of being easily fitted and removed and should give a level surface with the ladder placed at 75°. One disadvantage of platforms is that they can be difficult to climb past. Various hook-on tray attachments are available to enable tools and components to be readily accessible.

Cripples (ladder brackets)

A pair of ladder cripples enables a light working platform to be erected between two ladders (see Figure 2.16). Some are adjustable for angle while others have a fixed angle to suit a ladder at 75°.

Standoffs

These fitments hold the top of the ladder off from the wall (see Figure 2.17). They are particularly

Figure 2.14   Ladder staked and guyed

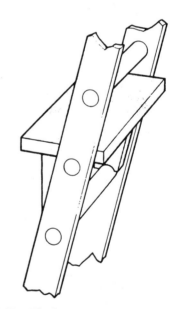

Figure 2.15   Platform

useful when working on gutters etc. as they overcome the need to lean outwards. It is advisable to secure them to the ladder to prevent side-to-side movement.

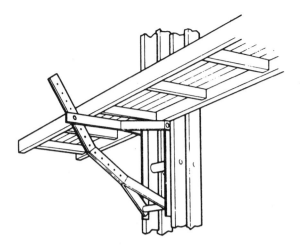

Figure 2.16   Cripples

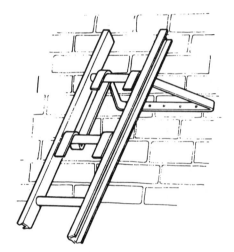

Figure 2.17   Standoff

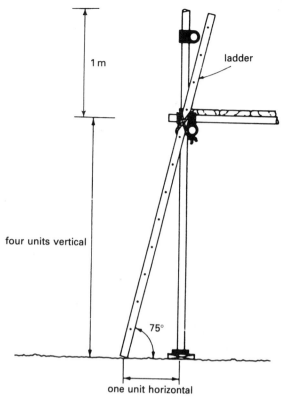

Figure 2.18   Correct positioning of a ladder

Correct positioning of a ladder

The recommended ideal working angle of a ladder is 75° to the horizontal or one unit out to four units up (see Figure 2.18). It is also recommended that the top of the ladder should extend 1 m past the working platform. The lift of a single ladder should not be more than 8–10 m.

Raising and carrying a ladder

Figure 2.19 illustrates the correct method of raising a ladder. Ladders should be carried vertically or with the front end elevated (see Figure 2.20). It takes two people to move a tall ladder.

Inspection and maintenance

Always inspect a ladder before use. Ladders should *not* be subjected to a severe test. Always check:

- the rungs, particularly at the point where they

Figure 2.19   Correct method of raising a ladder

enter the stiles (to test the rungs, tap each rung with a mallet – a dull sound indicates a defective rung)
- the wedges, which should be properly in position
- the stiles for warping, cracking or splintering
- the condition of the feet
- any ropes or metal attachments.

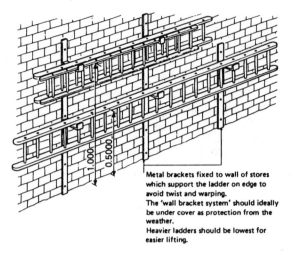

Metal brackets fixed to wall of stores
which support the ladder on edge to
avoid twist and warping.
The 'wall bracket system' should ideally
be under cover as protection from the
weather.
Heavier ladders should be lowest for
easier lifting.

Figure 2.21   Correct method of storage

Figure 2.20   Correct methods of carrying ladders

Take defective ladders out of service immediately, mark them defective and do not use them again until they are repaired. Destroy unfit ladders which cannot be repaired.

Treat new ladders with clear wood preservative, particularly round the end grain of the rungs and coat with clear varnish. Painting a ladder is not recommended as the paint may hide defects.

Storage of ladders

Do not leave ladders on wet ground or leave them exposed to the weather. Store at normal temperatures under cover to prevent warping. Support at intermediate points and not just the ends (see Figure 2.21).

Scaffolds

Scaffolding is a temporary structure which is used in order to carry out certain building operations at height. It must provide a safe means of access to heights and a safe working platform.

Scaffolding should only be erected, altered and dismantled by a trained scaffolder. Craft operatives have to work on scaffolding 'safely'. It is therefore essential that you have an understanding of scaffolding principles, types, materials and statutory regulations.

The following are some of the official publications which deal with scaffolding. They are recommended for further reading.

The Construction (Working Places) Regulations, 1966
The Construction (Lifting Operations) Regulations, 1961
BS 1139 1982: Metal Scaffolding
BS 2483 1981: Timber Scaffold Boards.

Scaffolds should be inspected before working on them. Check to see that all components are there and in good condition, not bent, twisted, rusty, split, loose or out of plumb and level. Also ensure that the base has not been undermined and is not too close to excavations. If in doubt do not use the scaffold, and have it looked at by an experienced scaffolder.

Trestle scaffolds

Figure 2.22 shows a trestle scaffold. Two pairs of trestles spanned by scaffolding boards provide a simple working platform. The platform must be at

Figure 2.22   Trestle scaffold

least two boards or 450 mm wide. At least one third of the trestle must be above the working platform. If the platform is more than 2 m above the ground, toeboards and guardrails must be fitted, and a separate ladder provided for access. The boards which form the working platform should be of equal length and should not overhang the trestles by more than four times their own thickness. The maximum span of boards between trestles is:

1.3 m for boards 40 mm thick
2.5 m for boards 50 mm thick

Trestles which are higher than 3.6 m must be tied to the building to give them stability. Where anyone can fall more than 4.5 m from the working platform, trestles may not be used.

Putlog scaffolds

These are often known as either bricklayers' scaffolds or single scaffolds. They are normally used when constructing new brick buildings and consist of a single row of vertical standards which are connected together by horizontal ledgers. Putlogs are coupled to the ledgers and are built into the wall as the brickwork proceeds. This type of scaffold obtains most of its support and stability from the building (Figure 2.23).

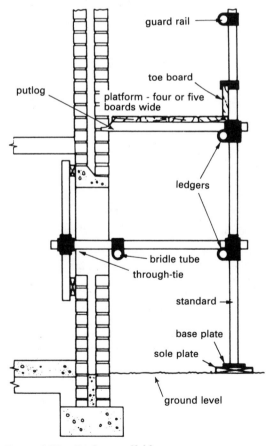

Figure 2.23   Putlog scaffold

Independent scaffolds

These are sometimes called double scaffolds as they are constructed using a double row of standards. This type of scaffold carries its own weight and the full weight of all loads imposed upon it, but it is not completely independent. It must be suitably tied to the building for stability (Figure 2.24).

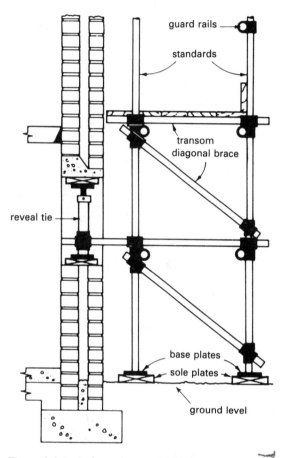

Figure 2.24   Independent scaffold

Tower scaffolds

These may be either static (Figure 2.25) or mobile. They are suitable for both internal and external use for work up to about 6 m in height. For work above this height the tower should be tied into the building or be fitted with counterweights to stabilise it.

Tower scaffolds must only be used on firm, level ground. Mobile towers must never be moved while people or equipment are on them.

Mobile scaffold towers may be constructed of basic scaffold components or made from light alloy tube. The tower is built up by slotting the sections together until the required height is reached.

If the working platform is above 2 m from the ground it must be close boarded and fitted with

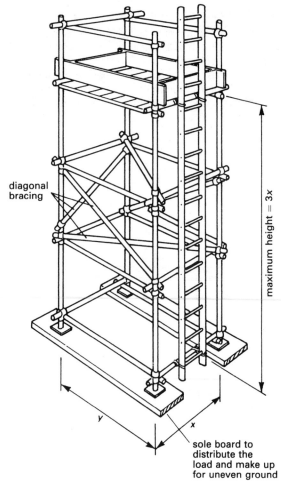

diagonal bracing

maximum height = 3x

sole board to distribute the load and make up for uneven ground

Figure 2.25   Static scaffold tower

guardrails and toeboards. When the platform is being used all four wheels must be locked. The platform must not be moved unless it is clear of tools, equipment and workers and should be pushed at the base of the tower and not at the top.

The stability of the tower depends upon the ratio of the base width to tower height. A ratio of base to height of 1 : 3 gives good stability. Outriggers can be used to increase stability by effectively increasing the base width. If outriggers are used then they must be fitted diagonally across all four corners of the tower and not on one side only.

Access to the working platform of a scaffold tower should be by a ladder securely fastened vertically to the tower. Ladders must never be leaned against a tower since this might push the tower over.

Working platform

This should be four or five 38 mm × 220 mm scaffold boards in width. Each board should normally have at least three supports in order to prevent undue sagging. Where there is a danger of high winds the scaffold boards should be clipped

down to putlogs or transoms. A clear passage of 440 mm (640 mm for barrows) must be maintained when loading materials.

Guard rails

These must be fitted to all working platforms where it is possible for a person or materials to fall 2 m or more. Fixed to the inside of the standards along the outside edge and the ends of the working platform, they are also required on the inside of the scaffold in the following circumstances:

- where the gap between the scaffold and the inside of an existing building exceeds 300 mm
- where the scaffold rises above a building
- where recesses occur in the building.

Guard rails must be between 910 and 1150 mm above the platform and not more than 765 mm above the top of the toe board (Figure 2.26).

Where materials are stacked on a scaffold the use of steel wire mesh panels is recommended.

Toe boards accompany the guard rail and must rise at least 150 mm above the working platform. They prevent items being kicked or falling off.

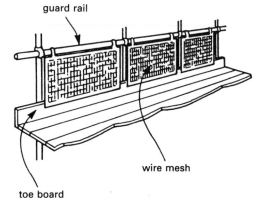

guard rail

wire mesh

toe board

Figure 2.26 Guard rails

Safe working at heights

When working on roofs or at heights:

- Check you have the correct tools and the right quantity of materials and fittings etc. before ascending.
- Keep to access points, ladders and walkways.
- Pay attention to warning notices and barriers.
- Stay alert to likely hazards such as uneven floors, overhead obstructions or changes in weather conditions which may make surfaces slippery.
- Do not stack materials above the level of toe boards or leave tools and materials lying about where they might cause somebody to trip and fall.
- Keep the working area clear of waste materials and clutter.
- Do not remove guard rails, toe boards, barriers or protective covers without permission.

Safety clothing and equipment

Always wear the correct protective equipment for the work in hand (Figure 2.27). Safety helmets and safety footwear should be worn at all times. Wear ear protectors when carrying out noisy activities, and safety goggles when carrying out any operation that is likely to produce dust, chips or sparks, etc. Dust masks or respirators should be worn where dust is being produced or fumes are present, and gloves when handling materials. Wet weather clothing is necessary for inclement conditions. Many of these items must be supplied free of charge by your employer.

Care should be taken with personal hygiene which is just as important as physical protection. Some building materials have an irritant effect on contact with the skin. Some are poisonous if swallowed, while others can result in a state of unconsciousness (narcosis) if their vapour or powder is inhaled. These harmful effects can be avoided by taking proper precautions: follow the manufacturer's instructions; avoid inhaling fumes or powders; wear a barrier cream; thoroughly wash your hands before eating, smoking and after work.

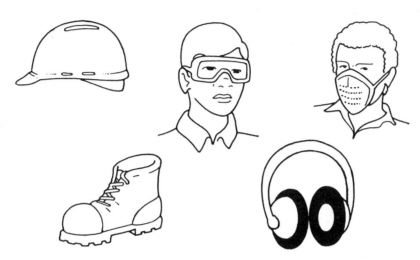

Figure 2.27   Safety equipment

In the event of an emergency

First aid

Despite all the safety precautions taken on construction sites to prevent injury to the workforce, accidents do happen and *you* may be the only other person able to take action to assist a colleague.

If you are not a qualified first aider, limit your help to obvious common sense assistance and call for help, *but* do remember that if a colleague's heart or breathing has stopped as a result of an accident, they have only minutes to live unless you act quickly.

The following first aid procedures should be practised under expert guidance before they are required in an emergency.

Bleeding

If the wound is dirty, rinse it under clean running water. Clean the skin around the wound and apply a plaster, pulling the skin together (Figure 2.28).

If the bleeding is severe, apply direct pressure to reduce bleeding and raise the limb if possible. Apply a sterile dressing or pad and bandage firmly before obtaining professional advice.

To avoid possible contact with hepatitis or HIV, when dealing with open wounds, first aiders should avoid contact with fresh blood by wearing plastic or rubber protective gloves, or by allowing the casualty to apply pressure to the bleeding wound.

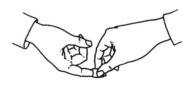

Figure 2.28   First aid for bleeding

Burns and scalds

Remove heat from the burn to relieve the pain by placing the injured part under cold clean water (Figure 2.29). Do not remove burnt clothing sticking to the skin. Do not apply lotions or ointments. Do not break blisters or attempt to remove loose skin. Cover the injured area with a clean dry dressing. Scalds are the result of wet heat such as steam, hot water, hot oil or other liquids.

Figure 2.29   Removing heat from a burn or scald

Broken bones

Make the casualty as comfortable as possible by supporting the broken limb either by hand or with padding. Do not move the casualty unless by remaining in that position they are likely to suffer further injury. Obtain professional help as soon as possible.

Eye injuries

Eye injuries must be treated seriously. The eye can be cut or bruised from a direct blow or by fragments of grit, metal or glass. Eye injuries can be very painful. The eye may be inflamed and bloodshot, and the casualty may be unable to see clearly.

Your aim should be to protect the eye by preventing movement. Get the casualty to lie down: support their head and keep it still. Ask the casualty to close their injured eye and cover it with an eye pad or sterile dressing (Figure 2.30).

Advise the casualty to keep their other eye as still as possible because movement of one eye will cause the other eye to move. If necessary, use a blindfold, but reassure the casualty before doing so.

DO NOT attempt to remove any foreign body from the eye yourself: this is best left to a qualified person. Get expert help as quickly as possible.

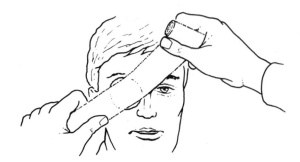

Figure 2.30   Protecting an injured eye with a dressing

Chemicals etc. in the eye

Chemicals, petrol, paints and corrosive substances can splash into the eye and cause serious injury. You should try to wash such substances away as soon as possible. Do not allow the casualty to rub the eye.

Try to wash the eye with gently running water (Figure 2.31), so that the water drains away from the face, or by pouring clean water over the eye from a bottle or jug. If possible, protect the uninjured eye with a pad or cloth.

Cover the damaged eye with a sterile pad or dressing and get expert help as quickly as possible.

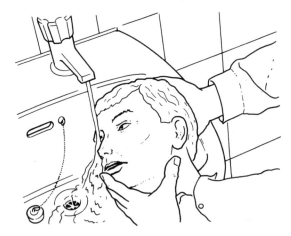

Figure 2.31   Washing chemicals from an eye

Skin contact with chemicals

Wash the affected area very thoroughly with clean cold water. Remove any contaminated clothing. Cover the affected area with a clean sterile dressing and seek expert advice. It is a wise precaution to treat all chemical substances as possibly harmful; even commonly used substances can be dangerous if contamination is from concentrated solutions. When handling dangerous substances it is also good practice to have a neutralising agent to hand.

Disposal of dangerous substances must not be into the main drains because this can give rise to an environmental hazard, but should be undertaken in accordance with Local Authority Regulations.

Exposure to toxic fumes

Move the casualty into fresh air quickly and encourage deep breathing if the casualty is conscious. Resuscitate the casualty if breathing has stopped. Obtain expert medical advice as fumes may cause irritation of the lungs.

Sprains and severe bruising

A cold compress can help to relieve swelling and pain. Soak a towel or cloth in cold water, squeeze it out and place it on the injured part. Renew the compress every few minutes. Make the casualty comfortable.

Unconscious casualty

Remove any restrictions from the face and ensure that the nose and mouth are clear. Loosen tight clothing around the neck, chest and waist. To ensure a good airway, lay the casualty on their back and support the shoulders on some padding. Tilt the head backwards and open the mouth. If the casualty is faintly breathing, lifting the tongue clear of the airway may be all that is necessary to restore normal breathing.

DO NOT leave an unconscious person unattended.

Heart has stopped beating

This sometimes happens following a severe electric shock. The signs of cardiac arrest are: the casualty's lips may be blue, the pupils of their eyes may be widely dilated and the pulse in the neck cannot be felt. Act quickly and lay the casualty on their back. Kneel down beside them and place the heel of one hand in the centre of their chest. Cover this hand with your other hand and interlace the fingers. Straighten your arms and press down on their chest sharply with the heel of your hands and release the pressure. Continue to do this 15 times at the rate of one push per second. Check the casualty's pulse. If none is felt, give two breaths of artificial respiration and then a further 15 chest compressions. Continue this procedure until the heart beat is restored. Pay close attention to the condition of the casualty whilst giving heart massage. When a pulse is restored, the blueness around the mouth will quickly go away and you should stop the heart massage. Look carefully at the rate of breathing. When this is also normal, stop giving artificial respiration. Treat the casualty for shock (see below) and obtain professional help.

Electric shock

Electric shock occurs when a person becomes part of the electrical circuit. The level or intensity of the shock will depend upon many factors, such as age, fitness and the circumstances in which the shock is received. The lethal level is approximately 50 mA, above which muscles contract, the heart flutters and breathing stops. A shock above the 50 mA level is therefore fatal unless the person is quickly separated from the supply. Below 50 mA an unpleasant tingling sensation may be experienced or the casualty may be thrown across a room, or from a roof or ladder, with the resulting fall leading to serious injury.

To prevent anyone receiving an electric shock accidentally, all circuits contain protective devices. All exposed metal is earthed, fuses and miniature circuit breakers (MCBs) are designed to trip under fault conditions and residual current circuit breakers (RCCBs) are designed to trip below the fatal level.

Construction workers and particularly electricians and plumbers do receive electric shocks, usually as a result of carelessness or unforeseen circumstances. When this happens it is necessary to act quickly to prevent a fatality (Figure 2.32). The actions to be taken upon finding a colleague receiving an electric shock are:

- switch off the supply if possible *or*, stand on some insulating material and remove the person from the supply *without touching them*, e.g. push them with a piece of wood, or pull them with a scarf, dry towel or coat
- if breathing or heart have stopped, apply resuscitation or cardiac massage until they recover
- treat for shock
- call medical assistance.

Figure 2.32   Act quickly to break the circuit

Shock

Everyone suffers from shock following an accident. The severity of the shock depends upon the nature and extent of the injury. In cases of severe

Health and Safety Executive
Health and Safety at Work etc Act 1974
Reporting of Injuries,Diseases and Dangerous Occurrences Regulations 1985

Spaces below
are for office
use only

Report of an injury or dangerous occurrence

- Full notes to help you complete this form are attached.
- This form is to be used to make a report to the enforcing authority under the requirements of Regulations 3 or 6.
- Completing and signing this form does not constitute an admission of liability of any kind, either by the person making the report or any other person.
- If more than one person was injured as a result of an accident, please complete a separate form for each person.

A   Subject of report *(tick appropriate box or boxes)* — *see note 2*

Fatality		Specified major injury or condition		"Over three day" injury		Dangerous occurrence		Flammable gas incident (fatality or major injury or condition)		Dangerous gas fitting	
	1		2		3		4		5		6

B Person or organisation making report (ie person obliged to report under the Regulations) — *see note 3*

Name and address —

Post code —

Name and telephone no. of person to contact —

Nature of trade, business or undertaking —

If in construction industry, state the total number of your employees —

and indicate the role of your company on site *(tick box)* —

Main site contractor		Sub contractor		Other	
	7		8		9

If in farming, are you reporting an injury to a member of your family? *(tick box)*   Yes No

C Date, time and place of accident, dangerous occurrence or flammable gas incident — *see note 4*

Date [ ][ ] 19[ ]   Time —
day month year

Give the name and address if different from above —

Where on the premises or site —
and
Normal activity carried on there

ENV

Complete the following sections D, E, F & H if you have ticked boxes, 1, 2, 3 or 5 in Section A. Otherwise go straight to Sections G and H.

D The injured person — *see note 5*

Full name and address —

Age [ ]   Sex [ ]   Status *(tick box)* —
(M or F)

Employee		Self employed		Trainee (YTS)	
	10		11		12
Trainee (other)				Any other person	
	13				14

Trade, occupation or job title —

Nature of injury or condition and the part of the body affected —

F2508 (rev 1/86)   *continued*

Figure 2.33   Sample accident form

shock the casualty will become pale and their skin become clammy from sweating. They may feel faint, have blurred vision, feel sick and complain of thirst. Reassure the casualty that everything that needs to be done is being done. Loosen tight clothing and keep them warm and dry until help arrives. DO NOT move the patient unnecessarily or give them anything to drink.

E Kind of accident - *see note 6*

Indicate what kind of accident led to the injury or condition (*tick one box*) —

Contact with moving machinery or material being machined ☐ 1	Injured whilst handling lifting or carrying ☐ 5
Struck by moving, including flying or falling, object. ☐ 2	Slip, trip or fall on same level ☐ 6
Struck by moving vehicle ☐ 3	Fall from a height* ☐ 7
Struck against something fixed or stationary ☐ 4	*Distance through which person fell ☐ (metres)

Trapped by something collapsing or overturning ☐ 8	Exposure to an explosion ☐ 12
Drowning or asphyxiation ☐ 9	Contact with electricity or an electrical discharge ☐ 13
Exposure to or contact with a harmful substance ☐ 10	Injured by an animal ☐ 14
Exposure to fire ☐ 11	Other kind of accident (give details in Section H) ☐ 15

Spaces below are for office use only. ☐

F Agent(s) involved — *see note 7*

Indicate which, if any, of the categories of agent or factor below were involved (*tick one or more of the boxes*) —

Machinery/equipment for lifting and conveying ☐ 1	Process plant, pipework or bulk storage ☐ 5
Portable power or hand tools ☐ 2	Any material, substance or product being handled, used or stored. ☐ 6
Any vehicle or associated equipment/ machinery ☐ 3	Gas, vapour, dust, fume or oxygen deficient atmosphere ☐ 7
Other machinery ☐ 4	Pathogen or infected material ☐ 8

Live animal ☐ 9	Ladder or scaffolding ☐ 13
Moveable container or package of any kind ☐ 10	Construction formwork, shuttering and falsework ☐ 14
Floor, ground, stairs or any working surface ☐ 11	Electricity supply cable, wiring, apparatus or equipment ☐ 15
Building, engineering structure or excavation/underground working ☐ 12	Entertainment or sporting facilities or equipment ☐ 16
	Any other agent ☐ 17

Describe briefly the agents or factors you have indicated —

G Dangerous occurrence or dangerous gas fitting — *see notes 8 and 9*

Reference number of dangerous occurrence ☐

Reference number of dangerous gas fitting ☐

H Account of accident, dangerous occurrence or flammable gas incident - *see note 10*

Describe what happened and how. In the case of an accident state what the injured person was doing at the time —

Signature of person making report ☐   Date ☐

Employer's responsibilities

An employer must provide adequate first aid equipment and on large sites, appoint a qualified first aider. Where only a few people are employed, someone should be nominated to take charge in the event of an accident occurring.

Accident reports

Every accident should be reported to the employer and the details of the accident and treatment given entered in an 'accident book'. Failure to do so may influence the payment of compensation later. Figure 2.33 illustrates a typical accident report form.

Hazardous substances, materials and processes

Most substances and materials are safe providing they are handled or worked on sensibly and with proper precautions. Almost anything can be dangerous of course if handled or used irresponsibly. The same is true of processes, which in general covers the things done (often with the aid of tools and equipment) to materials. Some materials and processes require extra care; a few need extreme caution. It is important to know what the hazards are, when they occur, and how they can be prevented. Usually prevention will involve the use of protective clothing and equipment.

Your responsibilities

Your employer will provide most items of protective equipment (though not protective clothing unless you are lucky) and will make sure you know when and how to use them. It is your responsibility to use the equipment provided for your safety and to take care of it. Failure to do so may mean you are breaking not only company rules, but the law; and it could result in accident and injury to yourself, and others.

Fumes and vapours

Fumes and vapours are most hazardous in confined spaces. In the open air they will usually disperse. Adhesives, resins, solvents, paints and paint stripper all produce fumes and vapours. When these substances are used inside buildings, doors and windows should be opened to create a through draught if possible. If this cannot be done or if it does not prevent a build up of fumes, it may be necessary to use breathing equipment.

Vapours are often inflammable. The substances which produce inflammable vapours should not be stored, opened or used near naked lights or any equipment (such as blowlamps or power tools) which might produce a spark. Make sure stoppers and caps are replaced after use and mop up spillages immediately. Keep in the workplace only the quantity of liquid needed for the job and return any not used to the flammable liquids store.

Fumes and vapours can also be produced by the heating of metals (in welding and flame-cutting for example).

Lead dust and fumes

Lead poisoning is usually caused by breathing in lead dust, fumes and vapours, though it may be caused by consuming food which has become contaminated. In certain circumstances, lead may be absorbed through the skin. Since the major hazard is lead dust or vapour it can affect anybody nearby – not just those working with the materials or substances from which these are released.

Lead-based paints are one source of this hazard.

Care is needed both in applying and removing them. Respiratory (breathing) equipment should be worn when applying lead-based paint and it must not be sprayed on. The safest method of removing old coatings of paint is with 'wet and dry' abrasive paper, using plenty of water to reduce the amount of dust produced. Removing the paint with a blow-lamp will produce poisonous fumes, and 'dry' rubbing releases excessive amounts of dust.

Lead in its more familiar form is used in roofwork, for chimney flashings and guttering. This involves a process called 'lead-burning' in which the material is heated before being formed into the shape required. Lead-burning produces fumes and may require the use of breathing apparatus.

Lead poisoning can occur through contamination – dust being carried from clothes or hands on to food and into the mouth. Overalls should be removed and hands washed before touching food or drink. Smoking should also be avoided where there is any risk of contamination.

Dusts and fibres

Dust and fibres are released when certain materials are worked on or handled and can harm eyes, lungs, and in some cases the skin. Brick, masonry, concrete, timber, plastics and other hard materials release dust when worked on with cutting or drilling tools. If there is any danger of material entering the eyes or lungs, protective equipment and clothing will be required.

The harmful effect of asbestos dust on the lungs is now well-known, and blue asbestos is considered so harmful that it is no longer used in building work or building products in this country. It was widely used before the dangers were recognised, particularly for lagging and insulation of pipework. Everyone, especially those engaged in demolition or maintenance work, should be alert to the hazards of this material and should not deal with it on their own initiative, but seek advice.

Other types of asbestos are still found, for example in asbestos cement roofing materials, in insulation boards and in the braking mechanism of vehicles. The main dangers occur when asbestos is cut or drilled, or when it is otherwise disturbed – as during repair or demolition work. It is then that the harmful dusts are released. The handling and use of asbestos is controlled by law under The Asbestos Regulations, 1969. Anyone involved in this work should be fully trained and protected against dust hazards.

Flame-producing equipment

Fire hazards exist in processes or operations employing flame-producing equipment such as welding and cutting equipment, gas torches and blow lamps. Butane gas torches are used for a variety of purposes by most trades and often form part of the tool kit.

A few precautions are necessary before and after using this equipment. Before beginning work, check there are no combustible materials in the work area (Figure 2.34). Clear away any rubbish or litter and make sure adjacent timbers and anything else which cannot be removed and might catch fire is protected from heat and flame. This can be done by shielding it with non-flammable material.

Figure 2.34 Check there are no combustible materials in the work area

Remember that metalwork (such as pipes and conduits) can conduct heat to combustible materials such as floor and ceiling joists. For this reason it is essential to make a further check when the job is done to ensure that nothing has been left smouldering.

Blow lamps and torches must not be left burning when they are not in use. Finally, make sure a means of extinguishing any outbreak of fire is kept readily to hand.

Welding and flame-cutting

These processes should only be undertaken by those fully trained in the use of the equipment. They are likely to produce splattering of hot metals, sparks and fumes, all of which can be harmful to anybody without the necessary protective equipment. Unless under instruction in the use of the apparatus, stay clear of the area in which it is being used.

Liquified petroleum gas

Liquified petroleum gas (or LPG) is widely used in construction and building work as a fuel for burners, heaters and gas torches. The liquid, which comes in cylinders and containers, is highly flammable and needs careful handling and storage.

Whether in use or stored, cylinders must be kept upright, i.e. with the valve uppermost. When the cylinder is not in use the valve should be closed (check that it is before storing a cylinder) and the protective dust cap should be in place. When handling cylinders, do not drop them or allow them to come into violent contact with other cylinders. When using a cylinder with an appliance ensure it is connected properly in accordance with the instructions you have been given, and that it is at a safe distance from the appliance or equipment it is feeding.

When not in use, the cylinders will be stored with other flammable gases in a special storage area. Usually a stock of cylinders will be grouped together, with empty cylinders separated from those containing gas. If you are asked to store empty or full cylinders, make sure you understand the arrangement of containers inside the storage area and follow it. Do not smoke in this area.

It is essential to make sure the gas does not leak. LPG is heavier than air; if it leaks, it will not disperse in the air but sink to the lowest point and form an explosive concentration – which could be ignited by a spark. Leakages are especially dangerous in basements, trenches and excavations because the gas cannot flow out if it is below ground level.

Other hazardous substances and processes

Skin contact with pitch, bitumen and tar should be avoided; these substances are also applied hot and involve the use of heating equipment. They require care in handling especially when filling boilers and pouring into buckets – which should never be overfilled. Similar care is needed when working with molten metals.

Highly flammable liquids and petroleum mixtures

These substances and liquids will be kept in the flammable materials storage area. They will include cellulose thinners, adhesive solutions, solvents and paint strippers. The hazards involved in using such substances have already been described. In the store, a considerable quantity of them will be kept in one place, and the danger of releasing inflammable vapours, with the consequent risk of fire, is greatly increased. Keep this in mind if you visit the store to obtain a supply of one or other of these substances.

Safety check

The following rules should be observed:

- check the labels on the containers and make sure you use the correct substance for the job you have to do

- if you have to decant the liquid into another container, do it outside the store
- make sure caps and stoppers are replaced on the containers used
- return containers to their proper place in the store – do not muddle them up with other containers
- never return inflammable liquids to the store in unmarked containers; nobody else will know what is in them, and you yourself may forget
- if you intend to use a substance in your work, read any manufacturer's directions, instructions and warnings on the container first
- in the event of fire, raise the alarm immediately.

Fire prevention and control

Fires do a great deal of costly damage every year on construction sites and in other places where building work is done. They destroy property and materials, injure people and sometimes cause loss of life. Every effort must be made to prevent fires. Those which do break out must be controlled and extinguished.

In case of fire

You will be told about emergency procedures at your place of work. The point of such procedures is that in the event of a fire everyone should know what to do, *immediately*. These procedures will cover such matters as the location of alarms, fire-fighting equipment, emergency exits, escape routes and assembly points, and will name the person responsible for taking charge and summoning the fire brigade. The procedures must be known and followed in an emergency; it will be too late to learn them once a fire has started.

Emergency exits and escape routes must always be kept clear of obstruction, as must the signs indicating where they are. Fire extinguishers should be in their correct locations; if they are moved somebody will have to waste time looking for them. Remember that the whole point of having emergency procedures is that everyone knows what they have to do immediately the emergency arises.

General procedure

In the event of a fire:

- raise the alarm
- turn off all machinery and power
- close doors and windows, but *do not* lock or bolt them
- try to deal with the fire if you can do so safely but do not risk becoming trapped
- if you are not involved in fighting the fire, leave calmly using the emergency exits and go to your assembly point.

Nature of fire

A fire will continue to burn as long as three factors are present in combination (Figure 2.35).

Fuel – any substance (liquid, solid or gas) will burn given oxygen and a high enough temperature.

Figure 2.35   Removing any one of these factors will extinguish the fire

Heat – every fuel will begin to burn at a certain temperature. It is called the 'minimum ignition temperature' and varies, depending on the fuel. Solids and liquids give off vapour when heated and it is this vapour which ignites. Some liquids, however, do not have to be heated – they give off vapour at normal room temperature: petrol and white spirits are common examples.

Oxygen – usually exists in sufficient quantities in air to keep a fire burning.

Isolating or removing any one of these factors from the combination will extinguish the fire. There are three basic ways of achieving this:

- starving the fire of fuel by removing this element
- smothering, i.e. isolating the fire from the supply of oxygen by blanketing it with foam, sand etc.
- cooling – using water to lower the temperature.

Preventing fires

The majority of fires begin with small outbreaks which burn unnoticed until they have a secure hold. Most fires could be prevented with more care and by following some simple common sense rules. The main precautions to be taken and methods of prevention are outlined below.

Bonfires

It is dangerous to light bonfires of waste materials where they cannot be attended to or where nobody can keep an eye on them. Likewise it is asking for trouble to leave fires smouldering when everyone has left work. Waste material should be burnt well away from boundary fences, buildings, storage areas, and in fact anything that might accidentally catch fire.

Combustible refuse

Any rubbish which will burn is 'combustible refuse', including rags soaked with oil, paint or spirits, scraps of wood, paper, packaging and other materials. These materials are a fire risk and should not be allowed to pile up in odd corners, especially not in buildings. Cloths and rags soaked with inflammable substances should be placed in metal bins (with lids) kept for the purpose. Other refuse should be removed to collection points as soon as possible.

Heating appliances

These are usually provided to heat site huts and similar places. Because they provide heat, they can also be a cause of fires. Clothing and anything else which might catch fire should be kept well away from heaters, particularly those with burners. Fuel supplies must be kept outside the building. Oil heaters should never be filled while alight. If you are made responsible for a heater, make sure it is shut off at the end of the working day.

Electrical equipment

The most common cause of fire in electrical equipment is misuse or neglect. Circuits are often overloaded by using too many pieces of equipment or wrongly rated fuses, causing overheating which may in turn lead to fire. Equipment which is constantly in use, particularly portable equipment such as power tools, can become damaged or worn in ways which increase the risk of electrical faults and fires. Cables are especially vulnerable to damage; if the sheath is split the insulation and conductors will be exposed.

Flammable gases and vapours

Because they are highly inflammable and can ignite with a spark, concentrations of gases and vapours are extremely dangerous. It is worth emphasising the importance of ventilating the areas where these substances are being used, and of not using any spark or flame-producing tools or apparatus in these areas. (See also p. 40)

Flame-producing equipment

The important points are to check (before beginning the job) for combustible materials which might be ignited by the equipment, to work carefully, and to check that nothing is left smouldering when the job is finished. (See also p. 41)

Other causes of fire

Carelessly discarded cigarette ends and matches cause fires on building sites as elsewhere. Throwing hot ashes, caustic materials and inflammable substances into waste bins or on to rubbish dumps can also start fires.

When a fire does break out, the seriousness of the blaze and the amount of damage it does may depend on how much attention has been given to fire precautions; for example, whether refuse has been cleared away, and flammable liquids placed in fireproof lockers, or whether access to the area has been kept clear, and fire extinguishers are available in known locations, etc.

Types of fire extinguishing agents

Different types of fire have to be dealt with in different ways and with different extinguishing agents (Figure 2.36). An 'agent' is the material or substance used to put the fire out, and is usually (but not always) contained in a fire extinguisher with a mechanism for spraying on to the fire. It is important to know the right type of agent for particular types of fire; using the wrong one can make things worse.

Extinguishing fires

Wood, paper, cloth etc.

Cooling with water is the most effective way of extinguishing fires involving these materials. The jet of water should be played on to the base of the fire and then gradually upwards.

Flammable liquids

Fires involving flammable liquids should be smothered. The aim is to cover the entire surface of the burning liquid; this has the effect of cutting off the supply of air (and thus oxygen) to the fire and stifling the flames. Foam, dry powder or carbon dioxide extinguishers, fire blankets or sand may be used on fires of this type. Water should never be used on burning liquids – it merely spreads the fire further.

Gas and liquefied gases

Extreme caution is necessary in dealing with liquefied gases. If an appliance fed from a cylinder catches fire, the supply of gas should be turned off at the cylinder. When the cylinder itself is endangered by fire there is a risk of explosion: the safest course is to raise the alarm and leave the fire to be dealt with by someone who understands the dangers. Dry powder extinguishers are used on this type of fire, although overheated gas cylinders must be cooled with jets of water.

Electrical equipment

Carbon dioxide, dry powder and vaporising liquid (BCF) extinguishers can be used to deal with fires in electrical equipment. Dry sand or fire blankets may also be suitable in some circumstances. Portable fire-fighting equipment should not be used, however, on electrical apparatus which has not been disconnected from the supply. Foam or liquid (e.g. water) extinguishers must not be used on electrical equipment at all.

USE OF FIRE EXTINGUISHERS						
	Red	Cream	Black	Blue	Green	Red
TYPE OF FIRE RISK	water	Foam	Carbon dioxide	Dry powder	Vaporizing liquid	Fire blanket
Paper, wood and textiles	✓	✓	✓	✓	✓	Can be used for smothering all types of fire
Flammable liquids and gases	✗	✓	✓	✓	✓	
Electrical hazard	✗	✗	✓	✓	✓	
Machinery and vehicles	✗	✗	✓	✓	✓	
Suitable ✓			Unsuitable ✗			

Figure '2.36   Types of fire extinguishing agents

Where fires in sensitive (and expensive) electronic equipment have to be dealt with, the use of dry powder extinguishers should be avoided if possible; although suited to the type of fire, the powder could seriously damage the equipment. BCF extinguishers need to be used with care in confined spaces, since they produce fumes which can be dangerous.

In extinguishing electrical fires, the jet should be directed to the edge of the fire and with a sweeping motion to the far edges until the flames are extinguished.

Burning clothing

Dry powder extinguishers may be used on burning clothing. Alternatively a fire blanket can be used, the person wearing the clothing being laid on the blanket which is then wrapped around them to extinguish the flames. The blanket should be left in place while medical assistance is sought.

General measures

Gas and electricity supplies in the area of the fire should be turned off as quickly as possible. Combustible materials will provide the fire with fuel and should be moved out of reach of the flames if this can be done safely. Closing doors and windows (but *not* locking them) will limit the amount of oxygen fed to the fire and also help to prevent it spreading.

Anybody not engaged in fighting the fire should leave the building or area immediately the fire alarm is raised and go to the designated assembly point. Failure to do this may mean that person will be unaccounted for – and others may have to put themselves at risk searching for him or her.

When leaving buildings make sure fire doors are closed. If there is a lift in the building, do not use it; it may fail and you might be trapped.

Reporting of fires

All fires, however small, must be investigated. The purpose of an investigation is to ensure that the causes are learned and steps can then be taken to prevent the same kind of accident occurring again. Fires must be reported so that this investigation can take place.

Questions for you

1. State *three* of the main objectives of the Health and Safety at Work Act.
   (a) _____
   (b) _____
   (c) _____

2. State *two* duties of employees under the Health and Safety at Work Act.
   (a) _____
   (b) _____

3. Name *three* notices or certificates that must be displayed on a building site.
   (a) _____
   (b) _____
   (c) _____

4. Name *four* types of safety sign that may be displayed on a construction site.
   (a) _____
   (b) _____
   (c) _____
   (d) _____

5. Name *five* plumbing work operations where it is essential to use protective equipment. Name the item of protective equipment in each case.
   (a) _____
   (b) _____
   (c) _____
   (d) _____
   (e) _____

6. Name *three* types of fire extinguisher which may be used on a fire caused by flammable liquid or gas.
   (a) _____
   (b) _____
   (c) _____

7. To avoid injuries when lifting heavy weights from ground level, a plumber should:
   _____
   _____

8. Describe the basic difference between a burn and a scald.
   _____
   _____

9. What do the initials LPG stand for?
   _____

10. Name the *three* factors essential for a fire to continue to burn.
    (a) _____
    (b) _____
    (c) _____

11. By law an industrial accident must be reported without delay if it involves:
    (a) hospital treatment
    (b) two or more persons
    (c) site visitors
    (d) absence from work longer than three days.

12. Mobile scaffolding should be fitted with:
    (a) locking wheels
    (b) lifting handles
    (c) wheels at one end only
    (d) an independent ladder.

13. Which one of the following groups of materials is potentially the most dangerous to health?
    (a) brick, plaster, cement
    (b) sawdust, steel, PVA adhesive
    (c) timber, plastic, glass paper
    (d) asbestos, lead, mercury

14. Before operating a machine, an employee must:
    (a) know the installation cost of the machine
    (b) be able to carry out all necessary repairs and maintenance
    (c) have training in the safe use of the machine
    (d) have written permission from the foreman.

15. The purpose of timbering trenches dug for drains is to:
    (a) provide fixings for drain pipes
    (b) assist workers in getting in and out of the trench
    (c) support the walls of the excavation
    (d) ensure that the drains are laid to the correct gradient.

16. Which fire extinguisher should *not* be used on electrical fires?
    (a) dry powder
    (b) carbon dioxide
    (c) foam
    (d) vaporizing liquid

17. Tilting the head backward when giving mouth-to-mouth resuscitation ensures:
    (a) an effective breathing position for the rescuer
    (b) a clear airway into the lungs of the victim
    (c) a good supply of blood to the victim's brain
    (d) the victim's chest will rise and fall automatically.

18. When treating an unconscious person for electric shock a number of steps need to be taken immediately:
    (1) switch off the supply
    (2) seek medical help
    (3) treat the burns
    (4) carry out artificial respiration
    (5) keep the patient warm
    What is the corrrect sequence of events?
    (a) 2, 1, 3, 5, 4   (c) 3, 5, 1, 2, 4
    (b) 1, 2, 3, 4, 5   (d) 1, 4, 2, 5, 3

19. When an accident victim is suffering from shock, the correct initial treatment would be to keep them:
    (a) sitting down in the open air
    (b) lying down in a cool place
    (c) lying down warm and quiet
    (d) mobile by walking.

20. Before mounting an abrasive wheel, the operator should
    (a) be at least 16 years of age
    (b) be trained and certified to do so
    (c) consult the Woodworking Machines Regulations
    (d) get permission from his or her supervisor.

21. Which one of the following is the correct procedure to be adopted for severe external bleeding from an arm wound if no dressing is available?
    (a) wash the wound thoroughly
    (b) appy a splint
    (c) hold the sides of the wound firmly together
    (d) apply an antiseptic lotion.

22. In order to develop an awareness of safe working practices on site, it is essential that all personnel know the:
    (a) dangers that exist
    (b) building regulations
    (c) first-aid procedures
    (d) safety officer's name.

23. Before applying a dry dressing to a simple burn, it is essential to:
    (a) apply ointment
    (b) cool the burn area with cold water
    (c) apply a cold cream
    (d) clean the burn area with antiseptic lotion.

24. If solvent cement has a flash point of 7 °C, this indicates that the cement:
    (a) cannot be used when the temperature is lower than 7 °C
    (b) has a constant temperature of 7 °C
    (c) gives off a vapour that will ignite when the temperature is above 7 °C
    (d) must not be used when the temperature is above 7 °C.

25. An improvement notice issued by the Health and Safety Executive requires the contractor to comply with the notice within:
    (a) 24 hours
    (b) 21 days
    (c) 28 days
    (d) 3 months.

26. Spontaneous combustion is caused by:
    (a) reduction
    (b) chemical action
    (c) combustion ratio
    (d) vapour pressure.

27. Whilst at work, all employees have a duty at all times to:
    (a) ensure site security as required
    (b) service plant and equipment
    (c) maintain their own safety and that of fellow employees
    (d) provide the necessary waterproof clothing.

28. To comply with safety regulations, a record book must be kept on site containing records of all:
    (a) hours of work
    (b) accidents
    (c) safety equipment
    (d) potential safety hazards.

29. Wooden ladders are treated with clear wood preservatives and varnish to:
    (a) give the ladder added flexibility
    (b) give a better grip on the stiles of the ladder
    (c) keep the surfaces smooth and allow the wood to breathe
    (d) enable any cracks or flaws in the wood to be seen.

30. The main function of a guard rail on a tubular scaffold is to:
    (a) provide a hand hold whilst working on the scaffold
    (b) prevent the loosening of the vertical standards of the scaffold
    (c) prevent persons from falling off the working platform

Basic plumbing and electrical principles

In the pages that follow you will gain an understanding of:

- Materials
- Properties of materials
- Pipes, joints and fittings
- Pipe fixing
- Cold water storage
- Hot water storage
- Corrosion
- Tools and equipment
- Water supply
- Electricity supply

Materials

Introduction

The installation of pipework systems for the supply of cold and hot water, heat and gas, together with the systems for the removal of surface, waste and foul water, form the major part of day-to-day work for plumbers. Included in the operations must be the manufacture and fitting of weathering components to roofs and the outsides of buildings. This means that it is essential for the competent plumber to have a comprehensive understanding of the characteristics, properties and performance of materials in current use.

British Standards

The British Standards Institution was founded in 1901 to standardize industrial activities such as design, installation and manufacturing practice. The British Standards Specifications refer to standards of manufacture, for example low carbon steel tube is made to conform with the specification contained in BS 1387.

British Standard Codes of Practice are recommendations related to methods of good practice in installation work, for example CP 5572: 1978 deals with sanitary pipework. By having standards which have been agreed by manufacturers and industrial experts, the process of obtaining the right materials and correct design and installation techniques or procedure is made easier, and leads to a better quality of completed job. Architects and others involved with design work need only to specify that material must conform to the relevant British Standard and that work is to be undertaken and installed in accordance with the relevant British Standard Code of Practice, to ensure that materials used and work undertaken is of a satisfactory and

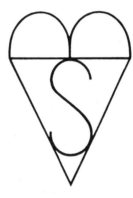

Figure 3.1   British Standard kitemark

acceptable standard. Figure 3.1 shows the British Standard kitemark.

It is likely that as Great Britain moves closer to Europe, both economically and politically, that British Standards will become integrated in a system of European Standards.

Categories of materials

Materials can be divided into different categories in a variety of ways. The easiest division is into: *metals* and *non-metals*.

Metals differ from non-metals in chemical properties as well as in the more obvious physical properties. There is not a rigid dividing line between the two categories. Some metals possess characteristics of both groups, while some non-metal materials behave like metals in some respects, for instance the conducting of electricity.

Table 3 gives examples of some of the differences between the two categories.

Table 3

Metals	Non-metals
Characteristic appearance, 'metallic' sheen or gloss	No particular characteristic apearance
Good conductor of heat	Usually poor conductor of heat, may be insulator
Good conductor of electricity	Usually poor conductor of electricity, may be insulator (except carbon, silicon)
Electrical resistance usually increases as temperature rises	Electrical resistance usually decreases as temperature rises
Density usually high	Density usually low
Melting point and boiling point usually high	Melting point and boiling point usually low

Table 5

Pure metal	Alloy
Aluminium	Brass
Chromium	Bronze
Copper	Chrome-vanadium steel
Gold	Duralumin
Iron	Gunmetal
Lead	Invar
Magnesium	Nickel silver
Mercury	Pewter
Nickel	Rose's alloy
Platinum	Solder
Silver	Stainless steel
Sodium	White-metal (bearing metal)
Tin	
Tungsten	
Zinc	

Metals can be subdivided into *element metals* and *alloys*.

The element or pure metals are those which do not have any other metal or materials mixed with them.

Alloys are produced when two or more metals, or a metal and a non-metal, are blended together, usually by melting (see Table 4). Many alloys have useful properties which their parent metals do not possess. For example, a much lower melting point, as in the case of solders.

Table 4 Composition of common alloys

Alloy	Main elements
Brass	Copper and zinc
Bronze	Copper and tin
Gunmetal	Copper, tin and zinc
Pewter	Tin and lead
Steel	Iron and carbon
Steel (stainless)	Iron, chromium and nickel
Soft solder	Lead and tin

Table 5 lists many metals which are used by the plumber.

Metals may be further classified as:

- ferrous metals, that is those which contain iron
- non-ferrous metals, i.e. those that do not contain iron.

The basic difference between the two categories is that, with the exception of stainless steels, ferrous metals will rust when in contact with water and oxygen. Also, ferrous metals may be magnetized.

Non-ferrous metals do not rust, although they may corrode under certain circumstances, and they are non-magnetic.

Ferrous metals

Grey cast iron

This is a mixture of iron with 3.5 to 4.5 per cent carbon and very small amounts of silicon, manganese, phosphorous and sulphur. The carbon is in the form of 'flake graphite' and it is these flakes which make the material very brittle. The iron fractures easily along the lines of the flakes.

Cast iron is hard and has a much higher resistance to rusting than steel. It is used for drainage and discharge system pipework, appliance components, access covers and frames. Its melting point is 1200 °C.

Ductile cast iron

This has approximately the same carbon content as grey cast iron. The difference is in the shape, size and distribution of the carbon particles which are changed from flakes into ball-like nodules or 'spheroids'. The change is due to alloying the iron and carbon with magnesium compounds before casting. Subsequent heat treatment at 750 °C changes the brittle iron carbide into softer, ductile ferrite.

Used to make pipes for gas mains and drainage pipelines, ductile cast iron has the strength and ductility of lower grade steel and the high corrosion resistance of cast iron.

Wrought iron

This is the purest commercial form of iron, containing very little carbon. Made from heat-treated cast iron, it is rolled or hammered to give it the required grain structure. It is still used for chains, horse-shoes, gates and ornamental iron-work. Because of its high cost it is no longer used for pipes or fittings.

Malleable iron (malleable cast iron)

Malleable iron is white cast iron in which the carbon has combined with the iron to form iron carbide. This results in a very hard and brittle material which is annealed to soften it for commercial use.

Most of the ferrous pipe fittings used in conjunction with low carbon steel pipe in internal installations are malleable iron.

Low carbon steel (LCS)

This is another mixture of iron and carbon. Its carbon content is between 0.15 and 0.25 per cent. The material has a wide use and is commonly known as mild steel, although its correct title is low carbon steel (LCS). In building, it is used for general structural work, pipes, sheets and bars. It can be pressed, drawn, forged and welded easily.

The LCS tube used by plumbers is manufactured to BS 1387 in three grades of weight: light, medium and heavy.

The outside diameter of each grade of tube is similar, the difference being the tube wall thickness. The grades are identified by 50 mm wide colour band coding: brown, red and blue, to correspond with light, medium and heavy grades. Low carbon steel tubes used for domestic water supplies must be protected with a zinc coating; they are said to be 'galvanized'.

Tubes are generally available in 3 m and 6 m lengths, with bore size ranging from 6 mm to 150 mm.

Stainless steel

This material is mainly used in plumbing in tube form for domestic water and gas services or for the manufacture of sanitary appliances such as sink units, urinals, WC pans etc.

The metal is an alloy and has a composition of chromium (18 per cent), nickel (10 per cent), manganese (1.25 per cent), silicon (0.6 per cent), a maximum carbon content of 0.08 per cent, the remainder being iron with small amounts of sulphur and phosphorous. The chromium and nickel provide the material with its shiny appearance and its resistance to corrosion, this being due to a microscopic film of chromium oxide, which forms on the tube surface and prevents further oxidation.

Stainless steel tube is manufactured to BS 4127 and is available in nominal bore sizes ranging from 6 mm to 35 mm in one grade only (light gauge) with an average wall thickness of 0.7 mm. The outside diameter of the tube is comparable to copper tube manufactured to BS 2871 Table X so that most types of capillary and compression fittings can be used. The mechanical strength of stainless steel is much higher than that of copper giving it greater resistance to damage and a better ability to support itself. It therefore will require less fixing positions during installation. Stainless steel tubes of 15 mm to 35 mm diameter are supplied in 3 m and 6 m lengths.

Non-ferrous metals

Aluminium

This is a useful metal because it is so light. It is much lighter than steel, and some of its alloys are as strong as steel. It is also a good conductor of heat and electricity. Aluminium and its alloys are therefore widely used where lightness and strength are needed. The material does not rust as ferrous metals do when exposed to the atmosphere. Although the surface does oxidize, this oxide film acts as protection against corrosive attack. Aluminium is primarily alloyed with copper, magnesium and silicon.

Aluminium is the most common metal in the earth's crust. It is found in common clay, although removal is a difficult and expensive process. The only suitable ore is bauxite, which contains alumina, or aluminium oxide. Producing aluminium from bauxite is very different from the usual methods of obtaining metals from their ores. Firstly the bauxite is crushed and heated with caustic soda. The alumina dissolves and leaves behind the impurities. The pure alumina obtained is then dissolved in molten cryolite, and aluminium is produced when electricity is passed through this solution.

Aluminium in a soft condition is malleable and ductile, thus giving it good working properties, although it will work harden if cold worked. Annealing is easily completed, but because of its low melting point, care must be taken to avoid overheating.

BS 1470 specifies five grades of aluminium, but only two (S1 and S1B) are recommended for roofwork. Grade S1 is known as super purity aluminium.

The two grades of aluminium (S1 and S1B) used for roofworks are obtainable in standard rolls of 8 m length, with widths of 150 mm, 300 mm, 600 mm and 900 mm. Two thicknesses are available, these being 0.7 mm (standard), generally used for flashings, and 0.9 mm (heavy duty), which is suitable for bays and situations where foot traffic may occur.

Antimony

This is a hard, grey, crystalline metal which expands slightly when it solidifies. It is principally used in alloys of lead and tin (solder) to produce a degree of hardness and make the alloy more resistant to corrosion.

Bronze

True bronzes are alloys containing copper and tin as the basic metals, but the name bronze has been so loosely applied that certain alloys containing no tin at all are sold as bronze.

The useful bronzes contain not less than 65 per cent of copper. As the tin content is increased the alloys become progressively harder, although bronzes containing above 25 per cent of tin become weak and brittle. On the other hand, if too much copper is present, the cast metal becomes porous. The properties of many bronzes may be greatly improved by the addition of a third element – lead. When zinc is present in this alloy the material is known as 'gunmetal'.

Phosphorous is added to some copper/tin alloys to deoxidize the metal prior to casting. These alloys are termed 'phosphor bronze' although the percentage of phosphorous added may be very low.

Chromium

This metal is plated on other metals and materials to protect them. It is hard and does not lose its shine through corrosion. Steel is made stainless by the addition of chromium and nickel. Nickel and chromium together form important alloys much used for plating and the manufacture of tools. Chromium is found as chromite, or chrome iron ore.

Copper

Copper is obtained from the ore copper pyrites. The USA is a very large producer, although most of the copper used in Great Britain comes from Canada, Chile and Zambia.

This metal is probably the most important of the non-ferrous metals and is used extensively in sheet, strip, rod, wire, tube and other fabricated forms. It is also employed in the making of a wide range of alloys, of which brass and bronze are best known.

Although copper is a comparatively inexpensive metal, physically and chemically it is closely allied to silver and gold, and there are many similarities in the properties of the three. The outstanding features of copper are its high malleability (particularly when in a soft or annealed state), its electrical and thermal conductivities and its good resistance to corrosion.

Copper exposed to air forms on its surface a natural protective skin or 'patina' which effectively prevents corrosive attack under most conditions. On copper exposed to the atmosphere the patina takes the form of a green covering of copper salts (mainly sulphate or carbonate). The formation of a some-what similar protective film also takes place on the interior surface of copper water pipes. This film is insoluble in water, making copper an ideal material for carrying water.

The first British Standard for copper tube was issued in 1936 to standardize the various sizes of tube on the basis of their outside diameter. Prior to this, copper tube had been used since the turn of the century, when jointing was achieved by screwed and socketed fittings which required a tube wall thick enough to thread. As time progressed and methods of jointing which did not require threading of the tube developed, the wall thicknesses of the tube were reduced, and tubes were identified as 'light gauge'.

Copper tube for use in the construction industry is manufactured to BS 2871. Part 1 defines three specifications of tube, which are denoted as Tables X, Y, and Z. Table X specifies the requirements for light gauge tube of half-hard temper. Table Z refers to tubes of hard temper, with an increased hardness which allows for reductions in wall thicknesses, but makes the tube unsuitable for bending. Tubes complying with Tables X and Z are not intended for below ground use. Table Y covers tube of either half-hard or fully annealed temper; this is tube that can be laid underground for the conveyance of water or gas.

The basic differences between these tubes is their temper and wall thicknesses, the wall thickness factor affecting the mass. A comparison of 15 mm diameter tube manufactured to the three different specifications is given in Table 6.

Table 6

Specification	Mass (kg/m)	Wall thickness (mm)
Table X	0.2796	0.7
Table Y	0.3923	1.0
Table Z	0.2031	0.5

Copper tubes to BS 2871 Part 1 Table X and Z (half-hard and hard tempered respectively) are available in standard lengths of up to 6 m. Tubes to Table X can be bent with the aid of a bending machine or spring or by sand loading. Tubes to Table Z are hard drawn and thin walled and should not be bent – changes of direction must be achieved with the use of fittings.

Tubes to BS 2871 Part 1 Table Y (annealed condition) can be obtained in standard coil lengths from approximately 10 m to 30 m (depending on diameter size). This tube in its soft condition can be bent by hand and is most commonly used for below ground service pipes, it can be obtained with a protective plastic covering fitted during manufacture for use in soils which have a corrosive nature.

Sheet copper is malleable and highly ductile so it can be easily worked particularly when in a soft or fully annealed state. Work hardening, however, occurs with cold working so as little manipulation as possible should be done.

As soon as the material becomes hard it should be annealed. This is carried out by heating to a dull red colour. The metal can then be allowed to cool naturally or may be doused with water to assist the cooling process.

Copper for weathering is available in the form of rectangular sheets or in strip form.

Strip copper is usually supplied in rolls or coils of varying length and width. The standard strip widths are 114 mm, 228 mm, 380 mm, 475 mm, 533 mm, and 610 mm. The length is determined by the thickness and mass of the roll which is usually limited to 25 kg or 50 kg to assist safe handling.

Sheet copper is obtainable in a variety of sizes, although standard sizes of 1.83 m × 0.91 m and 1.83 m × 0.61 m are normally specified. All copper for weathering purposes is sold by mass.

Lead

Lead is obtained from the ore galena and is mined and processed in many different parts of the world, the main producing countries being Australia, the USA, Canada, Mexico and Russia.

The name 'plumber' derives from the Latin name for lead which is plumbum. Lead is one of the six metals known to humanity from the early days of history, and the development of the use of lead in building work for sanitary, roofing and weathering purposes was also the development of the plumber's trade.

The ore galena is a compound of lead containing, in the pure form, 86.6 per cent lead and 13.4 per cent sulphur. Galena has a cubic crystalline structure, is very lustrous and of a dark grey colour. The lead produced from the smelting process usually contains small quantities of other metals, for example antimony, tin, copper, gold and silver, and these are removed as required by refining processes. The lead which is obtained possesses a very high degree of purity – a good commercial lead being over 99.9 per cent pure.

Lead is the softest of the common metals and has a very high ductility, malleability and corrosion resistance. It is capable of being shaped easily at normal temperatures without the need of periodic softening (lead does not appreciably work harden). Lead sheet and pipe are therefore easily worked with hand tools, and can readily be manipulated into the most complicated shapes. Lead is very seldom corroded by electrolysis attack when in contact with other metals.

Lead pipe, because it is soft and heavy, requires frequent or even continuous support along its length. It also requires a high degree of skill to install, and this, coupled with high initial cost and public fears about lead poisoning, means that lead pipe is not widely used nowadays. However, it is still specified for certain uses and in specialist situations, and thousands of buildings still contain lead pipes which from time to time need repair or alteration, so it is necessary for plumbers to have knowledge and experience of the material.

Lead pipe for other than chemical purposes is manufactured to BS 602 and BS 1085, the essential difference being the composition of the lead, which is in fact a lead alloy. Pipe manufactured to BS 602 must contain not less than 99.8 per cent lead. Lead pipe up to 25 mm bore is usually sold in coils of 20 m length or 50 kg mass, pipes from 25 mm to 50 mm bore are obtainable in coils of 12 m length or 50 kg mass.

Lead sheet is produced by either casting or milling. Cast lead is still made as a craft operation by the traditional method of running molten lead over a bed of prepared sand. A comparatively small amount is produced by specialist leadworking companies, mainly for their own use, in particular for replacing old cast lead roofs and for ornamental leadwork. There is no British Standard for this material. The available size of sheet is determined by the casting table bed size.

Milled sheet lead is manufactured on rolling mills. The process involves passing a slab of refined lead about 125 mm thick backwards and forwards through the mill until it is reduced to the required thickness.

Milled sheet lead is manufactured to BS 1178 and is supplied by the manufacturer cut to dimensions as required or as large sheets 2.4 m wide and up to 12 m length. Lead strip is defined as material ready cut into widths from 75 mm up to 600 mm. Supplied in coils, this is a very convenient form of lead sheet for most flashing and weathering applications. The thickness of lead is designated by a BS specification code number, and by an identifying colour. These are shown in Table 7 which also includes the relative thickness.

Table 7

BS code no.	Thickness (mm)	Colour	Weight (kg/m²)
3	1.25	Green	14.18
4	1.80	Blue	20.41
5	2.24	Red	25.40
6	2.50	Black	28.36
7	3.15	White	35.72
8	3.55	Orange	40.26

The thickness of sheet chosen for a particular situation or application depends upon several factors, for example roof design, type of building, shape and location of component, money available. Cost is of course an important consideration and so the thinnest lead to suit the particular fixing position will usually be used.

The thicknesses of lead sheet for various situations as recommended by the Lead Sheet Association are set out in Table 8.

Table 8

Fixing situation	BS code no.
Damp proof courses	3, 4 or 5
Pipe weatherings, chimney flashings	4 or 5
Soakers	3 or 4
Cornice weatherings	4, 5 or 6
Small flats with no foot traffic	4 or 5
Large flats with or without foot traffic	5, 6 or 7
Gutters, valley, box, parapet etc.	5 or 6
Dormer cheeks and roofs	4 or 5
Hip, ridge and cover flashings	4 or 5
Vertical claddings	4 or 5

Zinc

This metal is obtained from several ores, the most common being zinc blende, sphalerite and calamine. Commercial sheet zinc has low ductility and is the least malleable of common roofing metals. This means that manipulation is difficult when compared with materials such as lead or aluminium, and jointing or shaping is achieved by folding, cutting or soldering. These disadvantages have led to the development of zinc alloys.

Zinc alloys have good ductility, and a linear expansion rate of less than two thirds that of commercial quality zinc sheet (overcoming the problems of creep often associated with zinc sheet). Two of these alloys are currently available, namely zinc/lead and zinc/titanium, these being produced under the respective trade names of Metiflash and Metizinc.

Metiflash is very malleable and is most suitable for flashings and small weathering details such as bay window tops, dormers and canopies. Metizinc is most suitable for covering large roof areas.

Metiflash (zinc/lead) is obtainable in 10 m length rolls, in widths of 150 mm, 240 mm, 300 mm, 480 mm and 600 mm and with a thickness of 0.6 mm. Rolls of 6 m length with a width of 900 mm are also available.

Metizinc (zinc/titanium) can be obtained in sheets up to 3 m long by 1 m wide, although the standard sheet is 2.438 m × 0.914 m. Various thicknesses are available ranging from 0.2 mm to 2 mm, the usual thicknesses being the same as those for commercial zinc.

Commercial zinc is obtainable in sheets 2.438 m × 0.914 m with a recommended thickness of 0.6 mm for flashings and 0.8 mm for other roof areas. Zinc sheet has a grain which runs through the length of the sheet, and although this occurs in all rolled sheet metals the effect is of more significance in zinc, making it more difficult to obtain a sharp fold or turn along the length of a sheet than across its width. For this reason it is advisable to arrange weathering details so that the majority of folds or turns are made across the sheet, i.e. across the grain. In cold weather zinc becomes brittle and should be warmed slightly before folding is attempted, otherwise cracking or fracture may occur. Such folds should not be too sharp – a rounded fold with a radius at least twice the thickness of the metal will be satisfactory.

An electrolytic action is set up when zinc is in contact with copper in the presence of moisture, and for this reason zinc and copper should never be allowed to touch each other in roofing or as water service piping.

Non-metallic sheet

One of the most popular non-metallic sheet roofing materials is Nuralite. The material is manufactured from dacron and rockwool fibres blended together with bitumen.

Nuralite is intended primarily to replace zinc, copper, aluminium and lead as a fully supported roofing material, and is particularly suitable for flashings and other types of weathering accessories.

The material was introduced in the mid-1940s by British Uralite Limited, 'Nuralite' being its trade name. The material is semi-rigid which means it has a degree of natural flexibility, although any attempt to bend or form it at normal outside temperatures will result in fracture or tearing.

Shaping and forming is usually achieved by the application of a gentle heat (optimum moulding temperature 182 °C). The material has a low tensile strength and will tear if attempts are made to stretch it. Compared with metals, Nuralite has a low density. This lightness coupled with its low creep characteristics makes it satisfactory for vertical or steeply pitched surfaces.

Nuralite is available in standard sheets 2.4 m × 1 m, and is approximately 2 mm thick. Its mass is 2.6 kg/m^2.

Solders

A better understanding of the nature of the solders, and how to select one for a specific application, can be obtained by observing the melting characteristics of metals and alloys. Melting of pure metals is easy to describe as they transform from solid to liquid state at one temperature. The melting of alloys is more complicated as they may melt over a temperature range.

Solders of the tin/lead alloys constitute the largest portion of all solders in use. They are used for joining most metals. Impurities in tin/lead solders can result from carelessness in the refining and alloying operations, but can also be added inadvertently during normal usage. The soldering properties of tin/lead solders are affected by small traces of aluminium and zinc. As little as 0.005 per cent of either of these metals may cause lack of adhesion and grittiness. Above 0.02 per cent of iron in a tin/lead solder is harmful and will cause hardness and grittiness. The presence of above 0.5 per cent of copper will have the same harmful effects.

Antimony can play a dual role in tin/lead solders. Depending on the purpose for which the solder is to be used, it can be considered as either an impurity or as a substitute for some of the tin in the solder. When the amount of antimony is not more than 6 per cent of the tin content of the solder, it can be completely carried in solid solution by the tin. If the antimony content is more than the tin can carry in solid solution, tin/antimony components of high melting point crystallize out, making the solder gritty, brittle and sluggish.

Antimony content of up to 6 per cent of the tin content increases the mechanical properties of the solder but with slight impairment to the soldering characteristics. The use of lead/antimony/tin solders is not recommended on zinc or zinc-coated metals, such as galvanized iron. Solders containing antimony, when used on zinc or alloys of zinc, form an intermetallic compound, causing the solder to become brittle.

Tin/zinc solders are used for joining aluminium.

Corrosion of soldered joints in aluminium (electro-galvanic) is minimized if the metals in the joint are close to each other in the electrochemical series. The addition of silver to lead results in alloys which will wet steel and copper. Flow characteristics, however, are very poor. The addition of 1 per cent tin to a lead/silver solder increases the wetting and flow properties and, in addition, reduces the possibility of humid atmospheric corrosion.

All solders are alloys, and as mentioned previously the melting point of an alloy varies with the different percentages of element metals comprising the alloy (see Table 9). The graph in Figure 3.2 illustrates the various melting points of tin/lead solders.

Table 9 Composition and melting characteristics of soft solders

solder type	% metal content	melting range solidus (°C)	liquidus (°C)	practical soldering temperature (°C)
Tin	100	232	232	350
Tin/antimony	95/5	236	243	340
Tin/silver	96.5/3.5	221	221	355
Tin/copper	99/1	230	235	350
Tin/lead	50/50	183	212	250

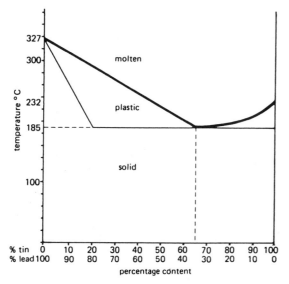

Figure 3.2   Tin/lead diagram

The soldering temperature when using lead solders is about 250°C, whereas for lead-free solders a temperature of about 350°C is required.

A solder with about 36 per cent lead and 64 per cent tin has the lowest melting point and changes from solid to liquid between 183 °C and 185 °C. This is known as the 'eutectic', which is the composition at which the alloy behaves as a pure metal. Adding either more lead or more tin raises the final melting point, although the alloy still begins to melt at about 185 °C. In its intermediate stage it becomes 'plastic' and may be 'wiped' or formed into its required shape or position before it becomes completely molten.

Plastics

The word 'plastics' came into being as a general description for many materials of a similar nature, such as celluloid, casein and bakelite. The name merely signifies that the material is capable of being moulded into shape. In this sense the word is not a suitable description for the many materials that have since been developed.

The term 'plastics' describes a group of man-made organic chemical compounds which can broadly be divided into two types – *thermoplastics* and *thermosetting plastics*.

Thermoplastics

Thermoplastics soften when heated and harden on cooling. They can be softened again afterwards provided that the heat applied is not sufficient to cause them to decompose. Among the thermoplastic materials used in plumbing work are polythene, polyvinyl chloride (PVC), polystyrene, polypropylene, acrylics (perspex) and nylon.

Thermosetting plastics

Thermosetting plastics are those which soften which first heated for moulding, and which then harden or set into a permanent shape which cannot afterwards be altered by the application of further heat. These are also called thermosetting resins. The most important of these are formaldehyde, phenol formaldehyde and polyester resins.

The advantages of plastic materials are their light weight, and the simple methods used in the jointing processes. Plastic materials used in plumbing have many common physical characteristics. Those used for pipes are invariably thermoplastics, all of which have a high resistance to corrosion and acid attack. They have a low specific heat, which implies that they do not absorb the same heat quantity as metals. They are also poor conductors of heat and electricity.

One of the disadvantages in the use of plastics is their high rate of linear expansion, although manufacturers make provision for this in the design of their components. Another disadvantage is that resistance to damage by fire attack is low. Plastics are not such stable materials as metals and are all, to some extent, affected by the ultra violet rays of the sunlight. This causes long term degradation or embrittlement of the material.

Most plastics in their natural state are clear and colourless, and to reduce the effects of degradation, manufacturers add a darkening substance or agent to give the material colour and body.

It is important for a plumber to be able to identify the type of plastics he or she is using, as the method of jointing suitable for one type may be unsuitable for another. Basic tests will be described which will enable him or her to correctly identify a particular material. Table 10 sets out typical properties of plastics used in building.

Polythene

Polythene pipes up to 150 mm nominal bore are manufactured to BS 3284 and are classified as 'low' or 'high' density. The low density pipe is comparatively flexible. High density polythene is more rigid and has a slightly higher melting temperature. Both types are resistant to chemical attack and are much used as a material for laboratory and chemical waste installations. Polythene is sufficiently elastic not to fracture if the water in the pipe should freeze, although normal frost precautions are recommended to prevent freezing and loss of supply.

Polypropylene

This material is in the same family group as polythene. It is tough, having both surface hardness and rigidity. It is able to withstand relatively high temperatures, and is in this respect superior to polythene, ABS or PVC.

Polypropylene can withstand boiling water temperature for short periods of time making it suitable material for the manufacture of traps. Methods of jointing are similar to those used for polythene, e.g. compression joints or 'O' ring couplings. Solvent welded joints are not suitable.

Polypropylene and polythene belong to the family of synthetic plastics, known as polyofins. They have a waxy touch and appearance, and if ignited burn with a flame similar to a paraffin wax candle.

Polyvinyl chloride

Generally abbreviated to PVC, this is possibly the most common plastic material used for drainage and

Table 10 Typical properties of plastics used in plumbing

Material	Density (kg/m)	Linear expansion per °C	Coefficient (mm/m)	Max. temperature recommended for continuous operation (°C)	Behaviour in fire
Polythene* low density	910	20×10^{-5}	0.2	80	Melts and burns like paraffin wax
high density					
Polypropylene	900	14×10^{-5}	0.14	104	Melts and burns like paraffin wax
Polymethyl methacrylate (acrylic)	1185	7×10^{-5}	0.07	80	Melts and burns readily
Rigid PVC (UPVC)	1395	5×10^{-5}	0.07	65	Melts and burns only with great difficulty
Post-chlorinated PVC (CPVC)	1300–1500	7×10^{-5}	0.07	100	Melts but burns only with great difficulty
Plasticized PVC	1280	7×10^{-5}	0.07	40–65	Melts, may burn, depending on plasticizer used
Acetal resin	1410	8×10^{-5}	0.08	80	Softens and burns fairly readily
ABS	1060	7×10^{-5}	0.07	90	Melts and burns readily
Nylon	1120	8×10^{-5}	0.08	80–120	Melts, burns with difficulty
Polycarbonate	1200	7×10^{-5}	0.07	110	Melts, burns with difficulty
Phenolic laminates	1410	3×10^{-5}	0.03	120	Highly resistant to ignition
GRP laminates	1600	2×10^{-5}	0.02	90–150	Usually inflammable Relatively flame-retardant grades are available

Key: UPVC = unplasticized polyvinyl chloride   GRP = glass-reinforced polyester   PVC = polyvinyl chloride   ABS = acrylonitrile/butadiene/styrene copolymer
*High density and low density polythene differ in their basic physical properties, the former being harder and more rigid than the latter. No distinction is drawn between them in terms of chemical properties or durability. The values shown are for typical materials but may vary considerably, depending on composition and method of manufacture.

discharge pipe systems. The material is a thermoplastic produced on the basic reaction of acetylene with hydrochloric acid in gas form in the presence of a catalyst. The material is rigid, smooth, light and resistant to corrosion.

PVC is often confused with polythene and polypropylene. One method of identifying the material is to drop a small piece of it into water, and if it sinks it is PVC which is heavier than water, whereas the other two materials are lighter and therefore float. PVC unlike many other plastics materials will not burn easily, another fact which can be used for its identification.

Unplasticized polyvinyl chloride (UPVC) is the basic material without softening additives. Plasticized polyvinyl chloride is produced by adding a small amount of rubber plasticizer to the basic material during the manufacturing process. The result is a slightly more flexible material which is more resistant to impact damage than UPVC. All UPVC pipes for cold water supply should comply with BS 3505.

Polyvinyl chloride for sanitary pipework should conform to BS 4514. This standard requires that the material should not soften below 70 °C for fittings and 81 °C for pipes and it should be capable of receiving discharge water at a higher temperature than these for short periods of time.

Jointing methods used include solvent welding, rubber 'O' ring joints and compression type couplings.

Acrylonitrile butadiene styrene

Known as ABS, this is a material used mainly for small diameter waste and discharge pipes or overflows. The material itself is a toughened polystyrene which can be extruded or moulded. It can withstand higher water temperatures for a longer period of time than PVC and for this reason some manufacturers produce full ABS waste systems. It also retains its strength against impact at very low temperatures thus providing greater resistance to physical damage. ABS has a duller matt appearance than PVC, and if ignited burns with a bright white flame. The material is slightly more dense than water and will therefore not float.

Acrylic (perspex)

This thermoplastic is tough and durable with good resistance to abrasion. The material can be transparent or opaque, it is easily machined and parts can be joined together by cementing. It is used mainly in plumbing for bathroom accessories.

Polystyrene

This is a white thermoplastic produced by the polymerization of styrene (vinyl benzine). This material is very light and brittle, and is mainly used for thermal insulation in granule, sheet or foam form.

Polytetra fluroethene (PTFE)

This material can be used at temperatures up to 300 °C, and because it is chemically inert it is used for lining pipes and components where chemical resistance is necessary. It is used by the plumber in tape or paste form as a sealant or jointing material.

Nylon

This is a thermoplastic material which is produced from phenol or benzine. It is rot proof and strong. Nylon is widely used in the form of a solid plastic, often as valve seatings, taps, gears and bearings. Moving nylon parts need no oiling because they slide easily over each other. The word nylon was made up by its inventors Du Pont.

Synthetic rubber

There are many forms of synthetic rubber, some of which contain a proportion of natural rubber. The most common synthetic rubber used in plumbing is called Neoprene which is generally used for the manufacture of 'O' ring seals for various jointing techniques. Neoprene is a trade name. The substance resists attack from oil, grease and heat, and is more stable against oxidation than natural rubber.

Ceramics

Sanitary equipment may be made from one of the three ceramic materials – fireclay, earthenware or vitreous china. These materials have different qualities and characteristics. Each is, therefore, suitable for different uses which may be divided broadly into public, industrial and private use.

Where rough or heavy usage is expected, strength is a most important factor, and this is the outstanding quality of both fireclay and vitreous china. For private purposes, where good appearance is important, vitreous china is used.

Fireclay

This ware is made from clay which can be fired at very high temperatures, resulting in an article both heavy and strong. Large articles can be made in fireclay with the minimum of distortion, due to the shrinkage which occurs during firing and is inevitable with all ceramic materials. Fireclay is used in the manufacture of large sanitary appliances such as sinks, urinal ranges, laboratory sinks and special hospital fittings. Fireclay is heavy in weight and has a buff coloured porous body protected by the hard glaze which covers it. It has the highest initial cost of the three ceramic materials.

Earthenware

Ball and china clays are the most important constituents of earthenware, which is considerably lighter in weight than fireclay. This material has a pleasing appearance due to the clean lines and sharp definition which characterize articles manufactured from it. Earthenware has a white porous body protected by a hard impervious glaze.

Vitreous china

This material is made from the same clays as earthenware but feldspar is also included. This gives two additional qualities, great strength and a vitrified body impervious to water. It is lighter in weight and less costly than fireclay, and has the same clean lines as earthenware. Apart from industrial use it is particularly good for hotel and household use since it combines pleasing appearance and strength.

Since the body is vitrified, vitreous china does not rely upon its skin of glaze for its sanitary properties, and is glazed only to give it a smooth, glossy finish and to allow easy cleaning. Should the glaze become damaged, the appliance remains impervious to water, and, therefore, completely sanitary. For this reason, and because of its strength and moderate cost, vitreous china is the most economic pottery material, both from the point of view of initial cost and maintenance costs.

During firing, vitreous china tends to distort more readily than either fireclay or earthenware, and for this reason great care has to be taken to ensure that the finished articles are of good shape. For this reason some of the larger sanitary appliances such as sinks, urinals and hospital equipment are not manufactured in vitreous china.

Vitreous china lends itself to the manufacture of articles of curved and rounded design, which minimizes the production problem of good shape and results in articles that are practical in use and conform to contemporary ideas of good practice in design.

Weight for weight, vitreous china is the strongest of the three ceramic materials used in the manufacture of sanitary appliances.

Properties of materials

Strength

One of the main properties of a material is its strength, i.e. its ability to withstand force or resist stress. Stress can be applied to a material in many ways (see Figure 3.3), for instance:

(a) Tensile, or stretching.
(b) Compressive, crushing, or squeezing.
(c) Bending, which is both (a) and (b) on either side of an axis.
(d) Shear, or cutting.
(e) Torsion, or twisting.

$$\text{Stress} = \frac{\text{load}}{\text{area}}$$

and this means that the stress can be increased by either increasing the *load* or by decreasing the *area*. So when a piece of material is cut out of a support, this has the effect of increasing the *load* acting upon the support. Therefore care must be taken when it becomes necessary to cut structural support such as a joist or beam.

Brittleness

This means that the material is easily fractured or broken. Brittleness in metals is usually associated with hardness, and it is often necessary to reduce the hardness of a material in order to make it less brittle.

Malleability

This means that the material is capable of being formed or shaped by the use of hand tools or machines (see Figure 3.4).

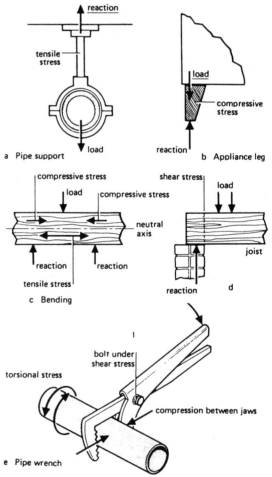

Figure 3.3 Types of stress: (a) tensile; (b) compressive; (c) bending; (d) shear; (e) torsion

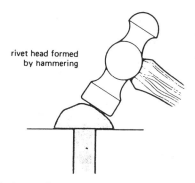

Figure 3.4   Malleability

Ductility

This is a property of many metals and enables them to be drawn out into a slender wire or thread without breaking (see Figure 3.5). Ductile materials are easily bent.

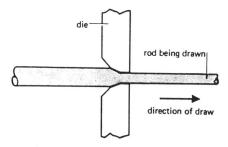

Figure 3.5   Ductility

Elasticity

The ability of a material to return to its original shape, or length after a stress (stretching) has been removed (see Figure 3.6) is termed elasticity. The 'elastic limit' is the greatest strain that a material can take without becoming permanently distorted.

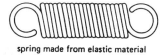

Figure 3.6   Elasticity

Hardness

The hardness of a material is its ability to resist wear or penetration. This is an essential requirement for the cutting edge of a tool. The hardest naturally occurring substance is diamond.

Tensile strength

The tensile strength of a material is its ability to resist being torn apart. Samples are subjected to increasing loads until breakage occurs. The loading which causes breakage is the ultimate tensile strength.

Temper

The temper of a metal is the degree or level of hardness within the metal and can vary from dead soft to dead hard. Copper is a good example related to temper, being in a dead soft condition following annealing its temper changes as it is hammered or worked into a dead hard, cold worked condition.

Work hardening

This describes the increase in hardness caused by hammering, bossing or other cold working techniques. These working techniques cause the grains or crystals which form the metal to become mis-shaped. This deformation of the metal structure reduces malleability and ductility which prevents further cold working.

Annealing

This is the description of the heat treatment applied to soften temper and to relieve the condition of work hardening. The metal is heated to a specified temperature, during which the deformed crystalline structure returns to its normal condition. This treatment softens the metal, thereby reducing internal stresses and allows further working processes to be carried out.

Corrosion resistance

Corrosion is a chemical or electrochemical action which causes the 'eating away' of some metals. Different metals react in varying ways to the different forms of corrosive attack, some having strong resistance, others needing protection where attack may occur.

Table 11   Properties of some common plumbing materials

	PVC	Copper	Aluminium	Brass	Steel
Strength	Very poor	Poor	Poor	Good	Very good
Hardness	Very poor	Poor	Poor	Good	Good
Conductivity	None	Very good	Good	Good	Fair
Corrosion resistance	Very good	Good	Good	Good	Poor
Magnetic properties	None	None	None	None	Good

Table 12 Properties of materials

Material	Chemical symbol	Density (kg/m³)	Coeff. linear exp. (°C)	Melting point (°C)
Aluminium	Al	2705	0.0000234	660
Copper	Cu	8900	0.0000160	1083
Iron (cast)	Fe	7200	0.0000117	1526
Iron (wrought)	Fe	7700	0.0000120	2200
Lead (milled)	Pb	11300	0.0000293	327
Non-metallic sheet	—	1021	0.0000188	not applicable
Tin	Sn	7300	0.0000210	215
Zinc	Zn	7200	0.0000290	416

Note: Properties vary according to condition, that is, whether the material is cold-worked, hot-worked, hard or annealed.

Electrical conductivity

Some materials easily allow the free passage of electric current and are said to have high electrical conductivity. Typical materials which have good electrical conductivity are copper and aluminium.

Materials which do not allow the free passage of electric current are called *insulators*. Typical insulators are glass, porcelain, rubber and plastics.

Heat conductivity

Some materials conduct heat easily. Copper, for example, is a good *conductor* of heat. Materials which do not conduct heat well are said to have good thermal insulation properties. Materials of this kind include glass, wood and some plastics.

Pipes, joints and fittings

Types of pipe

The following materials are used to make pipes to convey water in the domestic system.

Copper

This is by far the most popular metal used today for the manufacture of pipes for domestic use. It has many advantages:

1) It is neat in appearance;
2) It is strong;
3) It is easy to join;
4) It is cheap to install.

Copper can be jointed with compression fittings, capillary fittings, silver soldering, brazing and bronze welding.

Polythene

This material is not very widely used, because it has been superseded by some of the modern plastics such as polyvinyl chloride. It is interesting to note that the methods of jointing are similar to those for copper tube – both manipulative and non-manipulative fittings are used. Fusion welding can also be used.

Steel pipes

Steel pipes are not very popular for domestic work but are very extensively used for industrial work. They form an important part of the plumber's work.

Steel pipes are jointed by the threading (screwing) method and the use of purpose-made fittings.

Stainless steel

This extremely strong and attractive looking metal has been able to claim only a very limited share of the market. The method of jointing is by means of compression and capillary fittings as described in the jointing of copper tube.

Polyethylene

Polyethylene has proved to be an excellent material for cold water installations, particularly when used below ground. It is corrosion resistant, easy to lay and simple to joint. It can be obtained in long lengths permitting supply pipes to be laid with the minimum of joints. Its flexibility allows it to be bent around obstacles and threaded through ducts into buildings. It must not be used for hot water installations.

When laying polyethylene pipe below ground, it is advisable to bed and cover the pipe with a selected soil, or granular material such as pea shingle, to prevent damage from stones and flints, and to avoid deformation of the pipe when backfilling the trench.

Pipe sizes

Since about 1970 pipe sizes have gradually been changing from imperial to metric measurements. Pipes in some materials were metricated quickly, e.g. copper, while others even now retain their imperial identification.

With metrication came a move away from designating pipe sizes by the inside diameter towards the use of the outside diameter.

The result of these changes is a complicated system in which some pipes are designated by their inside diameter and others by their outside diameters, and some have been metricated and others have not.

Table 13 provides a comparison between the sizes of pipes of different materials, using inside diameters as a base, because it is the inside diameter which determines the water carrying capacity of the pipe.

Jointing of copper tube

Copper tube can be jointed in several ways. The most common methods are:

1) Compression fittings
2) Capillary fittings
3) Silver solder
4) Brazing
5) Bronze welding
6) Copper welding.

Compression joints

These are divided into two groups:

- manipulative fittings (Type B)
- non-manipulative fittings (Type A).

Manipulative fittings

These require the end of the tube to be cut square and to length. The nut is then slipped over the tube end and the tube opened to allow for a brass olive ring to be inserted or a ridge formed with a rolling tool. The nut is then tightened and the copper tube end trapped and squeezed between the fitting or olive and nut. This manipulation of the tube end ensures the nut fitting will not pull off. Many water authorities insist on this type of fitting being used on underground services. This type of joint is unaffected by vibration and withstands tensile and other stresses.

There are several types of manipulative fittings on the market. Their common factor is that some form of work (manipulation) is performed on the end of the tube before it is assembled with the fitting. The following are examples of two typical fittings.

Kingley fittings In this case a special tool is inserted in the end of the tube which, by means of a small ball bearing, forms a bead on the tube (see Figures 3.7 and 3.8).

Compression joint In this case the end of the tube is flared out so that it can be compressed between the inner cone of the fitting and the shaped compensating ring (see Figure 3.9).

Table 13 Equivalent pipe sizes

Comparative interval size (millimetres)	Copper* to BS 2871 (table X)		Stainless steel to BS 4127: Part 2		Steel (screwed) (galvanized or black)* to BS 1387 (medium grade)		Thread desig-nation	Grey iron to BS 4622		Ductile iron to BS 4772		Asbestos cement* to BS 484 (Class 25)	
	BS nominal size		BS nominal size		Bs nominal size			BS nominal diameter		BS nominal diameter		BS nominal diameter	
	ID (mm)	OD (mm)	ID (mm)	OD (mm)	ID (mm)	OD (mm)	BS21 (inches)	ID (mm)	OD (mm)	ID (mm)	OD (mm)	ID (mm)	OD (mm)
4.5	4.8	6	4.8	6	—	—	—	—	—	—	—	—	—
6	6.8	8	6.8	8	—	—	—	—	—	—	—	—	—
8	8.8	10	8.8	10	8	13.6	1/4	—	—	—	—	—	—
10	10.8	12	10.8	12	10	17.1	3/4	—	—	—	—	—	—
13	13.6	15	13.6	15	15	21.4	1/2	—	—	—	—	—	—
15	16.4	18	16.6	18	—	—	—	—	—	—	—	—	—
20	20.2	22	20.6	22	20	26.9	3/4	—	—	—	—	—	—
20	26.2	28	26.4	28	25	33.8	1	—	—	—	—	—	—
32	32.6	35	33	35	32	42.5	1 1/4	—	—	—	—	—	—
40	39.6	42	39.8	42	40	48.4	1 1/2	—	—	—	—	—	—
50	51.8	54	—	—	50	59.3	2	—	—	—	—	50	69
63	64.6	67	—	—	65	80.1	2 1/2	—	—	—	—	—	—
75	73.1	76.1	—	—	80	88.8	3	80	98	80	98	75	96
100	105	108	—	—	100	113.9	4	100	118	100	118	100	122
125	130	133	—	—	125	139.6	5	—	—	—	—	125	—
150	155	159	—	—	150	165.1	6	150	170	150	170	150	177
200	—	—	—	—	—	—	—	200	222	200	222	200	240
250	-	—	—	—	—	—	—	250	274	250	274	250	295
300	-	—	—	—	—	—	—	300	326	300	326	300	356
								†	†	†	†	†	†

Table 13 *continued*

uPVC* to BS 3505 (Class E)			Propylene copolymer to BS 4991		Polyethylene to BS 6572 medium density BLUE		to BS 6730 medium density BLACK		to BS 1972 low density Class C	to BS 1384 high density	Class C
BS nominal size			BS nominal size				BS nominal size			BS nominal size	
ID (inches)	OD (mm)	ID (mm)	ID (inches)	OD (mm)	ID (mm)	OD (mm)	ID (mm)	OD (mm)	OD (mm)	ID (inches)	OD (mm)
—	—	—	—	—	—	—	—	—	—	—	—
—	—	—	—	—	—	—	—	—	—	—	—
—	—	—	1/4	13.6	—	—	—	—	—	—	—
—	—	—	3/8	17.1	—	—	—	—	17.1	3/8	17.1
3/8	17.1	15.3	1/2	21.3	—	—	—	—	21.3	1/2	21.3
1/2	21.3	17.5	—	—	15.1	20	15.1	20	—	—	—
3/4	26.7	21.7	3/4	26.7	20.4	25	20.4	25	26.7	3/4	26.7
1	33.5	28.3	1	33.5	26	32	26	32	33.5	1	33.5
1 1/4	42.2	34.8	1 1/4	42.2	—	—	—	—	42.3	1 1/4	42.3
1 1/2	48.2	41.0	1 1/2	48.3	40.8	50	40.8	50	48.3	1 1/2	48.3
2	59.2	51.3	2	60.3	51.4	63	51.4	63	60.3	2	60.3
—	—	—	2 1/2	75.3	—	—	—	—	—	—	—
3	88.9	76.5	3	88.9	—	—	—	—	—	—	—
4	114.3	97.7	4	114.3	—	—	—	—	—	—	—
5	140.2	120	—	—	—	—	—	—	—	—	—
6	168.2	144	6	168.3	—	—	—	—	—	—	—
8	219.1	190.9	8	219.5	—	—	—	—	—	—	—
10	273	138	10	273.4	—	—	—	—	—	—	—
12	323.8	282.2	12	323.8	—	—	—	—	—	—	—
†	†	†	†	†	—	—	—	—	—	—	—

Note Some intermediate sizes have been omitted
*In some materials only one grade is shown.
†Larger sizes than 300 mm have been excluded

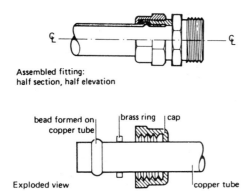

Figure 3.7   Kingley joint: manipulative fitting

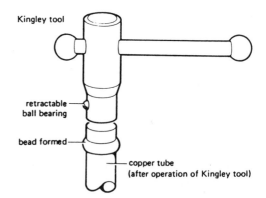

Figure 3.8   Copper tube with Kingley tool

Non-manipulative fittings

These require only the end of the tube to be cut square and to length. The nut is then slipped over the tube end followed by a soft copper wedge shaped ring or brass wedding shaped ring. The tube is then inserted into the fitting socket, the nut tightened and the ring compressed between the inside of the fitting and the outside of the copper or stainless steel tube (Figure 3.10)

This type of fitting is very popular due to its ease of application on both half hard and thin wall copper tube. They can also be used in certain cases

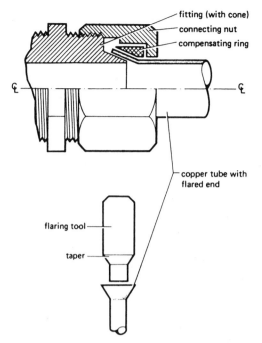

Figure 3.9 *Compression joint: manipulative (Type B)*

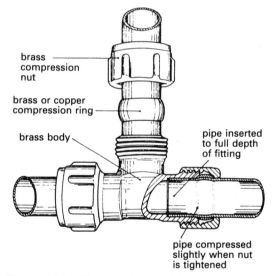

Figure 3.10 *Compression joint: non-manipulative (Type A)*

on soft copper tubes. It is important to remember that this type of fitting should never be used on copper tube buried in the ground.

Capillary joints

Capillary type fittings are also divided into two groups:

- fittings with integral solder rings
- end feed fittings.

Integral solder rings

This type of fitting can be used for both above and below ground work. It can be used extensively in construction, gas, refrigeration, marine and engineering pipelines conveying air and water. It is also without doubt an extremely attractive looking fitting and is also simple to make. The above points make this type of fitting the most popular, and the best known of all capillary fittings. Figure 3.11 shows an example of this type of fitting.

The joint relies on the phenomenon of capillary attraction in the making of the joint. Each fitting contains the correct amount of solder as an integral part. When heat is applied the solder turns from a solid to a liquid and is then drawn by capillary around the whole of the joint in the tight space between the outside of the pipe and the inside of the fitting.

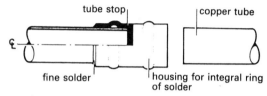

Assembled fitting: half section, half elevation

Figure 3.11 *Capillary joint (integral solder ring)*

End feed fittings

This type of fitting is used in exactly the same circumstances as for the integral solder ring fittings and is identical in all ways except that the solder has to be added to the end of the fitting. The jointing surfaces inside the fitting and outside of the pipe are first cleaned, fluxed and assembled. Heat is applied until the temperature is high enough to melt the solder which is then drawn by capillary attraction into and around the whole joint (Figure 3.12). All surplus flux residue should be removed, otherwise it will continue to act on the surface of the copper and so leave staining and corrosion marks.

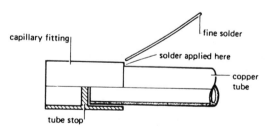

Figure 3.12 *Capillary joint (end feed type)*

Push-fit fittings

Jointing of copper pipes can be carried out much more quickly than with conventional methods and the fittings are suitable for domestic hot and cold water supply systems, and in domestic space heating systems. They are not at present recommended for gas distribution work.

The method of jointing is by manually push-fitting the copper pipe into the socket. The assembly force required, which takes the pipe end beyond a resistance within a fitting, is well within the physical capabilities of the average installer, and requires no special technique or tools (see Figures 3.13 and 3.14).

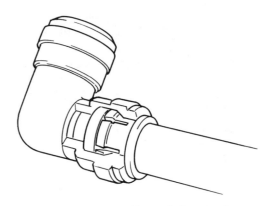

Figure 3.14   J.G. Speedfit push-fit joint for copper tube

The fittings have a polybutylene body, and incorporated within this is a special stainless steel grab ring. The body also houses a washer and rubber sealing ring. All are retained within the body by a screwed on end cap. Polybutylene is an advanced engineering plastic formulated specifically for resistance to high temperatures and pressures.

Jointing of polythene pipes

Polythene pipes may be joined by compression fittings, polyfusion, manipulative jointing or fusion welding.

Compression fittings

These require only the end of the tube to be cut square. The nut is passed over the tube end followed by a copper wedge ring or brass wedding shaped ring. Into the open end of the tube a copper liner is inserted to strengthen the tube walls and then the tube end is inserted into the socket of fitting. The nut is then tightened and the ring compressed into the polythene tube wall previously strenghtened by the copper insert (see Figure 3.15). Liquid jointing compound must not be used.

Polyfusion

In this method the end of the tube is cut square and to the required length. The end of the tube and the socket of the polythene fitting is placed inside a heater, until the polythene surfaces melt. The heater is then removed and the tube end (spigot) is pushed

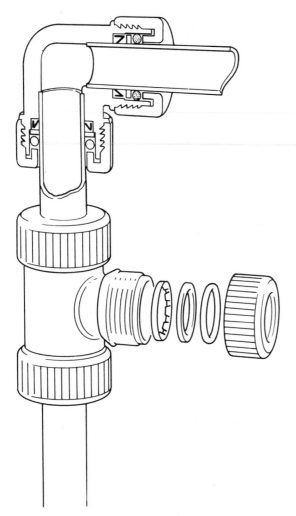

Figure 3.13   Acorn type push-fit joint

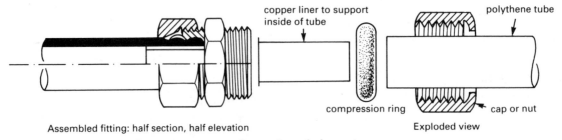

copper liner to support inside of tube

polythene tube

compression ring

cap or nut

Assembled fitting: half section, half elevation

Exploded view

Figure 3.15   Non-manipulative compression fitting for polythene pipe

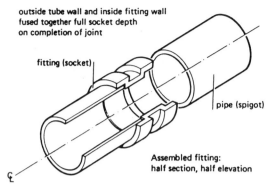

Figure 3.16   Polyfusion

into the fitting (socket) and held in place while the melted surfaces fuse (weld) together, thus making the joint (see Figure 3.16).

Manipulative jointing

The ends of the tube are cut square. The nut is then slipped on to the pipe followed by a brass washer. The pipe end is then placed in a special tool which heats and forms a jointing flange which exactly marries up to the inside surface of the fitting. The newly formed flange is now inserted into the socket of the fitting. The brass ring and the nut are then secured into place, making a water-tight joint.

Fusion welding

This term is used for the jointing of plastic by means of a special solution which has the property of melting the surface of the plastic. The tube and fitting must be thoroughly cleaned with spirit. The outside of the tube and the inside of the fitting is then quickly coated with the solution and assembled. The joint should be held together for a short time until the solution hardens. It takes approximately twenty-four hours for full maturity to take place. The two surfaces now form one homogeneous mass.

Jointing of steel pipes

It is usual for low carbon steel pipes to be jointed by fittings such as elbows, bends, tees, couplings, flanges etc. All these fittings are threaded with the British Standard Pipe Thread (BSPT) BS 21, thus making all fittings interchangeable irrespective of manufacturer. Steel tubing is usually supplied with a BSPT at each end plus a socket at one end (see Figure 3.17).

The tube is cut square and to the required length while held in a pipe vice. A thread is then cut on the end of the pipe with a tool called stocks and dies (see Figure 3.18). In one type there are four cutting dies housed in an adjustable stock head. This tool is set on the pipe end and rotated around the pipe. Long handles attached to the stock head provide the necessary leverage. A lubricant such as oil or grease must be applied to prevent possible thread tearing.

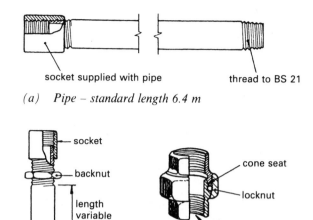

(a)   Pipe – standard length 6.4 m

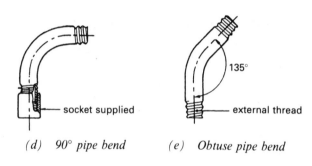

(b)   Longscrew connector   (c)   Union

(d)   90° pipe bend   (e)   Obtuse pipe bend

Figure 3.17   Pipe and fittings for steel tubes to BS 1387

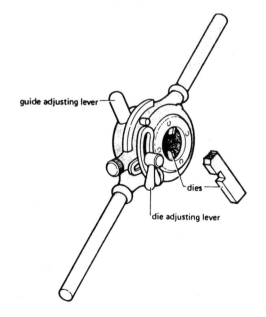

Figure 3.18   Hand stocks and dies

Method of jointing steel pipes

- Cut the end of the tube square.
- Remove internal burr with the reamer, external burr with a file.
- Set stocks and dies to the correct pipe size (for large size pipes it may be necessary to make the thread in two or more cuttings, the required adjustments being made after each cut).
- Cut thread to correct length.
- Remove the stocks by releasing the dies with the release lever.
- Try a fitting to check that the thread is correctly cut.
- Wrap the threads with a special plastic tape.
- The fitting is now screwed on to the pipe, trapping the tape between the threads and so making a water-tight joint.

Note: Care must be taken not to over-tighten the joint. Fittings can become distorted and can even split if over-tightened, causing leakage.

Jointing of polyethylene pipes

Polyethylene pipes can be jointed by:

- compression fittings (Figure 3.19)
- push-fit joints (Figure 3.20)
- thermal fusion (Figure 3.21)

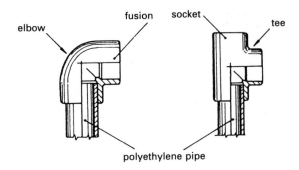

Figure 3.21   Thermal fusion joints

Thermal fusion joints

These joints, illustrated in Figure 3.21, are suitable for large diameter polyethylene (PE) pipes, but are not popular for small diameters because other methods of jointing are so much easier. They are also suitable for polypropylene (PP) pipes. In addition to the jointing method shown in Figure 3.22 polyethylene pipes can be jointed by 'electro-fusion' and butt fusion.

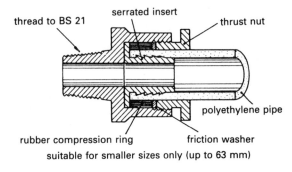

Figure 3.19   Compression fitting for polyethylene pipes

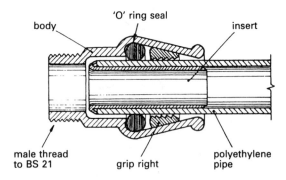

Figure 3.20   Push-fit joint for polyethylene pipe

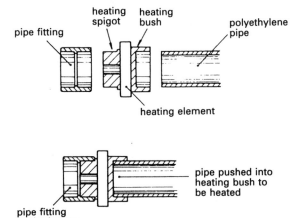

Also suitable for polypropylene pipe.

Pipes should only be joined with compatible fittings.

Correct heat is essential.

Follow manufacturer's instructions for jointing method.

Figure 3.22   Making thermal fusion joints

Pipe fixing

All pipework whether conveying hot or cold water should be correctly supported and fixed. Unless this is done the result could be mechanical damage and/or unnecessary pipe movement noises.

There are many types of clip, bracket and fixing some of which are illustrated in Figures 3.23–3.31.

The type chosen will be governed by several factors such as:

- the type and size of water pipe
- whether the pipe is conveying hot or cold water
- the type of background, i.e. brickwork, timber etc.
- whether the pipes are to be visible or hidden
- whether the pipes project from the surface or not, i.e. spacing clips or saddle

Recommended fixing distances for pipes are shown in Tables 14 (for steel and copper pipes) and 15 (for polyethylene pipes).

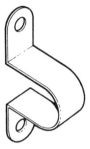

Figure 3.23   Saddle clip

Figure 3.24   Snap action PVC spacing clip

Figure 3.25   Screw-on bracket

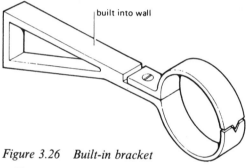

Figure 3.26   Built-in bracket

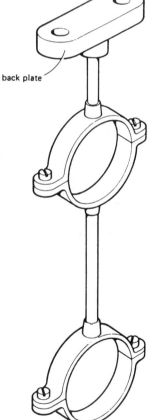

Figure 3.29   Variation of two piece pipe ring multiple carrying arrangement

Figure 3.30   Two piece pipe ring with extension rod and back plate

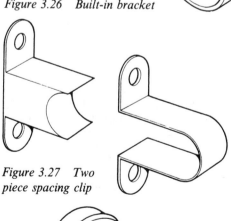

Figure 3.27   Two piece spacing clip

Figure 3.28
Single spacing clip

Figure 3.31   Alternative method of fixing two piece pipe ring

Table 14 Recommended fixing distances (nominal pipe sizes)

Material	Fixing position	Diameter in millimetres (nominal)								
		13	19	25	32	38	50	63	75	100
Low carbon steel	Horizontal (m)	1.8	2.4	2.4	2.7	3.0	3.0	3.6	3.6	3.6
	Vertical (m)	2.4	3.0	3.0	3.0	3.6	3.6	4.5	4.5	4.5
Copper	Horizontal (m)	1.2	1.8	1.8	2.4	2.4	2.7	3.0	3.0	3.0
	Vertical (m)	1.8	2.4	2.4	3.0	3.0	3.0	3.6	3.6	3.6

Table 15 Maximum spacing of fixings for internal polyethylene pipes

Type of piping	Nominal size of pipe	Spacing on horizontal run (m)	Spacing on vertical run (m)
Low density polyethylene to BS 1972 and medium density polyethylene to BS 6730 (see note)	$\frac{3}{8}$	0.30	0.60
	$\frac{1}{2}$	0.40	0.80
	$\frac{3}{4}$	0.40	0.80
	1	0.40	0.80
	$1\frac{1}{4}$	0.45	0.90
	$1\frac{1}{2}$	0.45	0.90
	2	0.55	1.10
	$2\frac{1}{2}$	0.55	1.10
	3	0.60	1.20
	4	0.70	1.40
High density polyethylene to BS 3284 Type 50	$\frac{3}{8}$	0.45	0.90
	$\frac{1}{2}$	0.60	1.20
	$\frac{3}{4}$	0.60	1.20
	1	0.60	1.20
	$1\frac{1}{4}$	0.70	1.40
	$1\frac{1}{2}$	0.70	1.40
	2	0.85	1.70
	$2\frac{1}{2}$	0.85	1.70
	3	0.90	1.80
	4	1.10	2.20
	6	1.30	2.60

Note: There are no spacings available for medium density polyethylene pipes, therefore use the spacings for the low density polyethylene pipes.

Cold water storage

Materials used in the manufacture of feed and storage cisterns

Galvanized mild steel

Cisterns manufactured in galvanized mild steel to BS 417 have been widely used for many years (see Figure 3.32). They are obtainable in many thicknesses and sizes. They are formed from black mild steel sheet, and then dipped into baths of acid to remove grease and scale. After this they are dipped into a bath of molten zinc and so coated with a corrosion resistant skin of zinc.

This protective hot-dip galvanizing treatment has been developed from experiments carried out by Galvani, a scientist after whom the process is named.

The cisterns are available in either riveted or welded construction. Their top edges are stiffened with an angled curb which is formed during manufacture and the open top corners are sometimes braced with corner plates which are riveted or welded depending upon the construction.

They are self supporting and can be situated directly on timber bearers. The holes are cut by means of a tank cutter or expanding bit and the jointing done by means of nylon washers.

It is good practice to ensure that no cuttings are left in the tank and that the inside is painted with an approved non-toxic paint prior to commissioning.

Plastic materials

Various plastics are now being extensively used for cold water storage cisterns: polyethylene, polypropylene and polyvinyl chloride (PVC), to mention just a few (see Figure 3.33). They are strong and resistant to corrosion of all types, virtually ever-

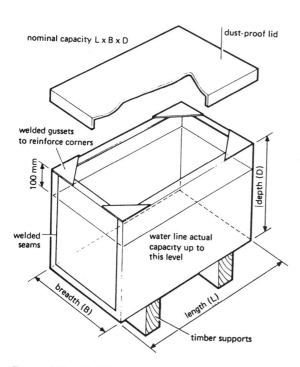

Figure 3.32   *Cold water cistern*

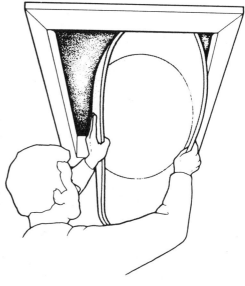

Figure 3.34   Flexibility of material enables the cistern to be passed through small openings

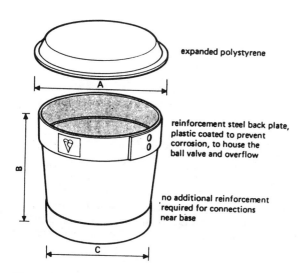

Figure 3.33   *Low density polyethylene cistern*

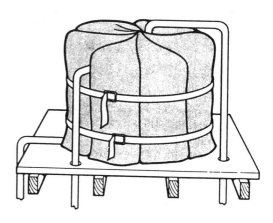

Figure 3.35   Base must be fully supported

Plastic cisterns are square, rectangular or circular in shape and are black to prevent algae growth. They must be fully supported by being placed on a solid decking (see Figure 3.35).

Holes to enable pipe connections to be made are cut by circular saw cutters. The jointing is by means of plastic washers but no oil-based paste of any description must be used, because this softens the material and causes it to break down.

Plastic materials are comparatively soft, so care must be taken in handling and fixing. Sharp instruments and tools can easily cut or puncture the cistern. Naked flames and excessive heat will also damage the material.

Siting and fixing cisterns

Siting and fixing any cistern will normally be governed by the following factors:

lasting, very hygienic and light in weight. They do not cause, nor are they subject to, electrolytic corrosion, and they have low rates of thermal conductivity – so the stored water retains its heat longer in cold weather.

These cisterns are quieter in filling than a metal cistern, and this is a useful advantage, particularly when the cistern is sited near bedrooms. Furthermore, they are easy to squeeze through small openings, which is an advantage when the cistern is to be placed in an attic or loft (see Figure 3.34).

Space available The space available in a loft, roof space, or cistern housing must be adequate to accommodate a cistern.

Head The cistern must be a certain height, or head, above the fittings, in order to provide sufficient water pressure.

Ease of access for maintenance Periodic inspection, cleaning and ball valve adjustment will be necessary.

Temperature The cistern and its contents must not be subjected to extremes of temperature.

Structural tolerances Water is heavy, 1 litre weighs 1 kg. 1 m³ of water weighs 1000 kg.

Figure 3.36 shows good siting of a storage cistern.

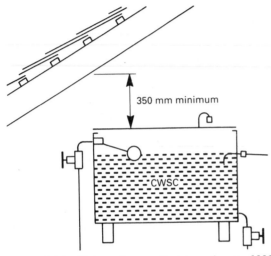

Figure 3.36 Siting of a small cistern (up to 1000 litres capacity)

It has already been pointed out that the storage cistern, which is fed from the service pipe, must be placed in an elevated position in order to give sufficient pressure at the draw-off points to meet the demand rates. If, however, the storage cistern is placed on the same storey as the draw-offs, larger sized pipes must be installed to compensate for the lack of height.

The distribution pipe, conveying the water from cistern to the draw-off taps etc., should be controlled by a control valve fitted close to the storage vessel. To minimize loss by friction, a full way gate valve is recommended.

Connections for these distribution pipes should be located in the storage cistern in such a way that silt cannot be drawn into pipes. This means that the outlet should be taken from the side, and located at least 30 mm above the bottom of the cistern (see Figure 3.37). In cases where the outlet is taken from the bottom of the vessel, a suitable connector, providing a 'stand up' above the bottom of the cistern of at least 30 mm, should be used (see Figure 3.38).

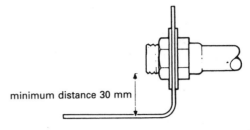

Figure 3.37 Outlet from side of storage vessel

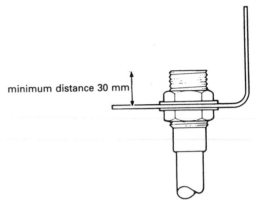

Figure 3.38 Outlet from bottom of storage vessel (not for plastic cisterns)

All cisterns used for storing water should be provided with an over-flow pipe. This should be at least one size larger than the incoming supply pipe, and situated to provide an approved type B air gap.

Regulations on cisterns

BS 6700 follows the Model Water Byelaws in specifying that water cisterns for domestic purposes must be of the 'protected' type (Figure 3.39) on the grounds that water is likely to be drunk from all taps in dwellings. This is a departure from past practice which should greatly improve cisterns hygienically.

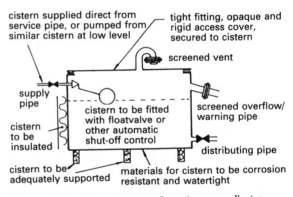

Figure 3.39 Requirements for a 'protected' cistern

Byelaw 30:

Cisterns storing water for domestic purposes

1. Every storage cistern for water supplied for domestic purposes, shall:

   (a) be installed in a place or position which will prevent the entry into that cistern of surface or ground water, foul water, or water which is otherwise unfit for human consumption; and

   (b) comply with paragraph (2).

2. Every cistern of a kind mentioned in paragraph (1) shall:

   (a) be insulated against heat and frost; and

   (b) when it is made of a material which will, or is likely to, contaminate stored water, be lined or coated with an impermeable material designed to prevent such contamination.

   (c) have a rigid, close fitting and securely fixed cover which:
      i is not airtight,
      ii excludes light and insects from the cistern,
      iii is made of a material or materials which do not shatter or fragment when broken and which will not contaminate any water which condenses on its underside,
      iv in the case of a cistern storing more than 1000 litres of water, is constructed so that the cistern may be inspected and cleansed without having to be wholly uncovered, and
      v is made to fit closely around any vent or expansion pipe installed to convey water into the cistern and

   (d) be provided with warning and overflow pipes, as appropriate, which are so constructed and arranged as to exclude insects.

   Figure 3.40 shows a cistern designed to meet the requirements of Byelaw 30.

Comment – Byelaw 30

Where a cistern storing water for domestic purposes is being replaced the replacement will be treated as a new and not as a replacement cistern.

Every water storage cistern from which cold water is drawn or may be drawn for domestic purposes must be insulated against heat and frost.

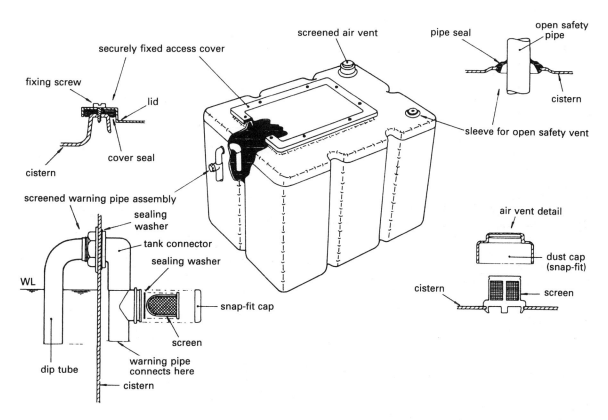

Figure 3.40   Cistern to meet the requirements of Byelaw 30

Hot water storage

Storage vessels should be large enough to contain sufficient hot water at suitable temperatures to supply the maximum anticipated demand over a specified period of time, and be strong enough to withstand the pressure of the water they contain as well as that exerted by the head of water in the feed cistern. They should be sited as near as possible to the boiler to reduce heat losses from the circulating pipes and 'dead legs' should be as short as possible. A dead leg is a run of pipe from the hot store vessel to a drain off point and most draw off pipes in small domestic properties are in fact dead legs. Long dead legs will result in waste of water and heat due to the amount of water having to be drawn off before hot water reaches the tap and the subsequent heat losses from the hot water remaining in the pipe gradually cooling when the tap is closed.

Hot water storage vessels may be cylindrical or rectangular in shape (Figure 3.41) although the use of the latter is confined mainly to replacement of

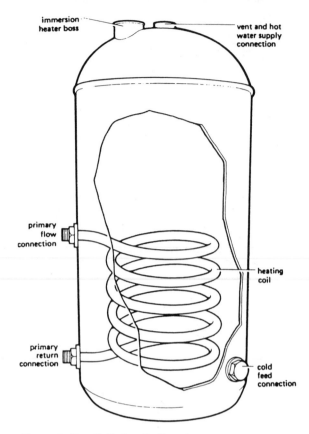

Figure 3.42   Cylinder (indirect), copper

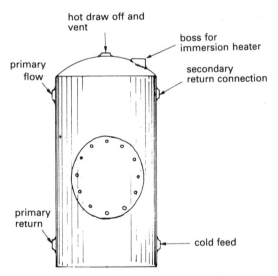

(a) Cylindrical, galvanized steel

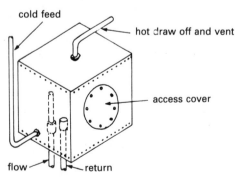

(b) Rectangular, galvanized steel

Figure 3.41   Shapes of hot water storage vessels

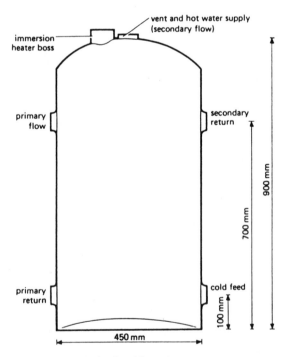

Figure 3.43   Cylinder (direct), copper

existing vessels. Both types of storage vessel are made of galvanized steel, although the smaller sizes of cylinders for domestic use are made of copper, due to its corrosion resistant properties and the fact that most domestic supplies are also run in copper tubes. It is not good practice to mix galvanised components and copper in the same system if it can be avoided due to the possibility of electrolytic corrosion (see pages 74 and 76).

Figure 3.42 shows an indirect hot water cylinder. Figure 3.43 shows a copper direct hot water cylinder with a capacity of approximately 112 litres.

Combined storage

Some manufacturers produce units which combine the cold water storage with that of the hot (Figure 3.44). These are suitable for small domestic properties such as flats and dwellings where the demand for hot water is not so high. Their main advantage is the limited space they occupy, and the fact that being a unit, the vent and feed pipes are built-in, which reduces the installation costs. They are also very useful in schemes involving the upgrading of older properties where space is limited.

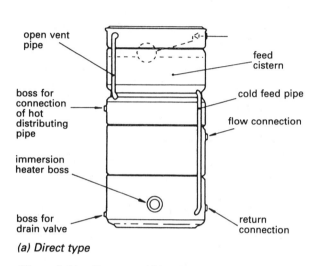

(a) Direct type

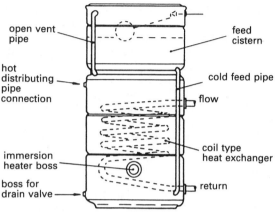

Also available:
• factory lagged or purpose made unit with lagging and metal outer casing;
• single feed indirect type.

(b) Double feed indirect type

Figure 3.44   Copper combination units

Corrosion

In plumbing, examples of corrosion of metals are not difficult to find. When we consider that pipes carrying water (which may itself be corrosive) are laid in soil with strongly corrosive properties, i.e. clays, clinker or ash, it is not surprising that corrosion takes place. What is sometimes difficult to determine is the cause of corrosion. The chief causes of corrosion are:

• the effects of air and water
• the direct effect of acids
• electrolytic action.

When metals are exposed to the atmosphere they form a layer of oxide on their surface. The speed at which the oxide forms varies with each metal. For atmospheric corrosion to take place it is not necessary for the metal to be constantly wet or even exposed to rain for long periods.

The gases present in the atmosphere that have the greatest effect on metals are oxygen, carbon dioxide,

sulphur dioxide and sulphur trioxide, together with the water vapour in the atmosphere.

Oxygen produces a film of oxide on metals. Carbon dioxide may mix with rainwater to form a weak solution of carbonic acid and in contact with metals it tends to promote the formation of carbonate films, as with sheet copper when it produces a basic carbonate film (patina). Sulphur dioxide is probably the greatest accelerator of atmospheric corrosion. It is a gas, ejected with flue gases, which when mixed with rainwater forms a weak sulphurous acid.

Sulphur trioxide also combines with water to form sulphuric acid. These gases are found in considerable concentrations in industrial areas and iron rusts 3–4 times as fast and zinc 6 times as fast in industrial areas as in rural areas. Seaside towns also suffer from atmospheric corrosion because of the sodium chloride (salt) particles present in the air and derived from the sea.

Copper

The bright lustre of copper sheet changes after a time to a greenish shade (patina). This discoloration is due to the combined effect of carbon dioxide, and sulphur dioxide which form carbonates and sulphates. Copper tubes that have been exposed to ashes containing sulphur exhibit the same hard green coating. The green covering on sheet copper is a hard and tough protective layer which prevents any further attack by the atmosphere.

Lead

Lead also forms a tough non-scaling film (lead oxide) on its surface when exposed to the atmosphere. If the atmosphere is an industrial one, the surface of the lead appears to be ingrained with sticky tar-like deposits.

Lead is also affected by the acids present in some timbers. Oak boards in particular contain acids that attack lead. The action of alkali in cement upon lead flashings or weatherings can also be detrimental in moist or permanently damp situations.

Zinc

This is a very stable metal in dry air, and in moist air forms a film of oxide and carbonate. The carbonate is formed from the carbon dioxide present in the air. It is liable to attack from sulphurous gases in the atmosphere – this results in the zinc being converted to zinc sulphate, a whitish compound. In addition, any solutions containing ammonia tend to attack the metal quite rapidly.

Aluminium

This metal also forms a hard and durable oxide film that protects the underlying metal from further attack. If exposed to alkali attack the material should be protected with bituminous paint.

Any weaknesses in the oxide film on aluminium are exploited by corrosive elements in the atmosphere. This results in 'pitting', which is a localized form of attack that is not serious: it does not remain as a steady rate of corrosion but falls off as the oxide film builds up. Alloys of aluminium are liable to attack by salt solution; seaside atmosphere is inclined to be aggressive because of its high salt content.

Electrolytic action

Almost any hot water system offers many examples of electrolytic action. The cold water cistern may be made of steel covered with zinc (galvanized), the hot water cylinder of copper, the pipework of lead, copper or steel, often with brass or gunmetal connections or wiped soldered joints. It has been found that certain types of water are capable of dissolving small quantities of copper in hot water systems. This copper-bearing water comes into contact with zinc coatings and some of the zinc is dissolved by electrolytic action between the two metals. Once the zinc coating has been perforated then the attack of the steel underneath proceeds at a rapid pace. The ability of the water to dissolve copper is important and it is known that any increase in the carbon dioxide content is liable to increase the copper-solvency of the water.

In hard water districts the formation of scale on pipes, boiler and cylinder, provided it is an unbroken film, often prevents attacks due to electrolytic action.

In general it is best therefore to construct the hot-water system of one metal only – unless previous experience in the district shows that corrosion problems do not arise from mixing metals in an installation. Before the introduction of the plastic flushing cistern, with nylon siphon and ball valve float, it was common to find a flushing cistern made of iron, with a brass ball valve; a copper ball float with a soldered seam and perhaps a lead-alloy siphon. It is not surprising that in this confined space the life of the soldered seam on the copper ball float was short, especially when the local water tended to be slightly acid.

The use of other metals in addition to lead as a roof covering have made it necessary for the plumber to be most careful when fixing roof coverings. An aluminium-covered roof provides a weathertight finish, but its efficiency would soon be affected if a copper or iron rainwater pipe discharged water on to it from an old lead- or zinc-covered roof. The aluminium roof would soon be pitted and perforated as a result of the electrolytic action between the dissimilar metals.

Corrosion in central heating systems

Steel is a man-made alloy and it is skill and knowledge that make it possible to convert the oxidic ore into iron and steel.

Common red rust is probably the best known of all the corrosion products of iron. Others are white, green and black. The black oxide, also known as ferrous oxide or magnetite, is most commonly found within central heating systems in the form of a black sludge (see Figure 3.45). Red rust requires moisture and generous supplies of free oxygen for its formation, while the black oxide of iron has a lower oxygen content in its molecule and it will form when there is very little free and dissolved oxygen available in the water.

Hydrogen gas is a by-product of this corrosion process, and the frequent necessity to bleed the gas from radiators (see Figure 3.46) clearly indicates that corrosion is taking place.

A simple way to determine if the water in a central heating system is corrosive is to carry out the corrosion test as shown in Figure 3.47.

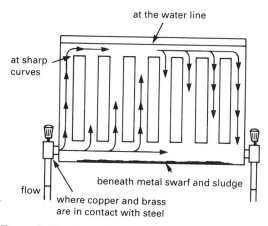

Figure 3.45   Corrosion attack in a radiator

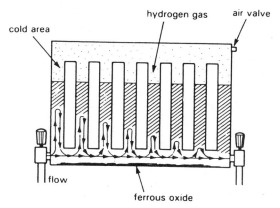

Figure 3.46   Build-up of hydrogen gas and reduced hot water circulation due to corrosion

(1) fill a small jar with water drawn from a radiator vent.

(2) add a few clean steel nails (not galvanised nails) to simulate the steel of the radiators. Close the jar and leave for three days.

if the nails rust, you can be sure that all steel within the system is corroding. In addition, when the system is heated, corrosion processes become more aggressive.

Figure 3.47   A simple test for corrosion

pH

pH is a numerical indication of the intensity of acidity or alkalinity of a solution. The pH scale is logarithmic and runs from 0 to 14, with 7 being neutral. Low numbers are acidic and high numbers, basic (alkaline). A pH of 4 is ten times more acidic than a pH of 5, and a pH of 3, one hundred times more acidic. Metals are affected differently by pH conditions, e.g. mild steel is most stable at pH 10.5 to 11.5, yet aluminium (always coated with a layer of aluminium oxide) is readily attacked above a pH of 8.7. Copper is adversely affected by a pH of greater than 9.5. The ideal pH for the domestic central heating system is between 6.5 and 8.0, when the corrosion rates for all metals are satisfactory.

Corrosion

Corrosion is the 'eating away' of a substance by an attacking influence, which is usually external. The term corrosion is often misapplied to cases of encrustation or deposition where no actual corrosion has occurred.

The more common corrosive agents with which we in the plumbing trade are concerned are:

- air containing moisture, carbon dioxide, sulphur dioxide, sulphuric acid, or combinations of these
- water containing dissolved air, mineral or vegetable acids, alkalis and certain salts.

All acids and the strong alkalis are corrosive, but as plumbers we are mainly concerned with those agents likely to attack plumbing pipework, roof work, sanitary fittings, etc.

Many soils are slightly acid or alkaline, and, with the inevitable moisture, have detrimental effects on many metals.

Atmospheric corrosion

Pure air or pure water acting independently has practically no corrosive action. Moist air and water with dissolved air attack iron and steel very quickly, producing the familiar oxide known as 'rust'. If this corrosive action is unchecked the metal will be completely destroyed.

If sulphur dioxide or carbon dioxide is present in the air, copper is attacked covering the metal with a film of basic sulphate and/or carbonate. This film protects the underlying copper; it is easily identified as the green coating seen on copper roofs. Zinc, while withstanding air and moisture, is subject to quick deterioration in the acid air of industrial towns, so also is brass – especially brass with a high zinc content.

Lead and tin withstand atmospheric corrosion well. Aluminium is corroded by the atmosphere to the extent of surface dullness, but is seriously damaged by alkaline solutions. This also applies to tin and lead solders.

Corrosion by water

The corrosive effects of impure water are very important. The case of iron and steel has already been referred to. So called 'soft' waters have a pronounced action on lead. The strength of a lead pipe is not greatly affected by this minute corrosion, but since a very small quantity of lead in domestic water supplies (plumbo-solvency) is highly dangerous to health, the matter assumes great importance.

Very few waters attack copper, but with highly

acidic waters, green staining of sanitary fittings may occur (cupro-solvency). Generally, in the case of neutral or hard waters, the tubes become coated internally.

Where the attack, however, is persistent, no harmful effects will occur to people consuming the water. Tin is sometimes used as a coating for lead and copper pipes, but commercial pure tin must be used, otherwise the coating is useless.

Corrosion resistance

Gold and the rare metals of the platinum group can be regarded as incorrosible for all practical purposes. To a lesser degree, nickel and chromium, much used for ornamental finishes, are resistant to corrosion.

The alloys of the 'stainless' steel group (steel and nickel) are reasonably immune to corrosion when blended together to form 'stainless steel'.

Electrolytic corrosion

This is caused when two very dissimilar metals, e.g. a galvanized tube and a copper fitting, are in direct metallic contact in certain types of water. This combination is in effect a primary electric cell and the currents induced, although small, cause one or other of the metals (in this case, the zinc) to be corroded and dissolved with considerable rapidity.

Specks of iron rust resting in a brass tube may cause perforation of the tube in certain types of water. This form of corrosion can take place in water systems or in damp soil. Electrolysis or 'galvanic corrosion' requires four things in order for it to take place. These are:

- an anode – the corroding area
- an electrolyte – the means of carrying the electric current (water or soil)
- a cathode – the protected area
- a return path – for the corrosion currents.

An electric current is generated at the anode and flows through the electrolyte to the cathode. The current then flows through the return path back to the anode again (see Figure 3.48).

The principal causes of electrolytic corrosion are:

1) Different metals joined together and both in contact with the electrolyte, for example, mild

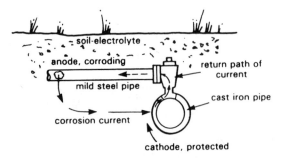

Figure 3.48 Electrolytic corrosion, dissimilar metals

steel radiators and copper pipe in a wet central heating system. Or a steel service pipe connected to a cast iron main. In both examples the steel is the anode or corroding area. The metals do not have to be completely different to set up electrolysis. It is sufficient to have clean, pure metal at one point and scale, impurities or scarring at another. Corrosion can take place between iron and particles of graphite or carbon in the same metal.

2) Differences in the chemical environment of the metal. For example, in buried pipes, a lack of oxygen or a concentration of soil chemicals or bacteria at the anode point (see Figure 3.49).

3) Stray electric currents. This may occur where bonding is ineffective and a gas service pipe acts as an electrical earth return. It happens on gas mains when in contact with other authorities' plant or electrified railway systems (see Figure 3.50).

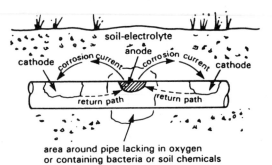

Figure 3.49 Electrolytic corrosion, difference in environment

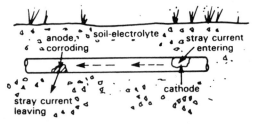

Figure 3.50 Electrolytic corrosion, stray currents

The electro-chemical series

The farther apart two metals appear in the electro-chemical series (Table 16) the more active the corrosion will be when they are placed in contact in a slightly aqueous solution.

Cathodic protection

Cathodic protection is a form of corrosion control designed and arranged to combat the chemical effect of electric current flows induced by electrolytic action. It is the protection of a cathodic metal (e.g.

Table 16 The electro-chemical series

		Metal	Chemical symbol
Cathodic	1	Gold	Au
	2	Platinum	Pt
	3	Silver	Ag
	4	Mercury	Hg
	5	Copper	Cu
	6	Lead	Pb
	7	Tin	Sn
	8	Nickel	Ni
	9	Cadmium	Cd
	10	Iron	Fe
	11	Chromium	Cr
	12	Zinc	Zn
	13	Aluminium	Al
Anodic	14	Magnesium	Mg

copper) by a sacrificial metal (e.g. zinc). The sacrificial metal is known as the anode and is destroyed over a period of time by the chemical effect of the electrical current.

Briefly summarized, the electro-chemical decomposition of metals is as follows:

1) Two dissimilar metals are involved.
2) The two metals or 'poles' must have contact so that current flow can take place.
3) The 'poles' must be immersed in an electrolyte, that is, a liquid or moist substance capable of conducting electricity.

The simplest example of electrolysis, or corrosion due to the chemical effect of electric current flow, is the voltaic cell. This comprises a jar to contain the electrolyte and the two 'poles' or dissimilar metals, say steel and copper. If the 'poles' are connected, by a wire or similar connector, outside the electrolyte then an electric current will flow around the circuit.

This simple arrangement (see Figure 3.51) produces an electric cell or 'battery' capable of producing electrical energy and this can be measured on suitable instruments. The current generated is very small, as also is the voltage, but if the current flow is allowed to continue, there will be evidence of the steel 'pole' seemingly being dissolved away. This electro-chemical decomposition is the form of corrosion which cathodic protection aims to inhibit or stop.

Zinc is said to be anodic to copper, or copper is cathodic to zinc, and a feature of electrolytic decomposition, or corrosion, is that the anodic metal is the one which is corroded by the chemical effect of the electric current passage as just outlined.

Different metals have varying capacities of current flow. These are referred to as their potential differences and enable a table to be drawn up to indicate the likely electro-chemical reaction one might expect when any two dissimilar metals are being considered.

An example is shown in Table 17, from which it

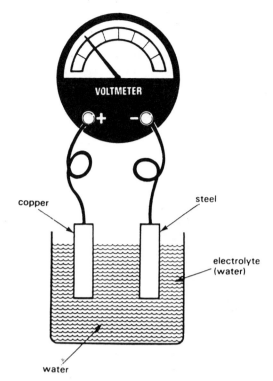

Figure 3.51 Example of electrolysis. Copper and steel, immersed in water, and connected to a voltmeter confirm that electricity is being generated. Steel is the 'sacrificial' element in this instance. Hot water, or the addition of impurities to the water, will increase electrolytic corrosion and thus the voltage.

Table 17

	Metal	Potential difference	Volts
Cathodic	Copper	0.35	positive
	Lead	0.13	negative
	Nickel	0.25	negative
	Chromium	0.71	negative
	Zinc	0.75	negative
	Aluminium	1.70	negative
Anodic	Magnesium	2.38	negative

will be seen that each metal is cathodic to all those metals listed beneath it.

Water pipes

1) Suitable for hard water: copper and galvanized low carbon steel.
2) Suitable for soft water: copper, stainless steel, galvanized low carbon steel.

Lead

Suitable for most waters except soft acid waters, where plumbo-solvency may occur. (WRC water supply by-laws prohibit the use of lead as a water supply pipe material.)

Galvanized steel

Galvanized low carbon steel pipes are given an additional protection against corrosion by the formation of a scale, 'calcium carbonate', from hard waters. However, some hard water with a high free carbon dioxide content will form a loose deposit (see Figure 3.52) which gives no protection.

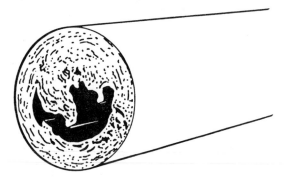

Figure 3.52   Galvanized steel water pipe blocked by corrosion deposits

Copper

Most types of water will dissolve minute particles of copper from new pipes. This may be sufficient to deposit green copper salts in fitments. Where this occurs (neutral and hard waters) it will usually cure itself as it forms a protective film over the internal surface. These small copper particles may also cause corrosion to galvanised steel cylinders, etc. and pitting in aluminium kettles.

Corrosive soldering flux residues can often cause pitting. No more flux than is necessary should be used in making capillary soldered joints, and all surplus flux should be removed on completion of jointing process.

Corrosion by building materials

Some types of wood have a corrosive action on lead, and latex cements and foamed concrete will effect copper. Some wood preservatives contain copper compounds and can cause corrosion of aluminium. Copper is not affected by cement or lime mortar, but should be protected from contact with magnesium oxychloride flooring or quick setting materials such as Prompt cement.

Lead is not affected by lime mortar, but must be protected from fresh cement mortar. Galvanized coatings are not usually attacked by lime or cement mortars once they have set. Aluminium is usually resistant to dry concrete and plaster after setting, but it is liable to attack when they are damp.

Corrosion of water cisterns and tanks and the exterior of underground pipes may often be prevented by cathodic protection. This involves a natural small electric current passing through the water or soil between the metal to be protected and a suitable anode. If the anode is of magnesium or zinc alloy it is connected to the metal to be protected. The two metals, the pipe and the anode, act as an electric cell and a current passes between them, all the corrosion taking place at the anode (sacrificial metal), which has therefore to be replaced eventually. Permanent non-corrodible anodes are sometimes used, but the electric current has then to be provided from an external source, through a transformer and rectifier.

Fittings

Galvanized fittings should always be used with galvanized pipe. Brass fittings may be cast or hot pressed. Cast fittings are usually of alpha brass. Hot pressed fittings are of 'duplex brass' which some waters will affect with dezincification. Dezincification may cause:

- blockage by build up of corrosion products
- mechanical failure due to conversion of brass to porous copper
- slow seepage of water through the material.

In this case, gun metal or copper, fittings should be used.

Cisterns

Galvanized steel cisterns will be affected by soft water with a high carbon dioxide content or, where copper is present in the water, some waters are cupro-solvent. Where this is likely to occur the painting of the inside of the cistern with a suitable bituminous paint is recommended. They may also be protected by means of magnesium anodes, or other forms of cathodic protection.

Copper vessels should not be soft soldered as this may give rise to corrosion of the tin in the solder.

Ball valves

In certain areas with hard water, especially those with a high free carbon dioxide content, ball valve seatings may become eroded as well as corroded by the action of the fast-flowing water. Where this occurs, phosphor-bronze or non-metallic seatings should be used.

Hot water tanks

Galvanized steel is a suitable material in hard water districts but may be affected by soft water which has a high carbon dioxide content. Failure of this material is usually due to:

- high copper content in the water
- excessively high water temperature
- debris and metal filings, etc. on the bottom of the tank
- damage to the protective galvanised coating.

Copper circulating pipes or cold feed services should not be used with galvanized steel tanks, although magnesium anodes may be used to provide protection in areas where failure might occur.

Copper cylinders should not be brazed with any copper–zinc alloy which is susceptible to dezincification. Brazing alloys immune to this form of corrosion are required by BS 699.

Pitting may occur in the dome of a cylinder if the top connection protrudes too far into the vessel or if the cylinder top has been dented, thus forming an air pocket in which carbon dioxide liberated from the water during the heating process can accumulate. Fittings for cylinders should be manufactured from brass, or where dezincification may occur, of copper or gun metal.

Boilers

Domestic boilers are usually of cast iron, which resists attack from the water inside and combustion products outside. In soft-water areas, cast iron may be susceptible to attack. In this case Bower Barffed boilers should be used.

Copper boilers will resist corrosion in waterways, but are more readily affected by combustion products. In soft-water areas, copper–steel boilers are sometimes used. These have an internal surface of copper and an external one of steel.

Aluminium bronze boilers are claimed to have a high resistance to both corrosive waters and combustion products.

Radiators

Corrosion to light-gauge steel radiators depends upon the presence of dissolved oxygen in the water. In closed systems this is soon reduced to a very low quantity and therefore these radiators may be safely used. They should not, however, be used in open circuits where fresh water containing oxygen is replenished.

Towel rails are usually of chromium-plated brass or copper. Copper or arsenical brass to BS 885 is satisfactory but non-arsenical brass rails should not be used as they may suffer dezincification.

Impingement attack

The rapid flow of turbulent water (see Figure 3.53) has a characteristic form of damage, small deep pitting, often of horseshoe shape. It occurs more often in heating systems than cold-water systems due to rapid pumping or local turbulence set up by partially opened valves or abrupt changes of pipe size, sharp elbows etc.

Copper can suffer attack at speeds of above 2m/s. For marine work other materials have been developed to overcome this attack. Aluminium and brass will stand speeds of up to 3 m/s and cupronickels will stand still higher speeds.

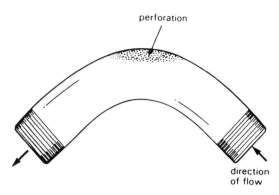

Figure 3.53   Impingement damage to a low carbon steel bend

Underground corrosion

Certain types of soil will affect pipes laid underground. Heavy clay may cause trouble, especially if waterlogged, as it may then contain sulphate-reducing bacteria which will corrode steel, lead and copper. Made-up ground containing cinders is very corrosive, and pipes laid in this or any other corrosive soil should be wrapped in one of the proprietary tapes sold for this purpose. Pipes should not be wrapped in hessian or similar material as this may lead to microbiological attack producing corrosive acids. Copper may be protected by the use of plastic covered tube.

Electric leakage

An electrical leakage from faulty apparatus earthed to the main water supply can cause severe corrosion to pipes.

Roofing
Lead

Lead will corrode if laid direct on oak or unseasoned timber. The corrosion will be on the underside in the form of a white powder and is due to the liberation of acetic acid from the wood. Lead should always be laid on approved underlays.

Copper

Once green patina – a form of corrosion on copper roofs – has formed, it affords protection against further attack.

Another form of corrosion may occur from water dripping from rusting steel, slates that contain pyrites, or lichen-covered slates or tiles as this water is highly corrosive.

Zinc

Zinc may suffer 'white rusting' on the underside if

condensation can occur there. It is also readily attacked by a polluted industrial atmosphere.

Aluminium

Aluminium is corroded by the soluble corrosion products of other metals. It is important that no drippings be received from any copper or copper alloy structure, e.g. copper gutters, lightning conductors, etc.

Soot

Soot deposits from chimneys will cause corrosion on all types of metal roofing (a) because a corrosion cell is set up between soot particles and the metal,

and (b) because the soot will contain sulphur acids formed by the combustion of the fuel.

Rainwater goods

Cast iron is generally satisfactory for carrying rainwater. Gutters should be cleaned and painted regularly both inside and outside.

Galvanized gutters and pipes have good resistance to corrosion, but should not be used in conjunction with copper roofing materials.

Aluminium gutters and pipes have good resistance except where allowed to receive drippings from copper.

Tools and equipment

Good tools are indispensable to the craftsperson and buying them can be an expensive business. Some tools can only be used for one specialized task, whilst others, like hammers and pliers, may be used for a variety of jobs.

Most trainee plumbers will buy their tools as experience grows and as they need them for the job they are doing. A kit of good quality tools, built up in this manner, is a sound investment. Some employers will buy tools for their employees, which helps to reduce the cost, payment often being made by an agreed weekly deduction from the employee's wages. The cost of the tool kit will, of course, depend upon the quality and quantity of tools bought.

Manufacturers produce such a wide variety of tools that there is no limit to the possible contents of a kit. Each tool has its own particular advantages and disadvantages and everyone has their own preferences and prejudices. Many plumbers also make or adapt tools to suit their own special needs. The following list has been agreed (1st July 1991) between the Joint Industry Board for Plumbing Mechanical Engineering Services in England and Wales and the Electrical, Electronic, Telecommunications and Plumbing Union to be a full kit of tools which should enable a plumber to complete a reasonable job:

- Allen keys – one set
- adjustable spanner – up to 150 mm
- adjustable spanner – up to 300 mm
- basin key
- bending spring – 15 mm
- bending spring – 22 mm
- blow torch and nozzle – complete (similar to Primus Type B)
- bolster, chisel – 65 mm
- bossing mallet
- bossing stick
- bradawl
- chisel – brick up to 500 mm
- chisel – wood

- dresser for lead
- flooring chisel
- footprints – 225 mm
- gas or adjustable pliers
- glass cutter*
- hacking knife*
- hacksaw frame
- hammer – large
- hammer – small
- hand drill/brace
- junior hacksaw/saw
- mole wrench
- padsaw/compass saw
- pipe wrench – Stillson – up to 400 mm
- pliers – insulated general type
- pocket knife (Stanley type)
- putty knife*
- rasp
- rule – 3 mm tape
- screwdriver – large
- screwdrive – small
- shave hook
- snips
- spirit level – 600 mm
- tank cutter
- tool bag
- trowel
- tube cutter
- wiping cloth

*Only if glazing is normally done by plumbers in the district.

Plumbers able to provide tools from the list when they are needed for a job are eligible for a tool maintenance payment for each day on which plumbing work is done. This money is used to maintain the kit in good working order, and to replace items as they wear out, or are lost.

The list does not include items such as pipe cutters, pipe vices, welding apparatus, stocks and dies, and bending machines – these and other larger and more expensive items of equipment are provided by the employer. Neither does the list contain various tools for specialized or unusual tasks such as may be encountered when working on sheet lead, copper, aluminium, zinc or non-metallic roof weatherings. Many of these tools are made by the plumber, and will be described as the need for them arises.

Plumbers are responsible for their tools and are dependent on them for their livelihood. They should:

- select, from the tool kit, the correct tool for the job
- ensure that it is in good working order
- use it correctly
- transport it safely.

Failure to do this can result in:

- use of more physical effort than is necessary
- waste of time
- damage to fittings, appliances or client's property
- injury to others.

The maintenance and care of tools is important from both the practical and safety point of view. This applies to all tools, whether they are your own or provided by your employer for your use. Damaged, blunt or worn tools will not produce good work, and they could prove dangerous to the user and others working nearby.

Metal saws

The hacksaw has a pistol grip and the frame is adjustable to take various lengths of blade, usually 250 mm or 300 mm (see Figure 3.54).

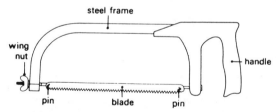

Figure 3.54 Hacksaw

Two types of blade are commonly used, one having 22 teeth per 25 mm of blade length and the other 32 teeth per 25 mm. The coarser blade is used for steel pipe and the finer blade for copper tube, although many plumbers use a junior hacksaw for cutting the smaller sizes of copper tube (see Figure 3.55).

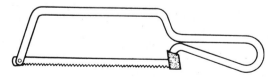

Figure 3.55 Junior hacksaw

Wood saws

There are many types of wood saw available; one of the most useful is the tenon saw. This can be used for cutting floorboards. These saws are generally 250–350 mm long and usually have about 12 teeth per 25 mm of blade. The blade teeth are 'set', that is folded outwards on alternate sides to provide clearance for the blade in the cut. A plumbers' saw has a double-edged blade and is suitable for wood or lead. The blade length is usually 400 mm.

The padsaw has a plastic or metal handle into which is fitted a blade (see Figure 3.56). The blade can be a tapered one with about 10 teeth per 25 mm of blade and used for cutting wood. Alternatively a hacksaw blade can be fitted for cutting metal. The padsaw is most useful in awkward corners or when cutting floorboards in position.

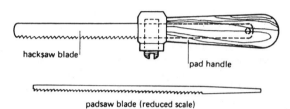

Figure 3.56 Padsaw

A flooring saw is used for cutting tongue and groove floorboards prior to lifting them. The saw has a convex blade which allows the tongue to be cut away from the floorboard while it is still in place. (Figure 3.57).

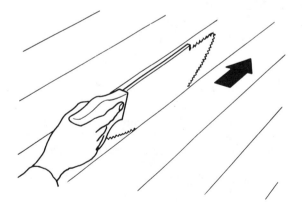

Figure 3.57 Flooring saw

Drilling tools

A ratchet brace can be used to hold a variety of drills or 'bits'. The ratchet allows the brace to be used close to a wall or corner. The chuck usually has two jaws and is most suitable for holding drills with a squared tapered shank. The jaws are called alligator jaws (see Figure 3.58).

The hand brace can be used in more confined

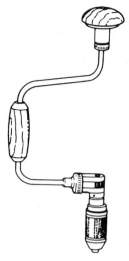

Figure 3.58   Ratchet brace

spaces than a ratchet brace. The hand brace has a three-jaw chuck and holds round shanked drills or bits. Its gearing enables it to turn much quicker than a ratchet brace and is most suitable for drilling holes up to about 7 mm in diameter in metal, wood or masonry. The hand and breast drill is a larger version of the hand brace (see Figure 3.59).

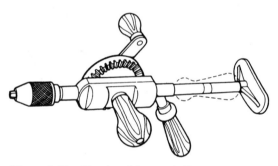

Figure 3.59   Hand and breast drill

The main types of power drill are the hand held electric drill (Figure 3.60), and the drill press or bench drill, which is a workshop machine. Drill bits are available in a wide range of types and sizes suited to a variety of purposes. The drill bit should generally be suited to the drilling speed and the material being drilled.

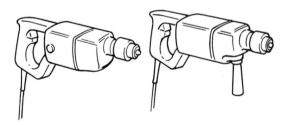

Figure 3.60   Electric drills

Rawlplug holder and bits

This is a percussion hole-boring tool, driven by a hammer. It consists of a rawldrill and the toolholder into which it fits. The tool is used to make holes in masonry for plug fixings.

Stardrill

This is a hand-held boring tool for use on masonry. It resembles a cold chisel, but has a fluted shaft tipped with four ground cutting faces. (see Figure 3.61). It is held in position and struck with a hammer, (while being turned between each blow) to produce a hole in the material.

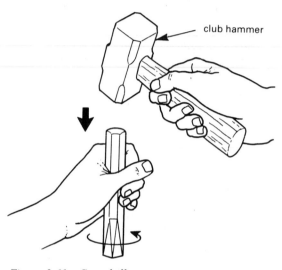

Figure 3.61   Star drill

Hammers

There are many different types of hammer and they are identified by their weight and head pattern. The 'pein' or 'pane' is the end of the head opposite to the face of the hammer. Hammer heads are usually made of cast steel and the handles or shafts are ash or hickory. A claw hammer is useful for removing nails from roof timbers or floorboards. The curved claw is used to lever and pull out nails. This function demands that the head be securely attached to the shaft. With steel shafted hammers, the head is permanently fixed to the shaft; hickory shafts are secured with wedges driven in to spread the shaft inside the eye. Work surfaces should be protected by placing a piece of hardboard under the head of the hammer when it is used as a fulcrum for levering.

The range of hammers is extensive and the choice will depend upon the particular work operation, personal opinion and experience (see Figures 3.62 to 3.64).

Figure 3.62   Cross pane hammer

Figure 3.63   Ball pane hammer

Figure 3.64   Claw hammer

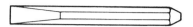

Figure 3.66   Plugging chisel

Figure 3.67   Flat cold chisel

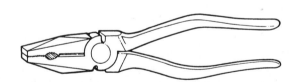

Figure 3.68   Floorboard chisel

Chisels for lifting floorboards are available (see Figure 3.68). These have a parallel blade about 75 mm wide. This blade is driven between the floorboards which are then raised by leverage via the chisel. This type of chisel is also used for cutting bricks.

Chisels

Wood chisels are made in a variety of types and sizes. In the past these chisels had a steel blade and wooden handle, but they are also available made completely of steel (see Figure 3.65). These are most useful to a plumber who will usually have a hammer in his tool kit but not always a wooden mallet to strike the chisel. Plugging chisels are used for cutting out slots or joints between bricks (see Figure 3.66).

Cold chisels are so called because they can cut mild steel when it is cold, although a plumber will also use this tool for cutting brick and concrete (see Figure 3.67). As with wood chisels, cold chisels are available in a variety of types, shapes and sizes, and for normal domestic work a selection of chisels ranging from 150 mm to 450 mm in length and 12 mm to 20 mm in diameter will be most useful.

Pliers

There are many types of pliers in common use, and most plumbers have several of these to enable them to perform different tasks.

Engineer's or combination pliers are available in several sizes, 150 mm to 200 mm are generally the most useful length (see Figure 3.69). Models are available with insulated grips for use on electrical circuits.

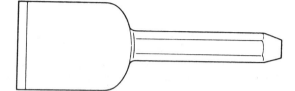

Figure 3.69   Engineer's pliers

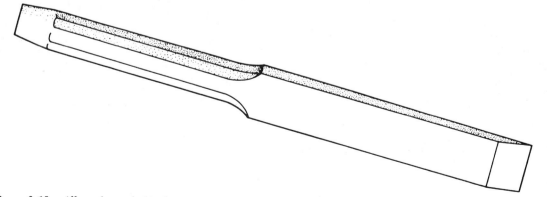

Figure 3.65   All steel wood chisel

Gas pliers are an essential item in any plumber's kit. Their circular jaws make them most useful for holding pipes or bulky components (see Figure 3.70).

Figure 3.70   Gas pliers

Long snipe pliers are useful when riveting sheet metal and on domestic servicing work. Seaming pliers are mainly used when working on sheet (aluminium, zinc or copper) weatherings to assist with folding and welting (see Figure 3.71). A variation of these have the jaws in line with the handle and formed into a 'V'. These are called dog earing pliers and are used for that operation.

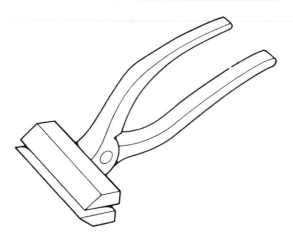

Figure 3.71   Seaming pliers

Gland nut pliers can be obtained in sizes from 100 mm to 350 mm and more than one size may be included in a tool kit (see Figure 3.72). They are extremely useful for many jobs, but like most pliers with serrated jaws can damage brass or chromium surfaces or fittings.

Figure 3.72   Gland nut pliers

Resembling pliers, wire strippers have the tips of their jaws turned inwards at right angles towards each other. When closed to a pre-adjusted setting over a cable, the cutting tips sheer off the insulation from the core, leaving it prepared for termination (see Figure 3.73).

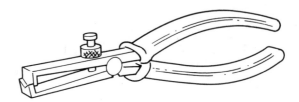

Figure 3.73   Insulation stripper

Files and rasps

Files and rasps are made of cast steel. One end is formed into a tang, on to which fits a wooden or plastic handle (see Figures 3.74 and 3.75).

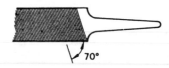

Figure 3.74   File

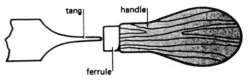

Figure 3.75   Handle for file

Some files and rasps are available with the tang formed into a handle. Files and rasps are identified by their:

Length 100 mm to 350 mm, in 50 mm steps.
Shape and cross-section Square, flat, half-round, round, etc. (Figure 3.76).

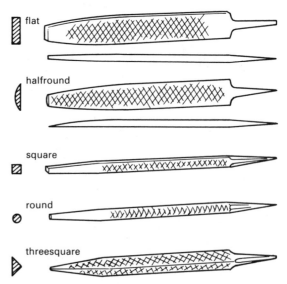

Figure 3.76   Shape of files

Cut single, double or rasp.
Grade rough, bastard, second cut or smooth.

The cut is standard for certain types of files. Flat files are double cut on the face and single cut on the edge. Hand files are similar, but have one edge uncut. Round files are usually single cut, and the half-round are double cut on the flat surface and single on the curved.

Spanners

Spanners are available in a variety of types. The most common are as follows:

Open ended
Ring
Box
Socket
Adjustable.

Open ended spanners are usually double ended, with each end taking a different sized nut (see Figure 3.77). They are described by the size of the thread on which the nut screws, or by the distance across the flats of the nut.

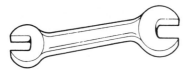

Figure 3.77   Open ended spanner

Ring spanners fit completely round the nut to hold it very securely (see Figure 3.78). Ring spanners are safer to use than open ended spanners as there is less risk of the spanner slipping off the nut. Also they are less likely to wear or open out. They are preferred for jobs where nuts must be tightened more securely.

Figure 3.78   Ring spanner

Box spanners are most useful for releasing or tightening recessed nuts, or nuts in inaccessible positions such as those securing taps to wash basins, baths and sink units. Most box spanners are double ended and are turned by a steel rod called a tommy bar (Figure 3.79).

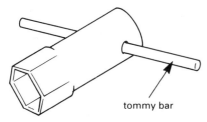
tommy bar

Figure 3.79   Box spanner

Socket spanners are a very robust type of tool. They may be used with a ring or open ended spanner or with a ratchet brace. Socket spanners are most useful for servicing work to boilers, water heaters etc.

Adjustable spanners are available in several sizes and different designs and most plumbers include at least two different lengths in their kit (see Figure 3.80). Thin jawed adjustable spanners are most suitable for assembly and disconnection work to pipework and components.

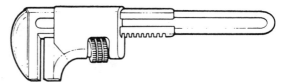

Figure 3.80   Adjustable spanner

Pipe grips or wrenches

There are four main types of wrench in use:

- Stillson pipe wrench
- footprint pipe wrench
- chain pipe wrench
- self grip wrench.

The Stillson wrench is a very robust tool and is most suitable for steel pipe work. These wrenches are available in a wide variety of lengths, ranging from 150 mm to 1.225 m. The most adaptable sizes for plumbers' work are 250 mm and 450 mm (Figure 3.81).

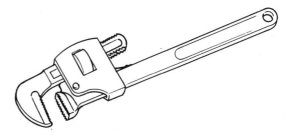

Figure 3.81   Stillson wrench

Footprint wrenches rely on hand grip pressure to secure the pipe or component. These are available in lengths ranging from 150 mm to 400 mm (Figure 3.82).

Figure 3.82   Footprint wrench

Chain pipe wrenches or chain tongs are usually associated with industrial work, but small models are available for domestic purposes. The length of lever handle may vary between 200 mm and 900 mm.

Self grip wrenches rely on hand grip pressure to secure the component although they also have a lock-on action to securely grip the wrench on to the component allowing the grip pressure to be released (see Figure 3.83). They are available with jaws of alloy steel and in lengths from 150 mm to 250 mm.

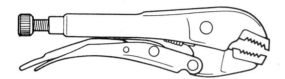

Figure 3.83   Self grip wrench or mole wrench

Wrenches for specialist tasks are produced by various manufacturers. The shetack basin wrench is specially designed for the difficult job of fitting back nuts and union nuts behind wash basins, baths and sink units. The tool may be used in the horizontal or vertical position enabling a nut to be tightened or loosened in the most inaccessible places. The spanner is approximately 250 mm long and fits standard size backnuts. A similar model is also available with a greater distance between the jaws for waste fittings and traps.

An adjustable wrench for use in similar locations to the shetack basin wrench overcomes the difficulty of non-standard size nuts and unions (see Figure 3.84). The serrated teeth give a ratchet action which is useful when space is limited.

Figure 3.84   Adjustable wrench

Screwdrivers

These are available in many types and sizes. Blades are made from high carbon steel and handles of wood or plastic. Some screwdrivers include a ratchet for ease of operation. Some manufacturers produce a set of screwdrivers of varying length with interchangeable blades having various widths and blade pattern, all fitting into a common handle. Screwdrivers are identified by their type and the length of the blade. Sometimes the width of the blade is also stated.

There are three main types of screwdriver tip in common use (Figure 3.85). The flared tip (designed

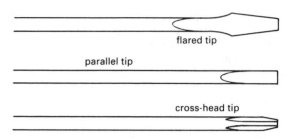

Figure 3.85   Screwdriver tips

to fit the familiar slotted screw) has a flat tapered tip which flares out from the blade. Parallel tips are tapered but not flared – so that the tip is no wider than the blade of the screwdriver, and can be used to drive screws recessed into holes. They are used on slotted head screws. The cross-head tip (Phillips, Posidrive) has four flutes ground on the head, formed to a point, which fits the corresponding crossed slots in the screw head. It has the advantage of giving extra purchase on the screw.

A cabinet screwdriver is used for bigger screws and has a large handle to provide gripping power to turn the screw. The most useful sizes are 200 mm and 400 mm.

Stubby or dumpy screwdrivers are used for larger screws which are located in awkward places. The blades are very short, usually about 25 mm long and available in a variety of widths, the most popular being 6 mm.

Electricians' screwdrivers are made for smaller screws. These screwdrivers have a plastics handle and some are available with a plastics sheathed blade.

Phillips and Posidriv screwdrivers both have cross-shaped blade points to fit cross-slotted head screws (see Figure 3.86). The Posidriv has superseded the Phillips type head, but the Phillips screwdriver is still retained because it will fit both screwheads, although the Posidriv cannot be used on Phillips screws. A Phillips screwdriver is more sharply pointed than the Posidriv, but the essential difference is in the square section between the slots of the cross which enables the Posidriv to fit closely between the blade and the screwhead. The corners of the square can be easily seen on the screwhead and are illustrated on the trade mark. Two sizes of blades are available. Cross-headed screws are common on certain plumbing components such as water heaters and boilers.

Figure 3.86   Phillips and Posidriv screw heads

Offset or cranked screwdrivers are very useful for getting at screws in awkward places. Blades may be flat or cross-slotted. These screwdrivers are usually all steel.

Gimlet and bradawl

These tools are used for forming holes in timber to enable a wood screw to start. The gimlet is used on hardwoods (see Figure 3.87) and the bradawl on softwoods (see Figure 3.88).

Figure 3.87   Gimlet

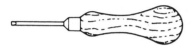

Figure 3.88   Bradawl

Punches

Several types of punch are available, varying in shape according to the job to be done.

The nail punch is for punching nails below the surface of the timber which is being secured (see Figure 3.89). This is essential practice on roof boarding which is to be covered with sheet weatherings. Another function is to punch nails through floorboards so that the boards may be raised easily. The punch is usually about 100 mm long, with a 3 mm diameter head which is slightly recessed to prevent the punch from slipping off the nail head.

Figure 3.89   Nail punch

Centre punches are used to mark the centre of a hole to be drilled in metal (see Figure 3.90). The punch provides a small indentation which locates the drill in the correct position and prevents it from slipping. These punches are usually 100 mm to 200 mm long and the point is tapered at 90°.

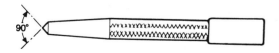

Figure 3.90   Centre punch

Hole punches are used to cut a small circular hole in soft materials such as sheet lead, so enabling washers to be made (see Figure 3.91).

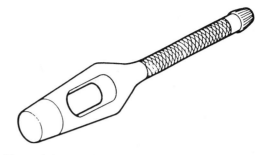

Figure 3.91   Hole punch

Taps

Taps are used for cutting internal screw threads in metal. There are three taps to a set (see Figure 3.92).

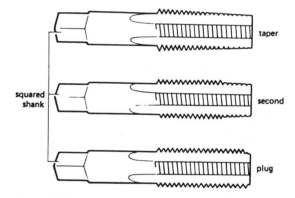

Figure 3.92   Taps

Taper tap

This is used to start the thread. It has no threads near its end so that it can enter the hole. This tap will cut a complete thread if it can pass right through the hole.

Second tap

This is used in a blind hole (a hole that does not pass right through the metal) to cut a thread near to the bottom of the hole, after preliminary cutting with the taper tap.

Plug tap or bottoming tap

This is used to complete the thread started by the taper and second taps, and cuts right through to the bottom of a blind hole.

Taps are turned by means of a tap wrench (see Figures 3.93 and 3.94).

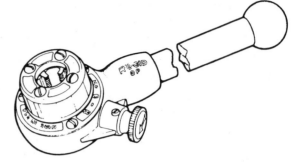

Figure 3.93   Tap wrench

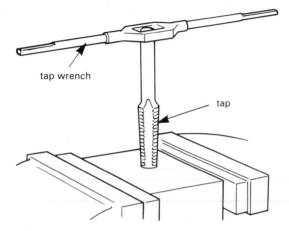

Figure 3.94   Tap and tap wrench

Dies

Dies are used for cutting external threads on circular sections of metal, plastic rod and pipe. Dies are available in a number of different forms and are held in 'stocks', so that they can be rotated around the rod or pipe. Figure 3.95 shows circular split pattern dies which are held in the stocks shown in Figure 3.96. The split allows for adjustment to be made to the size or depth of thread being cut.

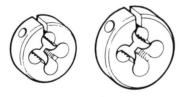

Figure 3.95   Circular split pattern dies

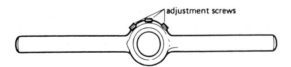

Figure 3.96   Circular die stocks

External threading of mild steel pipes is usually carried out using solid dies which have a ratchet included for ease of operation (see Figure 3.97).

Figure 3.97   Hand operated ratchet dies

Bending springs

Springs are used when bending copper tube or lead pipes by hand. The spring supports the tube and prevents it from kinking or losing its circular section. Springs for bending copper tube are made from square section spring steel and are available in two types: internal and external.

The internal spring is approximately 600 mm long and is most suitable for short lengths of pipe when a sharp tight bend is required (see Figure 3.98). The pipe is slightly over bent and then opened out to release the tension on the spring. The spring is then rotated in the direction required to reduce its diameter and withdrawn from the pipe.

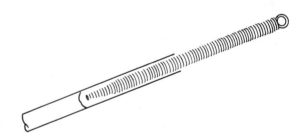

Figure 3.98   Internal bending spring

External springs for copper tube are shorter in length than internal springs and have one or both ends opened slightly to assist tube insertion (see Figure 3.99). They are most useful for long lengths of pipe or when bending *in situ*. Generally external bending springs do not allow such sharp bends to be pulled as with the internal spring.

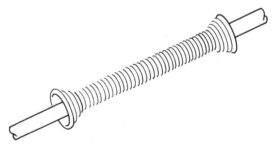

Figure 3.99   External bending spring

Pipe cutters

Pipe cutters operate by the rotation of a hardened steel cutting wheel around the outside of the pipe (see Figures 3.100 and 3.101). The wheel is gradually moved through the wall of the pipe as the adjustment is tightened until the pipe is cut. The cutting wheel is narrow and sharp, but the action of cutting produces a burr around the inside edge of the pipe which must be removed by a reamer (see Figure 3.102).

Cutters are generally used for cutting copper, stainless steel, mild steel and cast iron pipes. In the case of cast iron pipes, no internal burr is produced as the pipe shears at the cutting point before the cutting wheel reaches the inside edge of the pipe.

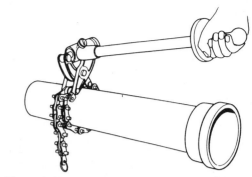

Figure 3.101   Snap action cast iron pipe cutter

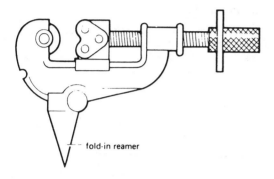

Figure 3.100   Copper tube cutter

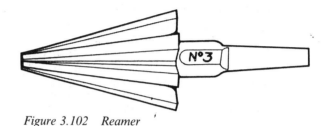

Figure 3.102   Reamer

Hole cutters

Hole cutters are used for cutting circular holes in cisterns, tanks and cylinders. The cutter shown in Figure 3.103 is used in a brace and the cutter is adjusted to the size of the hole required.

The cutter shown in Figure 3.104 is called a hole saw and resembles a circular hacksaw blade. These can be used in a brace or on an electric drill. They are available in a wide range of sizes and both the drill and blade are replaceable.

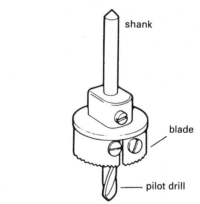

Figure 3.104   Circular blade hole cutter

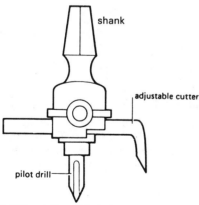

Figure 3.103   Adjustable hole cutter

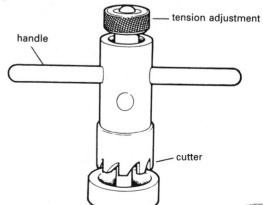

Figure 3.105   Hand operated cutter

Figure 3.105 shows a hand operated cutter which is most commonly used for cutting galvanized mild steel cisterns and tanks; a ratchet handle is available for easier operation in confined spaces.

Tools for expanding the diameter of copper tubes

Mandrel

This is used to open the end of a piece of tube (BS 2871 Part 1 Table X) to a 15° taper, making the tube suitable for use on certain tube fittings. The tool may be suitable for one diameter of tube, or may be a combination tool as shown in Figure 3.106 incorporating two sizes in one tool.

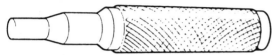

Figure 3.106   Combination mandrel

Socket forming tool

This is driven into the end of the copper tube opening it out parallel and forming a socket to receive another piece of tube (see Figure 3.107). If the end of the tube is annealed the opening process will be simplified. The capillary joint formed is easily made by soldering or brazing. It is suitable for use on tubes to BS 2871 Part 1 Table X.

Figure 3.107   Socket forming tool

Tools for sheet metal weatherings

Dresser

This tool is used for dressing copper, aluminium, zinc sheet and lead pipes and sheet (see Figure 3.108). Dressers are usually made from hardwoods or high density plastics.

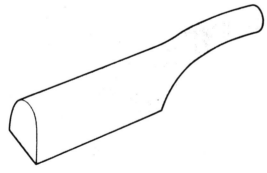

Figure 3.108

Bossing mallet

This is a useful tool when working on sheet roofing materials. The mallet head is made from a hardwood and the handle from malacca cane or high density plastic (see Figure 3.109).

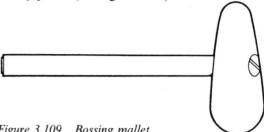

Figure 3.109   Bossing mallet

Tinmans mallet

This is used on sheet copper and aluminium weatherings to assist with joining together welts and seams, and may be used to strike another sheetwork tool, for example a setting-in stick, or dresser (see Figure 3.110).

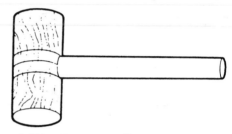

Figure 3.110   Tinmans mallet

Bossing stick

This is used mainly for bossing corners on sheet lead weatherings (see Figure 3.111).

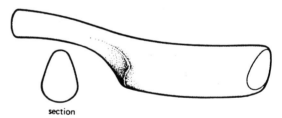

section

Figure 3.111   Bossing stick

Bending stick

This is an essential tool when bending lead waste pipes (see Figure 3.112). The stick is used to dress the lead around to the back of the bend. This tool may also be used on sheet lead weatherings.

section

Figure 3.112   Bending stick

Setting-in stick

This is, as its name implies, a tool used to reinforce or sharpen folds or angles which have been formed in sheet weatherings (see Figure 3.113).

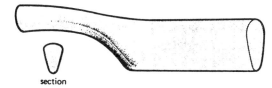

Figure 3.113   Setting-in stick

Chase wedge

This is a tool used for setting-in the corner of a fold or crease and is available in widths from 50 mm to 100 mm (see Figure 3.114).

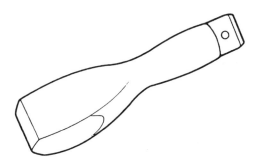

Figure 3.114   Chase wedge

Shavehook

This is used to remove a thin layer of shaving from the surface of lead pipe or sheet. The blade is held at 90° to the material and drawn along it to remove the surface layer. Shavehooks are available with different shaped blades to suit a variety of tasks (see Figure 3.115).

Figure 3.115   Shavehook

Tin snips

These are used for cutting thin sheet metal and are available in several sizes, the most popular being 150 mm and 250 mm long (see Figure 3.116). Straight and curved pattern blades are available. Universal snips are heavy duty pattern to cut either curved or straight and have open-ended handles to prevent nipping.

Figure 3.116   Tin snips

Soldering irons

These are used for soldering and tinning purposes, for example copper and brass unions or zinc and copper sheet. Soldering irons have a forged copper 'bit', steel shanks and a whitewood handle and are usually sold by weight.

Small electric soldering irons are available and are most suitable for workshop use, for example making electric wiring connections.

Pipe vices

Pipe vices are needed to grip and secure mild steel pipes which are to be cut or threaded. They may be of the hinged type or chain type, and may be secured either to a work bench or to portable tripod stand (Figure 3.117).

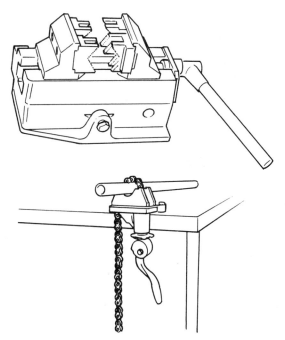

Figure 3.117   Pipe vices

Bending machines

These may be used for bending copper, stainless steel and mild steel pipes, and are necessary to bend pipes which are of large diameter or are too rigid to bend manually. They are also useful for prefabrication work, or when several bends have to be formed in a short length of pipe.

There are two types of machines: rotary (see Figure 3.118) and ram (see Figure 3.119).

Bending machines work by hand power or through a gear or ratchet action and employ special formers and back guides to ensure that the tube, when pulled to the required angle, maintains its true diameter and shape throughout the length of the bend. When using a machine it is advisable that the guides and formers should be lubricated and maintained in good condition.

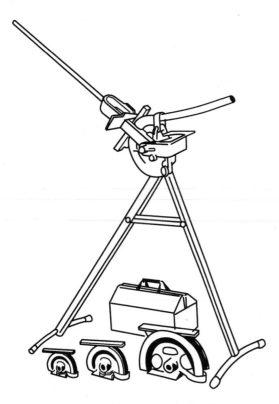

Figure 3.118   Portable rotary tube bender

Power tools

Although this title describes all kinds of tools driven by a variety of types of motor, so far as the plumber is concerned it is likely to include only a few tools, all of which are driven by electricity.

Electrical tools may be:

- mains voltage
- low voltage, with a step-down transformer
- double insulated
- fully insulated.

Mains voltage

Portable tools, like drills, usually have single phase universal motors and operate on 240 V. These tools have a three core cable with the casing connected to the earth connection. If this earthing becomes faulty, particularly in wet situations, the tool can cause a lethal electric shock. When working in premises where the earthing cannot be guaranteed, mains voltage tools should not be used.

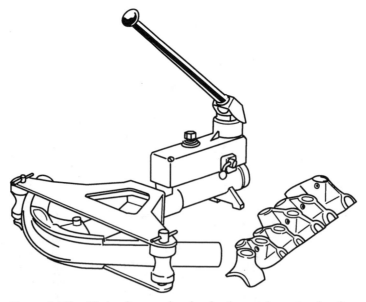

Figure 3.119   Hydraulic ram bender for heavy duty pipe bending. This type of bender is operated by a hydraulic pump and is commonly used for mild steel pipes

Low voltage

Transformers are used to step down the mains voltage from 240 V to 110 V for tools or 25 V for hand lead lamps. Usually both the live and neutral connections are fused on the transformer output. Low voltage tools can be fitted with special plugs so that they cannot be connected or used accidentally on full mains voltage.

Double insulated

These tools have additional insulation to eliminate risks from defective earthing. They are tested to 4000 V and may be used on 240 V supplies without an earth lead if they conform to BS 2769 and are identified by the appropriate BS symbols.

Fully insulated

This type of power tool is made entirely from shock-proof nylon and does not have a metal casing, therefore electricity cannot be conducted from any part, unless the casing becomes damaged. They are tested to 4000 V and may be used on 240 V without an earth like the double insulated tool.

The following notes are intended only as an introduction to power tools.

Drills

Portable electric drills generally have chucks to receive drills up to 10 mm in diameter. Two speed drills rotate at about 900 and 2400 revolutions per minute. Bench drills for larger work are usually fitted in workshops.

Percussion tools

These give the drill fast-hitting blows at the rate of about 50 per second. This hammer-action helps to penetrate hard materials such as concrete which are difficult to cut with an ordinary rotary drill. A special impact type of tungsten carbide tipped drill should be used with percussion tools to produce an accurate smooth hole.

Mechanical saws

These may be portable circular blade hand saws for cutting timber, or larger static machines for cutting mild steel pipes and rods. The item being cut must always be fixed or clamped securely and excessive pressure must not be used.

Screwing machines

There is a variety of types of machine for cutting similar to those on hand dies and many machines incorporate a pipe cutter and reamer. A suitable cutting lubricant must be used to keep the dies cool and assist with the cutting operation.

Cartridge tools

These tools act like a gun and shoot a hardened steel fixing stud into the material to which a fixing is required. Several types of fixing stud are available. Some are similar to wood nails for fixing timber, others have threaded ends to which a bracket, clip or nut can be screwed.

Water supply

Definition of water

Water is a chemical compound of the two gases hydrogen and oxygen. It is formed when the gas hydrogen or any substance containing hydrogen is burned.

One of the most important properties of water is its solvent power. It dissolves numerous gases and solids to form solutions. The purest natural water is rainwater collected in the open country. This contains small amounts of dissolved solids, mainly sodium chloride (common salt) dissolved from the air, and also dissolved gases: nitrogen, oxygen, carbon dioxide, nitric acid, and ammonia.

Rainwater collected in towns contains higher percentages of dissolved substances, and also soot, etc. In particular it may contain acids – sulphuric and carbonic – which may cause damage to certain stones and metals, particularly limestone and zinc.

Spring water usually contains more dissolved solids, the amount and kind depending on the type of soil and rocks through which it has passed.

River water is water which has passed through and over the ground and also contains some rainwater. Sea water contains the most dissolved matter.

Cold water supply

An adequate supply of pure water on tap is one of the prerequisites of modern living, a fact sometimes not fully appreciated by the average person. Local water authorities are required by law to provide a pure and wholesome supply of water, often referred to as 'potable' water, a term implying that it is fit for drinking and culinary purposes.

Before water is distributed through the water authority's distribution systems to individual premises, it must be collected and treated to rid it of any harmful waterborne bacteria and suspended organic and non-organic solids. Water authorities, through their bye-laws and inspectorates, constantly guard against pollution of main water supplies and every effort is made to ensure the supply of pure water to their consumers.

Because much of the work of a plumber is concerned with the supply of water and the fitting of appliances which are connected to the mains supplies, it is necessary that plumbers should have a good knowledge of water supply, an understanding of the methods used to prevent the possibility of pollution and also a good knowledge of (and the ability to interpret) the bye-laws relating to water supply.

Bye-laws

All the materials, i.e. pipes, fittings and appliances, used in water supply as well as the manner in which they are installed, are covered by *water bye-laws* and *codes of practice*. Before any work is carried out, the plumber must be conversant with all aspects of the work and the relevant regulations.

Water bye-laws are framed by various government bodies and give guidance about materials and methods of installation. They are accepted throughout the whole country.

The chemical properties of water

The chemical properties of water are not so constant or easily recognized as the physical ones. This is a fact which plumbers need to understand, since often these hidden properties are not discovered until their ill effects show in the form of corroded pipework, furred or scaled boilers and plumbing components that are not working properly. The chemical properties of water vary according to area and district, which is one reason why they are not constant. Water in its natural state as rainwater is not pure as it absorbs gases and dust from the atmosphere. It picks up other substances as it soaks through the ground before being collected and used.

Impurities dissolved in water may be gases, organic matter, minerals or a combination of these. As water falls as rainwater, it dissolves and absorbs atmospheric gases such as oxygen, sulphur dioxide and carbon dioxide; all of these tend to make the water aggressive and therefore *corrosive* to iron and steel pipework, storage vessels, radiators and boilers.

Water can also dissolve mineral solids that are present in the ground. One of these is calcium, which can be absorbed in the form of limestone or chalk. Water containing calcium is called 'hard' water and, when used in plumbing systems, forms a layer of scale or fur called an *encrustation*, which reduces the diameters of pipes and clogs the fine outlet holes in spray mixer taps and shower roses.

Figure 3.120 indicates the hardness of distributed water supplies in England and Wales.

Water can be classified as soft or hard.

Soft water

A water is said to be soft when it lathers readily. It is not very palatable as a drinking water, and has a

detrimental effect on most metals. It can cause rapid corrosion particularly of those metals which contain organic solutions.

Hard water

A water is said to be hard if it is difficult to obtain a lather. A hard water can be temporarily hard, permanently hard or both, depending upon the type or earth strata through which the water has passed.

Measurement of hardness

Hardness of water is expressed in parts per million (weight/volume) or in milligrams per litre, which is the same figure. At one time, degrees of hardness were classified according to Clarks scale in which 1° represents one grain of calcium per 4.5 litres.

Table 18 gives the accepted classifications of water according to their total hardness (both permanent and temporary).

Table 18

Designation of water	Parts per million or mg/litre
Soft	0 to 50
Moderately soft	50 to 100
Slightly hard	100 to 150
Moderately hard	150 to 200
Hard	200 to 300
Very hard	over 300

pH

pH value is a measure of how acid or alkaline a water is. The pH scale goes from 1 (strongly acidic) to 14 (strongly alkaline). Water with a pH of 7 is classified as neutral.

Sources of water supply

Rainfall

Rainfall is the source of all natural fresh water. When rain falls on the surface of the earth part immediately runs off to ditches or natural water courses (streams and rivers). The remainder soaks into the ground, some to remain underground for the whole of its journey until it mingles with salt water in the seas, some to break forth as springs, and some to be artificially extracted from wells (see Figure 3.121).

Whatever source of water is used – lakes, rivers, springs or wells – the available supply depends on the nature and size of the catchment area and the amount of rain that falls on it. The greatest supply is usually obtained where moisture-laden winds from the ocean pass over the mountain range which deflects them into higher and cooler regions where the moisture is condensed.

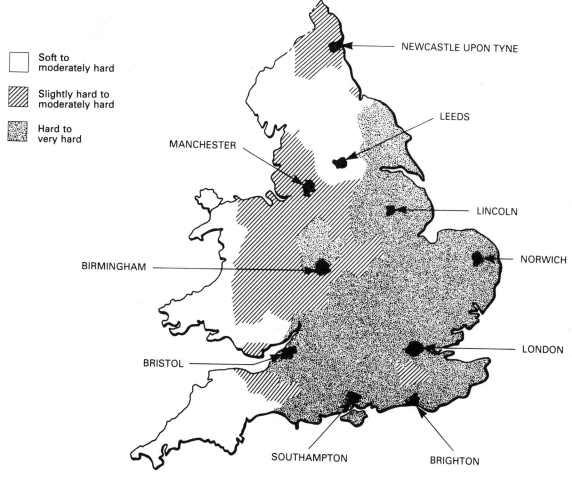

Figure 3.120   Hardness of distributed water

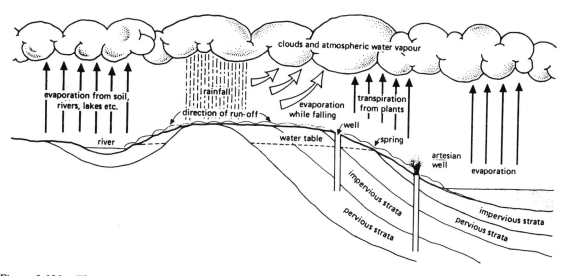

Figure 3.121   The water cycle

The average rainfall in England is about 0.875 m per annum, in Wales and Scotland 1.25 m, in Ireland 1.17 m and in the British Isles as a whole 1.15 m.

For purposes of water supply, rain which falls in autumn, winter and spring is the most important. A large proportion of the summer rainfall is lost by evaporation. Summer supplies from wells are not reliable because summer storms are so short and intense that more runs off the surface, instead of collecting in the way that long steady winter rainfall does.

Surface sources

Upland catchments

Water from upland catchments is usually of excellent quality, being soft and free from sewage or animal contamination or suspended matter. It is liable to be acid in character if it contains water from peat areas, and corrosive to lead pipes (a condition known as plumbo-solvency). As lead is poisonous such water must not be conveyed in lead pipes in an untreated state.

Lakes

Supplies from natural mountain lakes are similar in nearly all respects to those from upland catchments with artificial storage. Pond water cannot usually be regarded as a fit source of domestic water supply.

Rivers and streams

The quality of river water varies. A moorland stream which is not unduly peaty will generally be wholesome. Downstream a river will usually collect drainage from manured fields, farmyards and roads and become progressively more contaminated. Most lowland rivers receive sewage from towns and industrial effluent from factories and have become heavily polluted.

Outside manufacturing districts most large rivers furnish water for the supply of one or more towns past which they flow, where the amount of impurity is not too great.

River water varies in hardness according to the proportion of water reaching it from springs and surface run-off. Water in the upland reaches of rivers is naturally soft, that in the lower reaches is generally hard.

Collection tanks

Rainwater can be collected from roofs of buildings into tanks, in order to be stored over dry periods.

Slate roofs are best for collecting rainwater: tile or galvanized iron roofs will also serve. Roofs covered with lead, copper or tarred material are unsuitable.

Rainwater is the softest natural water, but after collection on a roof it may contain leaves, insects and bird droppings. If required for domestic purposes it should always be filtered, and before drinking it should be subjected to a suitable purification process – boiling is sufficient where small quantities are involved.

Underground sources

Public water supplies from underground sources are usually drawn from water-bearing formations deep in the earth and covered by impervious strata. The water is often derived from gathering grounds several miles away, and the long journey underground provides a very thorough filtration.

Springs

Spring water is water that has travelled through the ground and come to the surface as a result of geological conditions. Its qualities are similar to those of a well in the same circumstances.

Spring water may vary considerably in quality. When it has travelled long distances through a stratum of rock it may be free from contamination, but hard. When a spring is fed by local rainfall organic pollution is possible, but the water may be soft.

Wells

Well are classified as shallow or deep according to the water-bearing strata from which they derive their water. A well that is sunk into the first water-bearing strata is classified as shallow. A deep well is one sunk into the second water-bearing strata. Since the earth's strata vary in thickness, it is possible to have a shallow well deeper than a deep well.

Artesian wells

An artesian well or borehole is one which pierces an impervious stratum and enters a lower porous zone from which water rises as a 'gusher' above ground level. A similar borehole where water rises part of the way but does not reach the surface is called 'sub-artesian'.

Table 19 gives a summary of the quality of water from various sources.

Table 19 River pollution commissioners' classification table

Wholesome	1	Spring water	Very palatable
	2	Deep well water	
	3	Upland surface water	
Suspicious	4	Stored rainwater	Moderately palatable
	5	Surface water from cultivated land	
Dangerous	6	River water	Palatable
	7	Shallow well water	

The physical properties of water

Expansion of liquids

Different liquids have different thermal expansions (see Figure 3.122) and unlike solids have no fixed length or surface area, but always take up the shape of the containing vessel. Therefore in the case of liquids we are only concerned with volume changes when they are heated.

Definition

The coefficient of expansion of a liquid is the fraction of its volume by which it expands per degree rise in temperature.

Any attempt at very accurate measurement of the expansion of a liquid is complicated by the fact that the vessel which contains the liquid also expands.

However, since all liquids must always be kept in some kind of vessel or container it is just as useful to know the apparent expansion of a liquid. This is the difference between its real expansion and the expansion of the vessel, and is accurate enough for plumbers' work.

The unusual expansion of water

Not all substances expand when they are heated. Over certain temperature ranges they contract. Water is an outstanding example. If we take a quantity of water at 0 °C and begin to apply heat the water contracts over the temperature range 0–4°C.

At about 4°C the water reaches its smallest volume which means it is at maximum density. If we continue to apply heat to raise the temperature the water expands.

The peculiar expansion of water has an important bearing on aquatic life during very cold weather (see Figure 3.123). As the temperature of a pond falls, the water contracts, becomes denser and sinks. A circulation is set up until all the water reaches its maximum density at 4°C. If the temperature continues to drop, any water below 4°C will stay at the top due to its lower density. In due course ice

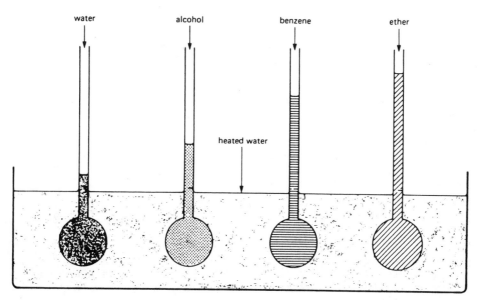

Figure 3.122   Comparison of expansion for different liquids

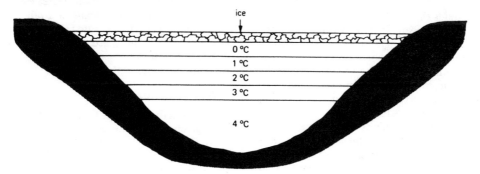

Figure 3.123   Temperatures in an ice covered pond

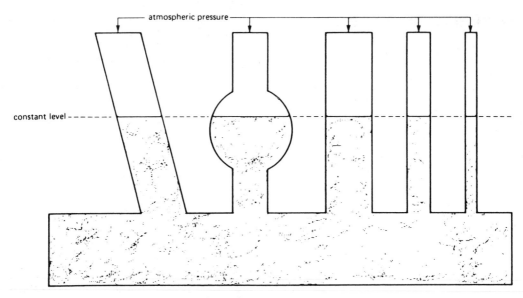

Figure 3.124 Apparatus used to show that water flows to find its own level

forms on the top of the water, and after this the water beneath can only loose heat by conduction. This explains why only very shallow water is likely to freeze solid.

As mentioned previously a rise in temperature causes objects to expand and a fall in temperature causes contraction. This rule applies to gases, most liquids and solids, but the effect is much more marked in the case of gases than in the case of the other two.

Pressure in liquids

Pressure is defined as the force acting normally per unit area. (Here the word 'normally' means vertically.)

The SI unit of pressure is newtons per square metre (N/m^2).

Water pressure

Water pressure is caused naturally by the weight of water which, under the influence of the earth's gravitational force, exerts pressure on all surfaces on which it bears (atmospheric pressure).

The molecules of which water is composed are held together by cohesion. This cohesive force is stronger in liquids than in gases but not as strong as in solids. This fact means that water molecules can move with relative freedom, and the force of gravity tends to pull them down in horizontal layers so that the surface of a liquid subject to the pressure of the atmosphere is horizontal. Therefore water flows to find its own level in irregular shaped vessels, pipes and cisterns (see Figure 3.124).

The fact that the liquid stands at the same vertical height in all the tubes whatever their shape confirms that, for a given liquid, the pressure at a point within it varies only with the vertical depth of the point below the surface of the liquid.

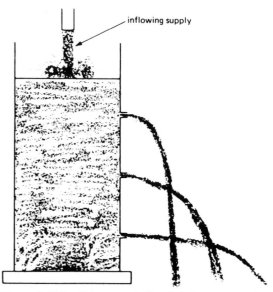

Figure 3.125 Spout can, indicating that pressure in a liquid increases with the depth of the liquid

Liquids exert a pressure in the same way that air does. The pressure in a liquid increases with depth. This may be shown by means of a tall vessel full of water with side tubes fitted at different heights (Figure 3.125). The speed with which water spurts out is greatest for the lowest tube, showing that pressure increases with depth.

Intensity of pressure

This is defined as that force created by the weight of a given mass of water acting on 1 unit of area (m^2). Or:

$$\text{intensity of pressure} = \frac{\text{force}}{\text{area}}$$

and, since force is measured by newtons:

$$\text{intensity of pressure} = \frac{\text{newtons}}{\text{area}}$$

The newton is of very small value in numerical terms, and it is generally more practical to use the kilonewton (kN = 1000 newtons) when dealing with pressures.

1 litre of water weighs 1 kg and the force produced by this mass of water equals 9.8 newtons. If we consider a cube of water measuring 1 m × 1 m × 1 m (1 m³), this volume of water contains 1000 litres and weighs 1000 kg. Therefore, the intensity of pressure on the base of this cube which has an area of 1 m² will be 1000 × 9.8 newtons or 9.8 kN/m².

So, if we visualize a column of water 1 m in height or depth and call this distance 'head' we can derive the following basic formula for calculating pressure:

$$\text{intensity of pressure} = \text{head (m)} \times 9.8 \text{ kN/m}^2$$

Example 1

Calculate the intensity of pressure on the base of a hot water tank subjected to a head of 4 m.

$$\begin{aligned}\text{intensity of pressure} &= \text{head (m)} \times 9.8 \text{ kN/m}^2\\ &= 4 \times 9.8\\ &= 39.2 \text{ kN/m}^2\end{aligned}$$

The example shows that a 4 m head of water will exert an intensity of pressure of 39.2 kN on a base area of 1 m². What must be considered now are areas larger or smaller than 1 m² which leads us to the total pressure acting upon an area.

If the pressure shown in the example had been acting upon a base of 2 m² then the total pressure acting upon the whole area would be 2 × 39.2 kN or 78.4 kN. At this point it should be noted that the area symbol (m²) is left out of the answer because with total pressure calculations we are not relating the pressure to 1 m² but to an area larger. The same rule applies to areas smaller than 1 m², which leads to the formula for calculating total pressure:

total pressure = intensity of pressure × area acted upon

Example 2

Calculate the total pressure on the base of the hot tank in Example 1, if the base has an area of 0.3 m².

$$\begin{aligned}\text{total pressure} &= \text{intensity of pressure} \times \text{area}\\ &\qquad\qquad \text{acted upon}\\ &= 39.2 \times 0.3\\ &= 11.76 \text{ kN}\end{aligned}$$

Units of pressure

Pressure can be calculated either by measuring the force exerted on a unit of area or by measuring the height of a column of liquid supported by the force.

So its units are either those of force per unit area, e.g. Newtons per square metre, or they are metres or millimetres height or 'head' of liquid.

There are alternative units. In some areas of activity kilograms force per square centimetre may be used and in the gas industry, for example, pressure will be measured normally in 'bars' and 'millibars'. The symbols are 'bar' and 'mbar'.

Where liquids are used in pressure gauges, water is the most common for low pressures and mercury, which is 13.6 times as dense, for higher pressures. The gauges have scales graduated in millibars.

It may sometimes be necessary to convert a pressure reading from force/area units to height units or vice versa and Table 20 shows the comparison between them.

Table 20 Comparison of units of pressure

Height	Bars	Force/area
1 m head of water	98 mbar	9800 N/m²
10.2 mm of water	1 mbar	100 N/m²
1 atmosphere or 760 mm of mercury	1013.25 mbar (1 bar)	101.3 kN/m² or 101,325 N/m²

Pressure in water heating systems

Hydrostatic pressure

'Hydrostatic pressure' is simply the pressure exerted in the system by the weight of the water.

Figure 3.126 shows a domestic water heating system consisting of a cistern A supplying cold water to a cylinder B, heated by a boiler C and with bath, basin and sink draw off taps at D, E and F.

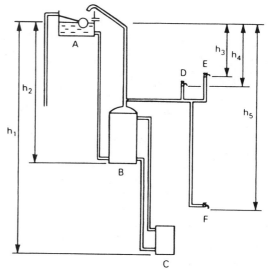

Figure 3.126 Pressures in a domestic hot water system

Table 21 Pressures of different heads of water

Head	Head (m)	Force/area (kN/m²)	Equivalent in millibars
h_1	5	49(50)*	490
h_2	2.5	24.5(25)	245
h_3	1.5	14.7(15)	147
h_4	2	19.6(20)	196
h_5	4	39.2(40)	392

*Figures in brackets are approximate.

Typical pressures in an average house are shown in Table 21. From the table the following points can be seen:

1) The pressure at the sink tap, F, is more than twice the pressure at the basin tap, E. So you would expect to get a much faster flow of water at the sink (depending on the pipes and the size of taps).

2) If the area of the base of cylinder was 0.8 square metres, then the force on the base would be:

   25 kN/m² (pressure) × 0.8 m² (area) = 20 kN or 20,000 Newtons

3) If the area of the base of the boiler was 0.5 square metres, then the force on the base would be:

   50 kN/m² × 0.5 m² = 25 kN

This shows why makers of boilers and water heaters always state a maximum head of water up to which their appliances may be fitted. If subjected to higher pressures the appliances could be damaged.

Circulating pressure

Water 'circulates' or goes round and round in water heating or wet central heating systems. The pressure which causes this circulation is naturally called 'circulating pressure'.

The circulating pressure in a system depends on two factors:

1) The difference in temperature between the hot water flowing from the boiler and the cold water returning to it,
2) The height of the columns of hot and cold water above the level of the boiler.

The example in Figure 3.127 shows part of a simple water circulation from a boiler to a radiator and back again.

Generally, central heating systems now rely on pumps to provide the main circulating pressure so that smaller bore pipes may be used. But gravity can be used and is still the motive force in many water heating systems. (Figure 3.126) shows the boiler connected to the cylinder by flow and return pipes, and the radiator in Figure 3.127 could be replaced by a cylinder. The principle is still the same although temperatures are lower.)

All fluids expand when heated and water is no exception. When a fluid expands, the same weight of fluid occupies a bigger volume. So its density (weight ÷ volume) is reduced. Put simply, a given volume of hot water weighs less than the same volume of cold water.

Tables are available giving the density of water at various temperatures and, if the flow and return temperatures and the circulation height are known, it is possible to calculate the circulating pressure in a system operating on gravity circulation.

Circulating pressure is proportional to the temperature difference between flow and return water and the circulating height.

Circulating pressure will increase:

1) If the temperature difference increases.
2) If the circulation height is increased.

The circulating pressure in Figure 3.127 is approximately 5 millibars. It can be obtained from the formula:

$$p = h\frac{(d_2 - d_1)}{d_2 + d_1} \times 196.1$$

where p = circulating pressure in millibars
h = circulation height in metres
d_1 = density of water in flow in kg/m³
d_2 = density of water in return in kg/m³ and
196.1 is a constant

From tables, d_1 at 82°C = 970.40 kg/m³
d_2 at 60°C = 983.21 kg/m³

Therefore $p = 4 \times \dfrac{983.21 - 970.40}{983.21 + 970.40} \times 196.1$

= 5.14 mbar (about 5 mbar)

Other tables are available which give a reading of circulating pressure per metre height directly from a temperature difference.

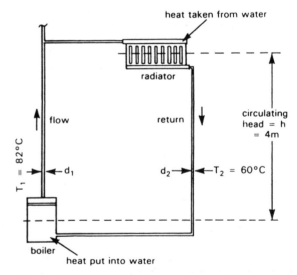

Figure 3.127 Circulating pressure. On a water heating system the cylinder would be in the position occupied by the radiator. T1 would be 60°C and T2 would be about 10°C when heating began.

Modes of heat transfer

Heat flows from a substance at a higher temperature to one at a lower temperature, and this effect is known as 'heat loss'. Heat loss continues until both substances are at the same temperature – unless some form of thermal insulation is used to isolate one substance from the other and thus prevent heat from being transferred.

Heat can travel as a result of one of the following 'modes of heat transfer': conduction, convection, and radiation, or by a combination of two or more of them.

Conduction occurs when heat flows through or along a material (see Figure 3.128) or from one material to another in contact with it. Conduction increases with the difference in temperature between the hot and cooler materials in contact. Some materials, such as metals, are good conductors of heat; others which resist the passage of heat by conduction are called poor conductors (thermal insulators). A good thermal insulating material must, among other things, be a poor conductor of heat.

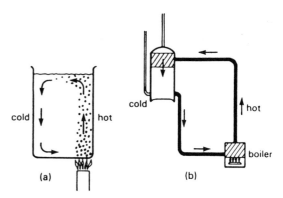

Figure 3.129   Convection currents in liquid: (a) in an open vessel; (b) in a closed water heating circuit

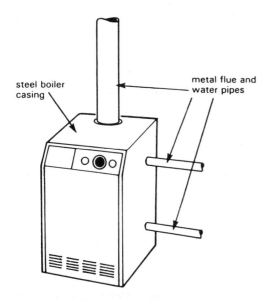

Figure 3.128   Conductors of heat

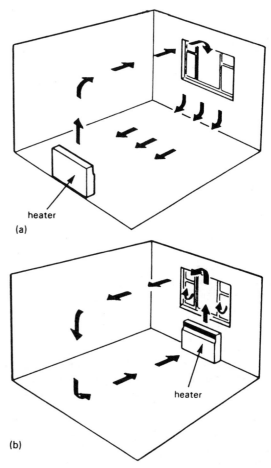

Figure 3.130   Convection currents in a room: (a) heater at opposite end to window – air cooled by the window becomes a cold draught across the floor; (b) heater under window – cold air is warmed and carried up by convection currents

Convection occurs in liquids and gases. When the liquid or gas is heated, the warmed particles expand and become lighter, the cooler heavier particles fall by gravity and push the ligher, warmed ones upward (see Figures 3.129 and 3.130). In this way convection currents will continue so long as heat is applied or so long as there is some difference in temperature in the liquid or gas.

Radiation heat is given off from a hot body to a colder one in the form of heat energy rays. Radiant heat rays do not appreciably warm the air through which they pass, but they do warm any cooler solid body with which they come into contact (see Figure 3.131). Radiant heat falling on a surface is partly absorbed and partly reflected. A dull black surface is a much better absorber of radiation than a polished surface. The latter is therefore a good reflector of heat.

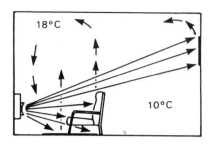

Figure 3.131   Room heated by radiation from a gas fire

Electricity supply

There is a growing need for mechanical engineering services operatives to have knowledge of electricity and electrical installation work. More and more plumbing systems and components depend on electricity to provide the energy for them to operate, and the NVQ plumbing scheme includes several objectives related to electrical systems and components.

It is necessary for operatives to acquire as quickly as possible an understanding of the relevant terminology which is described in the glossary at the back of this book. It must be mentioned that the glossary does not give a complete coverage of electrical engineering and electrical installation terminology but contains sufficient information to enable plumbing students to make reference to specific topics of interest to them and to the electrical technology covered in the following pages.

Electricity is a form of energy which is produced by generating equipment at power stations. These generators may be powered by coal, oil, or gas turbines or a nuclear reactor. The power of flowing water may also be used to drive these generators (hydro electricity). The Central Electricity Generating Board is responsible for the generation and primary distribution of electricity, while area boards handle the regional and local distribution and supply of electricity to individual properties.

Electricity from the generators is supplied into the national grid (network of overhead cables on pylons) at very high voltages (electric pressure). This is transformed down in voltage and fed into the regional grids, which consist of both overhead and underground cables. Substations in the regional grid again reduce the voltage to suit the power requirements of the user.

Electricity from the grid is brought into a building to the meter position either by an overhead service cable from the Board's supply pole (common in rural areas) or an underground service cable connected to the Board's main, which is situated under the road. The service cable terminates at a sealed fuse unit which is connected via two short lengths of cable

(live and neutral) to the meter fixed alongside. Electricity flows through the live wire and in order to complete the circuit returns along the neutral. In addition, an earthing connection is provided to an earth clamp, earth rod or an earth leakage circuit breaker. Some properties have a second meter which operates through a sealed time switch, to record the utilization of offpeak (cheaper) electricity.

The risks of electrocution and fire must be guarded against in all electrical installations. The precautions which are established practice are shown in principle in Figure 3.132.

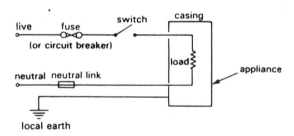

Figure 3.132   Established precautions

Supplies into consumers' premises

The *Electricity Supply Regulations* 1988 place a responsibility on all consumers of electricity to provide and maintain safe electrical installations. Such installations have to be designed to the requirements of the *IEE Wiring Regulations* for electrical installations. It is usually the practice for a domestic consumer to be supplied with a single-phase, two-wire a.c. supply at a nominal voltage of 240 V and a frequency of 50 Hz. The basic arrangement is shown in Figure 3.133 where it will be seen that the single-phase supply is actually derived from a three-phase, four-wire system which operates at 415 V between its supply lines. Sometimes this voltage is used in domestic premises but it is more suitable for larger types of premises such as

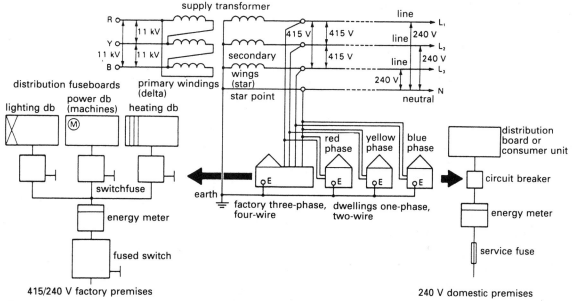

Figure 3.133 Supplies into consumers' premises

shops, offices and factories which demand more current and use a variety of three-phase equipment.

For single-phase supplies of 240 V and up to 100 A loading, the supply authority's low-voltage distribution cable will either be overhead or underground and will normally be installed along a public pathway or road, mostly at the front of consumers' property. The incoming supply to a particular consumer may be directly connected to the nearest point of the main distribution cable or it may be looped to an adjacent service point in nearby premises. This service termination will be accommodated either within the consumer's premises or in an external meter cabinet. It will consist of a 'cut-out' fuse and an energy meter to record the number of units (kWh) of electricity.

The 'cut-out' contains a solidly bolted neutral conductor or a combined neutral-earth conductor known as a PEN conductor and a single-pole fuse-link which is normally a BS 1361 Type II high breaking capacity cartridge fuse of 100 A rating. This fuse provides protection against overcurrent between the output terminals of the 'cut-out' and the supply terminals. Figure 3.134 shows one method of wiring a consumer's premises.

The electricity meter or energy meter is an integrating meter and records the number of units (1 kWh is 1 unit) of electricity a consumer uses. There are basically two kinds of energy meter, the *dial meter* and *digital meter*. When reading a dial meter, you should note that the adjacent dials revolve in opposite directions. You should read the meter from left to right, ignoring the dial marked $\frac{1}{10}$ which is used for testing purposes. Other points to note are: always write down the number the pointer has passed and if it is directly over a number, write this number down and underline it. If it is followed

by a 9, reduce the underlined figure by 1 (e.g. 234911 becomes 233911). In the digital meter, the units used are shown by a row of figures. If the premises are fitted with an Economy 7 meter, it will have two rows of figures, one for the lower-priced night-rate units and the other for the day-rate units.

Distribution arrangements

The connection between the supply authority's equipment and the next stage of protection is the responsibility of the consumer and it includes the meter tails, consumer unit and earthing and bonding arrangements. While the supply authority make every effort to provide an earthing terminal, where this is not possible the consumer has to install an earth electrode on the premises. This arrangement is known as a TT earthing system. Premises that have this system are supplied from overhead lines. Figure 3.135 shows this system, along with the supply authority's TN-S and TN-C-S systems. Both these latter systems allow the armouring of the service cable to be used as a means of earthing. The purpose of providing a good earth return from a TN-S and TN-C-S system is to encourage a large fault current to flow from the consumer's installation back to the supply transformer. If the earth loop impedance path is low enough then the returning fault current will automatically disconnect the circuit protective device. Protective devices for fixed circuits and socket outlet circuits have to meet two different disconnection times, namely 5 s and 0.4 s respectively. The faster operating time to disconnect socket outlets is because of the vulnerable nature presented by equipment connected through plugs and flexible leads. The *IEE Wiring Regulations* provide a number

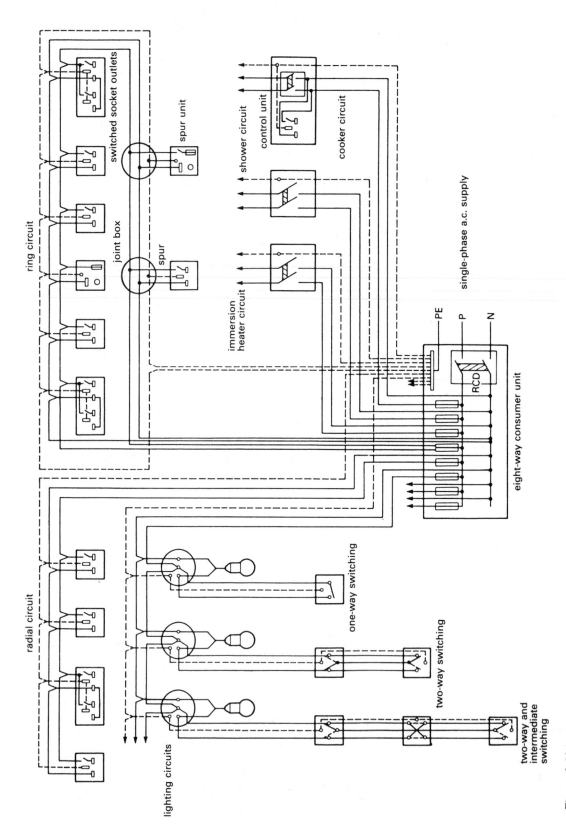

Figure 3.134 Final circuits

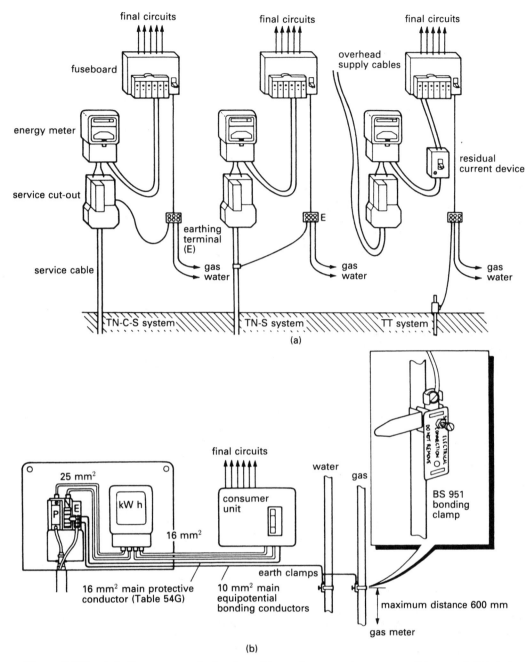

Figure 3.135   (a) Common methods of earthing a consumer's premises; (b) typical TN-C-S supply into a consumer's premises showing meter tails and earthing and bonding arrangements

of tables which give the maximum impedance values for different types of circuit protective device.

To address the fundamental requirements for safety, the supply of electricity into a consumer's premises must satisfy three important conditions, namely:

- control
- circuit protection and
- earth leakage protection.

The first condition is satisfied by isolation and switching so that the electrical installation can be cut off from its voltage source. The second condition is satisfied by circuit protective devices, designed to disconnect circuits automatically from excess current or overcurrent. The third condition may also be satisfied by circuit protective devices but is more favourably achieved using residual current devices which detect leakage currents to earth and act as a means of protection against electric shock and fire.

Figure 3.136 shows the sequence of control and protection in two distinct types of premises. Where separate buildings exist, it is essential they have their own means of control and protection.

There are numerous requirements in the *IEE Wiring Regulations* for isolation and switching (see Regulation 130–06, Chapter 46, Sections 476 and 537). Where electrical equipment is fed from a final

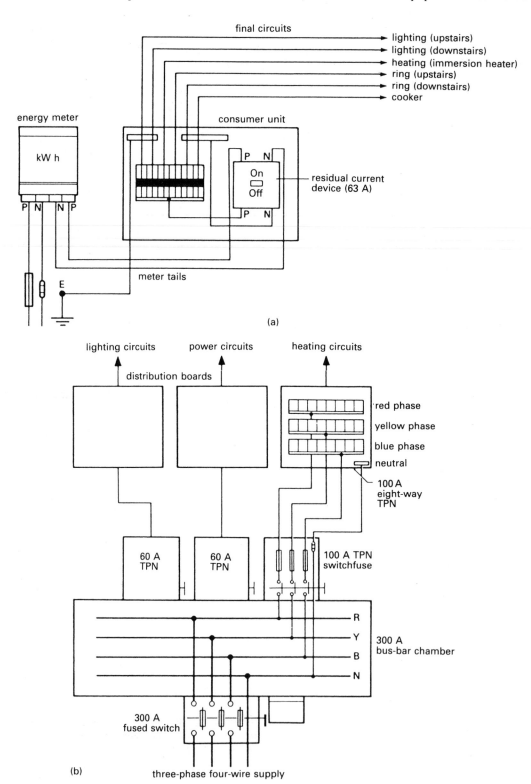

Figure 3.136 *Supplies into consumers' premises: (a) domestic premises; (b) factory premises*

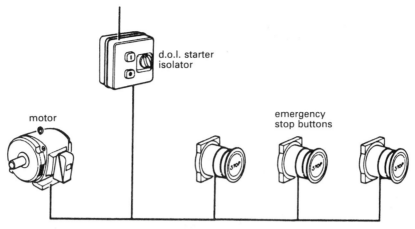

Figure 3.137   Control of motor showing emergency stop button

circuit, an isolator should be placed adjacent to that equipment but if the equipment is remotely placed, provision should be made to stop it being inadvertently closed during operation. This is often achieved with a padlock or removable handle. Besides functional switching for control purposes, some circuits might need switching off for mechanical maintenance or even emergency switching. The former is used to protect persons undertaking non-electrical tasks such as cleaning and maintenance, whereas the latter is used for the rapid cutting off of

a circuit in order to remove a hazard. It should be noted that a plug and socket cannot be used for emergency switching; it is best achieved with a single switch or combination of devices initiated by a single action such as emergency push buttons of the latched type. Such devices should be clearly identifiable and preferably red in colour and must be manually operated and placed in a position of accessibility. Figure 3.137 is a typical emergency stop button control circuit.

Wiring systems

Chapter 52 of the *IEE Wiring Regulations* concerns selection and erection of wiring systems. In practice, there may be several factors likely to influence the choice of wiring system for a particular electrical installation; for example, the type of building and its use. A *surface-type* wiring system may be acceptable in a factory or workplace but may be totally unacceptable in an office block or hotel or even domestic dwelling, simply on the grounds of appearance and aesthetic taste. Here, it is usual to install a hidden or *flush-type* wiring system, such as PVC-insulated cables, mechanically protected under plaster. There is also consideration for the environment, such as excessive temperature, as well as any particular external influence from a corrosive atmosphere such as salt or dust. Some of these factors have already been mentioned. Questions will need to be asked about the chosen system's durability, its mechanical protection and cost comparison with other favourable systems; not only might there be a material cost benefit but also an installation time benefit. Another important question is whether the chosen system needs to cater for any likely alterations and/or the installing of additional circuits. Fortunately, in many large premises, one is likely to come across numerous wiring systems and these are often integrated with each other so that alterations and modifications can occur.

Some common types of wiring system found today are:

- PVC-insulated PVC-sheathed cables;
- PVC-insulated armoured PVC-sheathed cables;
- mineral-insulated metal-sheathed cables;
- metal and plastic conduit systems (incorporating cables);
- metal and plastic trunking systems (incorporating cables);
- bus-bar trunking systems.

It should be pointed out that there are various support arrangements for the above systems, such as cable tray, ducting and cable trench; see the methods in Table 9A of the *IEE Wiring Regulations*.

PVC-insulated PVC-sheathed cables

This wiring system, shown in Figure 3.138, has a general use and will be found listed in Table 4D1–2 of the IEE Regulations. The common PVC/PVC/ c.p.c. is widely used for surface wiring, where it needs to be clipped and supported to meet the requirements of the Regulations. There are requirements for the internal radii of bends and supports. The wiring system can be hidden from view, above a false ceiling, in joists or buried under plaster. In a false ceiling, the cables should be kept clear of sharp edges and be adequately supported. Where they are run through holes in wooden joists, the cables must

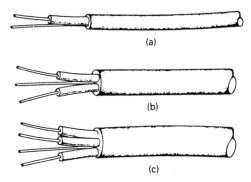

Figure 3.138   PVC-insulated, PVC-sheathed cables 600/1000 V: (a) single-core; (b) two-core; (c) three-core

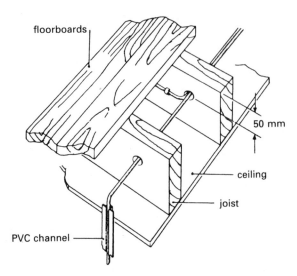

Figure 3.139   PVC cables under floorboards

be at least 50 mm from the top or bottom of the joist (Regulation 522–06–05). If cables are to be laid in existing notches, they should be provided with mechanical protection to prevent damage occurring from floor fixings. Figure 3.139 shows a typical arrangement through joists. It should be noted from Table 4D2 that these cables have a maximum conductor operating temperature of 70°C, and it will be observed that various correction factors apply for ambient temperatures in excess of 30°C. Chapter 42 of the IEE Regulations deals with *protection against thermal effects*. It is generally recognised that a group correction factor does not apply to domestic final circuits but, where this is the case in other instances. Table 4B1 has to be used. At terminations, the outer PVC sheath should not be removed any further than is necessary and all conductors should be identified by their appropriate colour coding. Sections 526 and 527 of the IEE Regulations cover *connections* and *selection* and *erection* to minimise the spread of fire, respectively. It is important to make sure that no mechanical stress is placed on the cables and that cable glands securely retain the outer sheath of the cable. On no account should conductor strands be cut in order to fit into a termination post.

PVC-insulated armoured PVC-sheathed cables

PVC armoured cables have a wide commercial and industrial application and there are several tables in the IEE Regulations concerning both the copper and aluminium conductor types. Figure 3.140(a) shows a diagram of a typical cable; the armouring consists of galvanised steel wire secured between PVC bedding and a tough PVC outer sheath. The armouring is often used as a protective conductor but this should be checked by calculation using Regulation 543-01-03. An alternative method is to apply the following table (Table 22) which is derived from BS 6346 and shows the nearest smaller

Table 22

Nominal area of conductor (mm²)	Nominal area of copper conductor equivalent to armouring (mm²)		
	Two-core	Three-core	Four-core
2.5	1.5	1.5	1.5
4.0	1.5	2.5	4.0
6.0	2.5	4.0	4.0
10.0	4.0	4.0	4.0
16.0	4.0	4.0	6.0
25.0	6.0	6.0	6.0
50.0	6.0	6.0	10.0

copper cable size equivalent to the armouring of the chosen cables.

The cables are often clipped on a surface using recommended wall cleats, or they can be installed on cable tray or run in a trench as outlined in Table 4A of the Regulations. Where they are buried in soil, one will find that the usual practice is to provide either cable tiles or yellow warning tape laid on top so as to denote their position. They must also be installed deep enough to avoid damage from any possible ground disturbance (see Regulation 522-06-03).

It is important to see that cable terminations are mechanically and electrically sound and that the cable gland and steel armouring make an effective earth connection. The use of an earth tag is recommended in order to give earth continuity between the gland and the steel enclosure to which the gland is fixed. All conductor cores of multicore cables should be identified properly using appropriate markers.

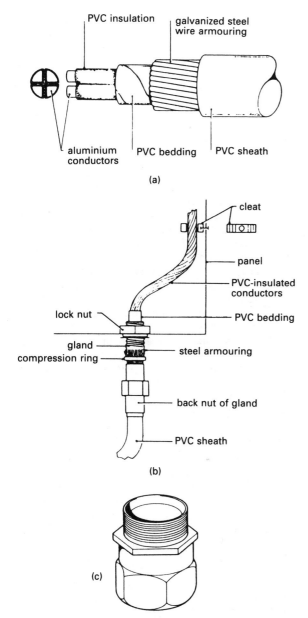

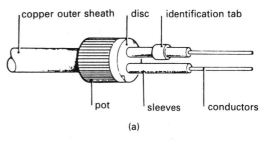

(a)

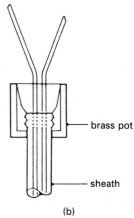

(b)

Figure 3.141 (a) Cable termination; (b) screw-on seal

Figure 3.140 (a) PVC-armoured, PVC-insulated cable; (b) termination; (c) gland

Mineral-insulated metal-sheathed cables

Mineral-insulated (MI) cables have a very wide commercial and industrial use. The common types are listed in Tables 4J1 to 4J2 of the Regulations, where they are divided between light-duty and heavy-duty use and the outer sheath either covered with PVC or not covered. These cables are ideal for 'hot' installations and their termination accessories such as sleeving, seals and compound can be designed for maximum sheath operating temperatures of 105°C. Figure 3.141 shows a typical MI cable termination. The cable conductors and sheath are generally constructed of high-conductivity copper or aluminium and, as already indicated,

both types may be provided with a PVC oversheath to give added protection against corrosion. The insulation medium between the conductor cores is a compressed mineral powder called magnesium oxide, and there have been improvements to reduce its hygroscopic nature (i.e. its ability to absorb moisture). Termination of the inner conductor cores involves several tools. The screw-on pot seal is widely used and this is attached to the sheath using a pot wrench. The correct temperature sealing compound is then inserted into the pot and the disc and insulating sleeving attached using a crimping tool.

The cables are often referred to as mineral-insulated metal-sheathed (m.i.m.s.) cables and are fireproof, waterproof and oilproof. They are also non-ageing and have higher current ratings compared with equivalent cable sizes. They are ideal for fire alarm circuits, boiler rooms and garage/petrol filling installations where dangerous atmospheres are likely to be present in Zone 1 hazardous areas. Here, they are fitted with flame-proof glands and the cables have an overall extruded covering of PVC. The metal sheath of these cables satisfies both shock protection and thermal protection requirements since it is approximately four times the cross-sectional area of the inside cores. To satisfy earthing connections, earth-tail pots are available having a cross-sectional area equal to the related size of the phase conductor(s). It is recommended that these should always be used for continuing the protective conductor function of the sheath through the earthing terminal at outlet points.

Metal and plastic conduit systems

Conduit systems are in wide use today either as surface or flush wiring arrangements. The common sizes are 16, 20, 25 and 32 mm. They provide the installed cables, such as the single-core PVC insulated or ethylene propylene rubber (e.p.r.) insulated cables, with additional mechanical protection. The advantage of conduit is the amount of flexibility it offers to final circuits, since cables can be added or withdrawn. It is important to see that the conduits are erected first before the cables are drawn in (Regulation 522-08-01) and it is equally or more important that *metal conduit* systems are both electrically and mechanically sound, even if it is decided to install protective conductors for additional safety (Regulation 543-02-04). Further requirements are made as shown in Figure 3.142.

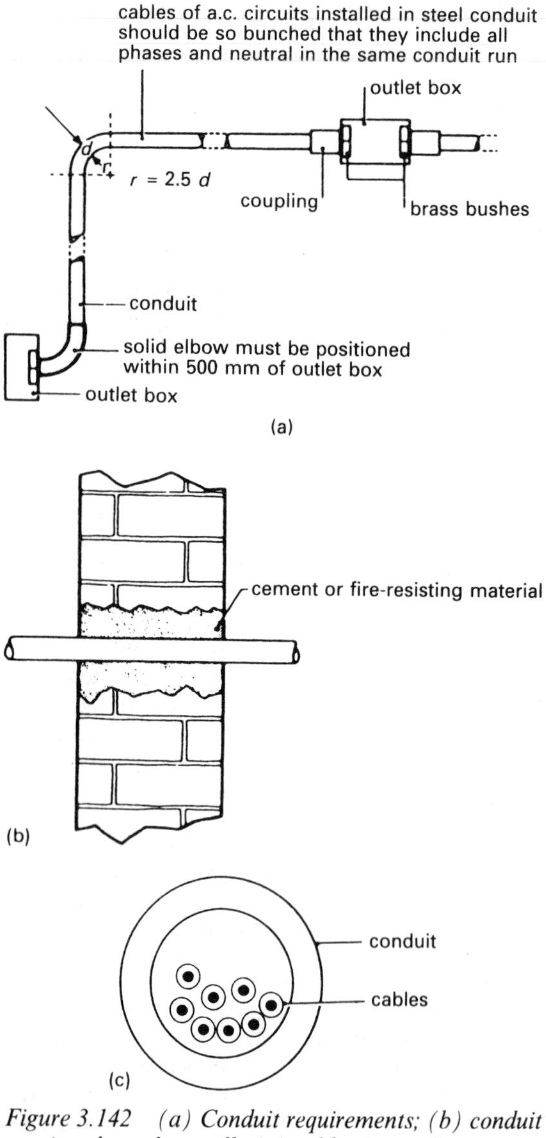

Figure 3.142   (a) Conduit requirements; (b) conduit passing through a wall; (c) cables in conduit

Conduits should be distinguished from other services by the colour orange (Regulation 514-03-01): in damp situations, galvanized conduit or plastic conduit should be used. With either method, it is essential to provide drainage facilities for the release of moisture (see Regulation 522-03-02). One of the most important requirements is Regulation 521-02-01 (*conductors of a.c. circuits installed in ferrous enclosures*): the reason behind this regulation is to stop *eddy currents* flowing in the metal conduit, which would result in them becoming hot and affecting the cables inside. It should also be pointed out that 3 m is the maximum length of span for heavy gauge steel conduit used for overhead wiring between buildings and it has to be a minimum size of 20 mm and be unjointed.

With regard to *plastic conduit*, the system is of course non-rusting and is a protective measure in itself against indirect contact. Despite this fact, separate protective conductors must be enclosed in the system and whilst rigid PVC conduit is suitable for normal ambient temperatures it must be remembered that it has a greater coefficient of expansion than steel and therefore provision must be made to allow for movement. It is recommended that expansion couplers be fitted in the worst affected areas. Regulation 522-06-01 should be noted with regard to plastic boxes used for suspending luminaires.

Insulation

All conductors are covered with insulating material or supported on insulators within an earthed casing with a clear air gap round each conductor. Standards of insulation vary with voltage. If a number of wires carrying different voltages are enclosed in a trunking they must all be insulated to the standard of the highest voltage. To avoid this, systems at different voltages are usually run in separate trunkings (e.g. British Telecom wiring and electricity supply wiring). Figure 3.143 illustrates different types of conductor.

Fusing

Each section of wiring must be protected by having in the circuit a fuse wire which will melt if a current passes higher than that which is safe for the wiring (see Figure 3.144).

This prevents overheating of wiring with the possible risk of fire. Fuses may be of the traditional type where a fuse wire is stretched between terminals in a ceramic holder, or of the modern cartridge type where the wire is held in a small ceramic tube with metal ends.

The cartridge types of fuse are much easier and quicker to replace. It is also possible to use circuit-breakers instead of fuses (see Figure 3.145. These operate by thermal or magnetic means and switch off the circuit immediately an overload occurs. They can be reset immediately by a switch. They are more

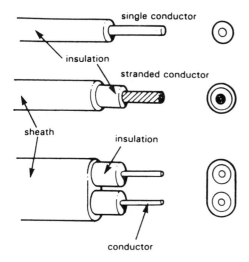

Single conductor, single core, insulated, non-sheathed.

Stranded conductor, single core insulated, sheathed.

Two-core flat, insulated and sheathed (also called flat twin).

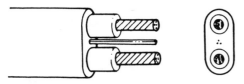

As above with an uninsulated earth continuity wire in the same sheath.

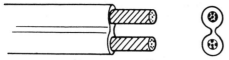

Parallel twin, cores easily separated without damage to insulation of either.

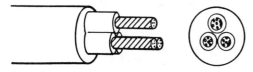

Three-core, insulated, sheathed, unarmoured.

Figure 3.143   Electrical conductors

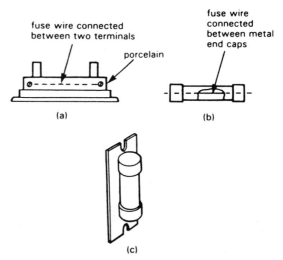

Figure 3.144   Types of fuse: (a) rewirable, BS 3036; (b) cartridge, BS 1362; (c) high rupturing capacity, BS 88

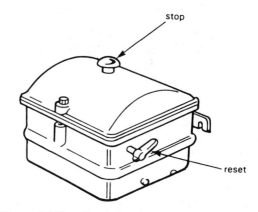

Figure 3.145   Circuit-breaker

Switch polarity

The position of the switch has the same effect upon safety as that of the fuse. If the switch is fitted on the neutral side of the apparatus this will always be live, even when the switch is turned off. Switches are therefore always fitted on the phase side of the apparatus they control.

Earthing

Any metalwork directly associated with electrical wiring could become live if insulation frayed or if wires became displaced. Anyone touching such a piece of apparatus would run the risk of serious electric shock. This is avoided by earthing the metalwork so that a heavy current flows to earth and the fuse is blown immediately the fault occurs. Although the neutral wire is earthed it will not serve for this purpose and a separate set of conductors for earthing are provided in almost all electrical installations. The earth connection itself is made locally in the building (see Figure 3.135 on p. 105).

expensive than fuses but have the advantage that they can also be used as switches to control the circuits they serve. They are particularly valuable in industrial uses where circuits may become overloaded in normal operation and the circuit-breaker will switch off but may be switched on again immediately the overload is removed. In domestic circumstances the blowing of a fuse or operation of a circuit-breaker usually indicates a fault.

Modern practice is to provide a fuse, or circuit-breaker, at the phase end of the circuit (called the line) and a simple link at the neutral end.

Bathrooms

In bathrooms and similar situations where water is present and metal fittings or wet concrete floors provide a good passage to earth, special safety precautions are called for. No socket outlets or switches may be provided in the area at risk. They must be sited outside the area, or on the ceiling, operated by non-conducting pulls. Where any electrical apparatus is present, all metal, including not only the casing of electrical apparatus but also pipework, baths, etc., must be bonded together electrically and earthed.

Terminations and connections

The type of termination used depends upon the type and size of cable and the kind of connection to be made. Figure 3.146 illustrates termination to a plug.

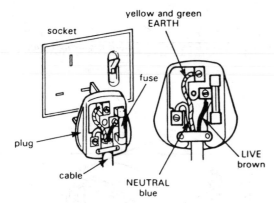

Figure 3.146   Terminations to a plug

Termination of cables and flexible cords

For flexible cords, the bare stranded conductors are usually twisted together and doubled back, if room permits, then screwed firmly in a pillar terminal, as shown in Figure 3.147.

For cables having single-stranded conductors which are to be terminated and connected under screwheads or nuts, it is convenient to shape the bare end into an eye to fit over the thread as shown in Figure 3.148.

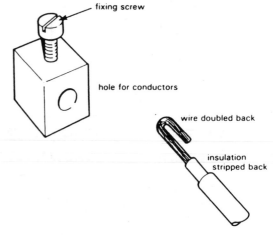

Figure 3.147   Connection to terminal

Cables with more than one stranded conductor may be terminated in a similar manner to that shown for the flexible cord.

Sockets (soldered and crimped)

For conductors of larger cross-sectional area, a socket may be used. There are two methods of fixing a socket to a cable end. One method is by soldering a tinned copper socket on the cable end. The other method is to fasten a compression-type socket on the cable end using a crimping tool. The two methods are shown in Figure 3.149.

The crimped socket is used to a large extent for terminating smaller cables. In smaller sizes they are

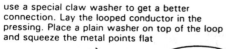
use a special claw washer to get a better connection. Lay the looped conductor in the pressing. Place a plain washer on top of the loop and squeeze the metal points flat

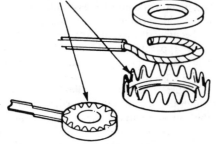

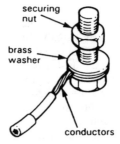

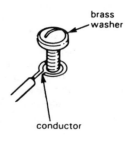

Figure 3.148   Termination under screwheads or nuts

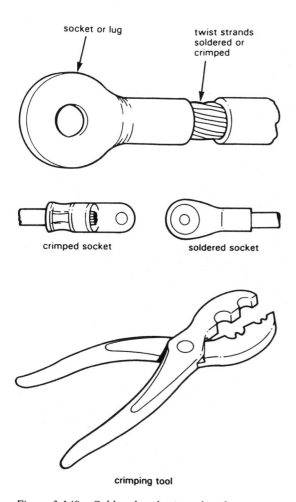

Figure 3.149   Soldered and crimped sockets

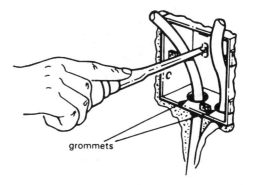

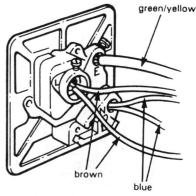

Figure 3.150   Wiring a socket outlet

even being used for flexible cords. Hand crimping tools are usually used for smaller size sockets which are capable of crimping a range of different sizes.

Termination of an aluminium conductor

Where an aluminium conductor is to be connected to a terminal it must be ensured that the conductor is not under excessive mechanical pressure. Further, an aluminium conductor must not be placed in contact with a brass terminal or any metal which is an alloy of copper. This may only be done if the terminal has been plated, otherwise corrosion would take place.

Other types of cables

When cables having metallic braid, sheath or tape coverings are used, the sheath must be cut back from the end of the insulation. This is done to prevent leakage from live parts to the covering. However, this is unnecessary for mineral-insulated cables. The ends of mineral-insulated copper-sheathed cables must be protected from moisture by sealing, ensuring that the mineral insulation is perfectly dry before sealing.

Wiring to socket outlets, spur boxes and junction boxes

Wiring a socket outlet (see Figure 3.150)

1) Cut the cable loop to make two tails 75 mm long and thread the cables through grommets in the mounting box.
2) Screw the mounting box to the wall and strip back the cable insulation.
3) Twist together and connect:
   (a) Brown wires to terminal L.
   (b) Blue wires to terminal N.
4) Fit green/yellow insulated sleeving over both earth wires.
5) Twist earth wires together and connect to terminal E.
6) Tighten all securing screws.

Note Ensure that the wires are pushed into terminals up to the insulation.

Spur boxes (see Figure 3.151)

These are fitted in a similar manner to socket outlets but have two sets of terminals. The lead to the appliance must be clamped in the cord grip.

Junction boxes

Junction boxes (Figure 3.152) have four knockout

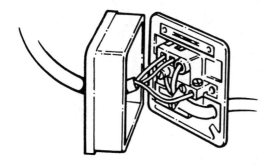

Figure 3.151   Spur box

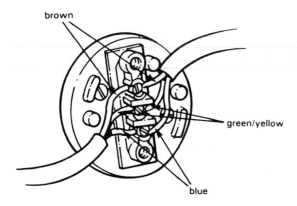

Figure 3.152   Junction box

sections for cable entry and exit. The central terminal is always used for the earth connection.

It is good practice to run spurs from the back of a socket but junction boxes can be used for this purpose.

Fuses for domestic appliances

The watt is the unit of electrical power, and can be calculated by multiplying volts by amps. If we know the voltage of the supply and wattage of an appliance we can calculate how much current the appliance will need by dividing watts by volts.

Most electrical appliances have a label fixed to them giving the voltage with which they must be supplied and the wattage of the appliance. This is very useful in deciding what value of fuse should be used for a particular appliance.

Example 3

An electric heater is rated at 3 kW and is designed to be used with a supply voltage of 240 Volts

$$= \frac{\text{watts}}{\text{volts}} = \text{amps} = \frac{3000}{240} = 12.5$$

Therefore the current required by this appliance is 12.5 amps, and a correct value fuse must be fitted. If a 10 amp fuse is used the heater will attempt to draw more current than the fuse will pass, the fuse will blow (melt), breaking the circuit and cutting off the supply. On the other hand a 13 amp fuse will permit the heater to operate normally and still provide a safety factor if needed.

Questions for you

1. Describe what is meant by the terms *element metals* and *alloys*.

   _____

   _____

   _____

   _____

2. Name the *two* basic types of plastic.

   (a) _____

   (b) _____

3. State *six* properties of plumbing materials.

   (a) _____

   (b) _____

   (c) _____

   (d) _____

   (e) _____

   (f) _____

4. Describe the basic difference between the two types of capillary joint used for joining copper tube.

   _____

   _____

5. What is the purpose of the metal insert incorporated into some types of joint used for connecting polyethylene pipes?

   _____

   _____

6. State *three* factors that will affect the type of pipe clip selected for a particular situation.

   (a) _____

   (b) _____

   (c) _____

7. Calculate the volume of a rectangular cistern which measures $950\,mm \times 840\,mm \times 780\,mm$ high.

   _____

   _____

8. Name the two organizations that produce the listing of tools that make up a plumber's tool kit.

   (a) _____

   (b) _____

9. Give *two* reasons why it would be wrong to use an oil-based jointing compound to seal a distribution pipe to a plastic cold water storage cistern.

   (a) _____

   (b) _____

10. Name the *two* tools used for cutting internal and external threads.

    (a) _____

    (b) _____

11. Steel cuttings left in a galvanized storage cistern are likely to cause
    (a) electrostatic action
    (b) plumbo-solvency
    (c) dezincification
    (d) electrolytic action.

12. The colour code indication for pipelines carrying drinking water is
    (a) green
    (b) yellow
    (c) blue
    (d) red.

13. A 3 m head of water will produce an intensity of pressure in kPa (kN/m^2) of
    (a) 2.943
    (b) 29.43
    (c) 294.3
    (d) 2943.

14. Water at normal atmospheric pressure will expand continuously if its temperature increases from
    (a) 0 to 4 °C
    (b) 0 to 100 °C
    (c) 3 to 40 °C
    (d) 4 to 100 °C.

15. Heating temporarily hard water above 65 °C will cause
    (a) electrolysis
    (b) erosion
    (c) incrustation
    (d) corrosion.

16. Potable waters are permanently hard if they contain
    (a) magnesium bicarbonate
    (b) calcium sulphates
    (c) ferric salts
    (d) calcium bicarbonates.

17. The most common material used for sacrificial anodes in relation to cathodic protection is
    (a) magnesium
    (b) zinc
    (c) copper
    (d) iron.

18. The type of water most likely to cause corrosion of metal water pipes and fittings is
    (a) temporarily hard water
    (b) permanently hard water
    (c) soft water
    (d) potable water.

19. Two equal volumes of water at an initial temperature of 15 °C are heated to 30 °C and 80 °C respectively. The water heated to 80 °C will
    (a) occupy a greater volume
    (b) have less mass
    (c) have a lower heat content
    (d) be heavier.

20. Which of the following is the correct method of jointing polyethylene tube used for water supply?
    (a) solvent welding
    (b) compression joints
    (c) socket joints
    (d) swayed joints

21. The byelaws of water authorities are designed to
    (a) prevent misuse, pollution and waste of water
    (b) ensure a high standard of workmanship
    (c) prevent variety of practice in the area
    (d) ensure compliance with government requirements.

22. Low carbon steel tube is made in three grades: heavy, medium and light weight. In the three grades the
    (a) outside diameter varies with the grade
    (b) actual internal diameter of the tube is the same
    (c) pipe wall thickness is the same
    (d) outside diameter of the tube is the same.

23. To obtain the capacity of a cylinder in litres, it is necessary to
    (a) multiply the diameter in metres by the height and divide by 1000
    (b) divide the volume in cubic metres by the area of an end
    (c) multiply the area of an end by the height in metres and multiply by 1000
    (d) square the radius and multiply by the height in metres.

24. The fuse used in a 13 A plug is intended to:
    (a) avoid the use of an earth wire
    (b) maintain a steady voltage
    (c) allow the use of double-insulated tools
    (d) fail as soon as the system is overloaded.

25. Which of the following earthing conductors is no longer recognised as satisfactory?
    (a) the supply authority's cable sheath
    (b) a buried earth electrode
    (c) a water pipe
    (d) an earth leakage circuit breaker

26. The correct colour code for flexible electrical wiring is indicated by

	Live	Neutral	Earth
(a)	blue	green/yellow	brown
(b)	green/yellow	brown	blue
(c)	brown	blue	green/yellow
(d)	blue	brown	green/yellow.

27. The purpose of the switch incorporated in some types of socket outlets in a.c. supplies for domestic systems is that
    (a) it provides a means of switching off the appliance without pulling out the plug
    (b) excessive arcing is promoted when a plug is withdrawn
    (c) it provides a better means of protecting the fuse
    (d) the socket itself is safer in the case of a plug being withdrawn by accident.

28. PVC and polypropylene are classified as being
    (a) thermosetting
    (b) thermostatic
    (c) thermoconstant
    (d) thermoplastic.

29. The chisel best suited to remove the mortar from the joints in the brickwork of a chimney stack to receive a stepped flashing is a
    (a) diamond point chisel
    (b) cold chisel
    (c) plugging chisel
    (d) bolster.

30. The 'set' of a hacksaw blade is provided in order to
    (a) give the blade body clearance when cutting
    (b) allow the blade to cut on the backward stroke
    (c) make the blade more flexible
    (d) increase the tensile strength of the blade.

Basic plumbing processes

In the pages that follow you will gain an understanding of:

- Measurement and marking out
- Building drawings
- Identification of pipelines
- Bending of pipes
- Drills and drilling
- Basic fixing techniques
- Jointing and installation of pipework
- Lifting and replacing flooring

Measurement and marking out

Measuring and marking off tools

Steel rule

Steel rules are graduated in metric scale and are usually available in lengths of 150 mm to 600 mm. They are very accurate, and necessary for any kind of metal work. Care should be taken not to damage the rule or impair its accuracy. They may be of fixed length, or made to fold.

Steel tape

This is a steel flexible strip rule coiled into its container and spring loaded. At up to 5 m long, it is compact and easily carried in the pocket. It is useful for measuring in restricted spaces and awkward locations.

Straight edge

This is a heavy steel or hardwood strip bevelled on one edge along which scribers or knives can be drawn to mark or cut material.

Try square

This is used for measuring and checking angles of 90°. It consists of two parts, the stock or base, and the blade. Good squares are made of cast steel, hardened and tempered, and are very accurate. Many types and sizes are in use; the most convenient for general use are 100 mm and 150 mm (Figure 4.1). They are used by plumbers for setting out sheet weatherings.

Spirit level

This is essentially a straight edge in which is set a glass tube filled with liquid and enclosing an air bubble. If the surface against which the straight edge is set is level or vertical, the bubble will centre itself between two lines on the tube (Figure 4.2).

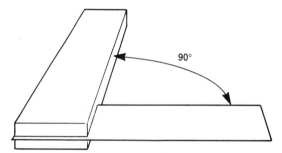

Figure 4.1   Try square

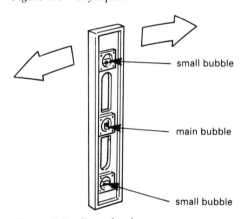

Figure 4.2   Spirit level

Scriber

This is a sharp, hardened and pointed metal tool used to inscribe lines on metal when marking out.

Dividers and calipers

These are measuring instruments used to transfer or verify a fixed dimension, the dimension being determined by the span of the legs (Figures 4.3 and 4.4). Dividers are also used for scribing this dimension.

119

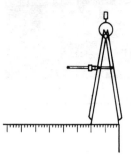

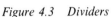

Figure 4.3   Dividers

Figure 4.4   Calipers

Marking off a horizontal

Where the horizontal is required in addition to the vertical a spirit level or water level can be used.

Spirit level

This consists of a level tube set in a straight edge which is usually 150 mm to 1 metre long. When the air bubble in the level tube is located centrally between the markings on the tube the straight edge is horizontal. A pencil line long the edge would mark the horizontal line.

Where longer lines are required, repeat the process in the direction required or position the spirit level centrally on a longer straight edge. This will transfer the level line as required.

Using a spirit level

1) Decide where you want the horizontal line to be drawn using dimensions from drawings and measuring off fixed features such as the floor or ceiling; make a single mark on the wall at the required height.
2) Hold the spirit level with both hands and line it up with the mark on the wall.
3) Check the position of the air bubble in relation to the markings on the tube. Move one hand up or down until the bubble comes to rest exactly in the centre of the two markings.
4) Firmly hold the level in this position with one hand and with the free hand draw a pencil line along the straight edge of the level (Figure 4.5).

Measuring off

Horizontal lines can also be drawn by measuring off from a common base. On walls this could be either the floor, top of the skirting board or ceiling surfaces provided these are reasonably level and even.

Identical measurements are taken at least 300 mm apart and marked off. A chalk line is stretched over these marks for the required distance and "plucked" to make the line.

Water level

A water level consists of two calibrated glass tubes which are connected together by a flexible (rubber or plastic) tube. Screw tops or other plugs are provided at both ends. The tube is filled with water until the level is half way up both glass tubes and then sealed when not in use. Screw tops are fitted to bleed the system to ensure that no air is trapped in the tube when in use.

Based on the principle that water finds its own level it is possible to use this apparatus to find *horizontal* levels over longer distances, i.e. on opposite sides of a room or wall, or around corners.

Using a water level

1) Decide where you want the horizontal line to be drawn using dimensions from drawings and measuring off fixed features such as the floor or ceiling. Make a single mark on the wall at the required height (Figure 4.6).

Figure 4.5   Using a spirit level

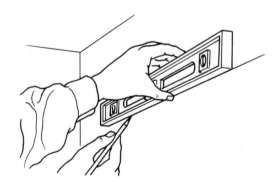

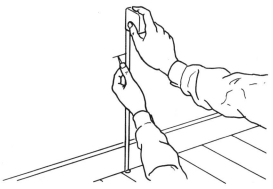

Figure 4.6

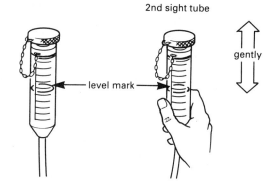

Figure 4.8

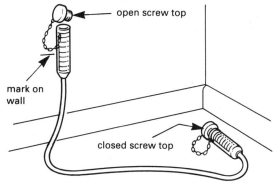

Figure 4.7

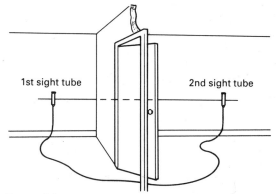

Figure 4.9

2) Lay out the two ends of the level on the floor so that there are no kinks or sharp bends in the flexible tube. This will help to get rid of trapped air and leave the level ready for use at the positions required.

3) Raise one of the calibrated 'sight' tubes until the middle mark is level with the mark on the wall (Figure 4.7). Open the screw top and arrange to have someone hold the sight tube in this position.

4) Now raise the second 'sight' tube to approximately the same height as the first and open the screw top slowly to prevent a sudden surge of water in the apparatus (Figure 4.8).

A few drops of detergent is known to help make the water 'runnier' by reducing the surface tension.

5) Raise or lower the second tube gently until the level of the water in the first sight tube is exactly in line with the level mark on the wall.

Holding both tubes steady, check that the level in the first sight tube is still correct and make a second level mark in line with the water level in the second sight tube (Figure 4.9).

Note: The water level appears to curve downwards and the lowest level must be used when marking off.

Building Drawings

These are the main method used to communicate technical information between all persons involved in the building process. They must be clear and accurate and easily understood by everyone who uses them. In order to achieve this, architects and designers use standardized methods for the layout of drawings, symbols, abbreviations and scales.

Scales

A suitable scale will often be necessary to either show the detail of a small object, or to accurately represent a large object on a smaller sheet of paper.

Scales use ratios to relate measurements on a drawing to the real dimensions on the actual job. Drawings using this method of representation are called *scale drawings*.

The main scales used in the construction industry are:

1) location drawings 1:2500
2) block plan 1:2500

Figure 4.10

3) site plan   1:500, 1:200
4) general location   1:200, 1:100, 1:50
5) component drawings   1:100, 1:50, 1:20
6) detailed drawings   1:10, 1:5, 1:1 (full size)
7) assembly drawings   1:20, 1:10, 1:5.

Scale rules are manufactured from plastic or boxwood, and have accurate dimensions along each edge (see Figure 4.10). The size of each division will depend on the ratio of the scale.

The following examples explain the relationship between the object's actual size and its scaled size.

Example 4: scale 1:100

If an object is 10 m in length and is measured to a scale of 1:100 and drawn on a sheet, it will be represented by a line of 0.1 m or 100 mm.

The formula used to calculate this is shown below:

$$\frac{\text{length of object}}{\text{scale}} = \frac{10}{1 : 100}$$

$$= \frac{1}{100} \times 10$$

$$= 0.1 \text{ m}$$

$$= 100 \text{ mm}$$

Example 5: scale 1:5

If an object is 0.85 m in length and is measured to a scale of 1:5 and drawn on a sheet, it will be represented by 0.17 m or 170 mm.

$$\frac{\text{length of object}}{\text{scale}} = \frac{0.85}{1 : 5}$$

$$= \frac{1}{5} \times 0.85$$

$$= 5\overline{)0.85}$$

$$= 0.17 \text{ m}$$

$$= 170 \text{ mm}$$

Graphical symbols and abbreviations

Graphical symbols and the appropriate abbreviations are used on building drawings in order that components installed within the building may be clearly identified. Figures 4.11 and 4.12 outline the main symbols and abbreviations used to show the plumbing and heating components.

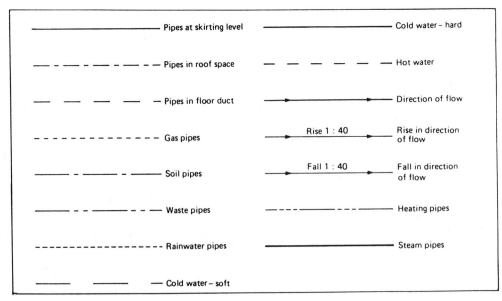

Figure 4.11   Graphical symbols for pipes

Symbol	Description	Application
	draining valve (BS 1192) (drain valve) (drain cock)	
	draining valve (abbreviated version used in this book)	
	line strainer	
	pressure reducing valve (small end denotes high pressure)	
	expansion vessel	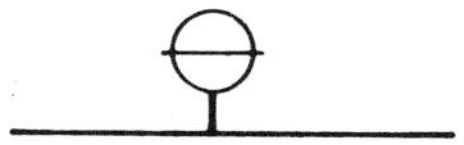
	pressure relief valve	
	check valve or non-return valve (NRV)	
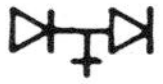	double check valve assembly	
	combined check and anti-vacuum valve (check valve and vacuum breaker)	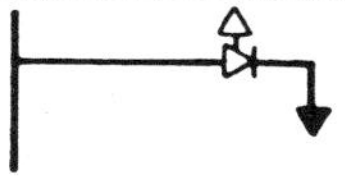
	air inlet valve	

Symbol	Description	Application
	draw-off tap	
	shower head	
	sprinkler head	
	float-operated valve	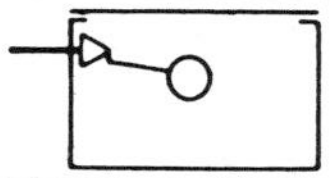
	float switch (hydraulic type)	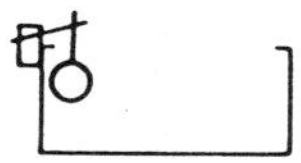
	float switch (magnetic type)	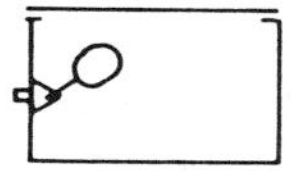
	filter or screen	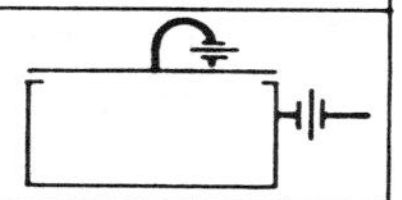
	supply stopvalve (SV)	
	servicing valve (SV)	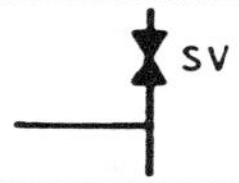
	water meter	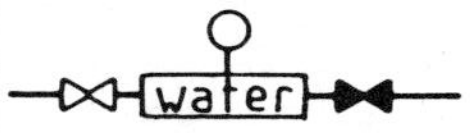

Figure 4.12 Other graphical symbols and abbreviations

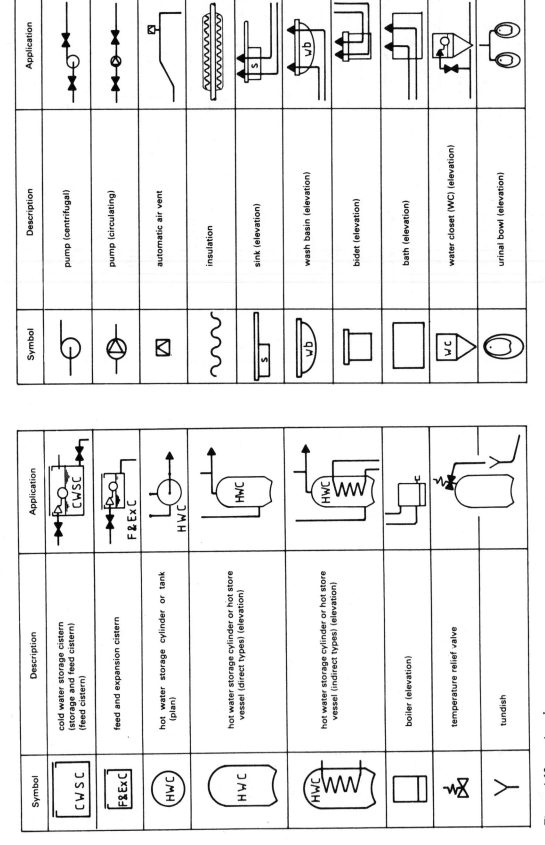

Symbol	Description	Application
	pump (centrifugal)	
	pump (circulating)	
	automatic air vent	
	insulation	
	sink (elevation)	
	wash basin (elevation)	
	bidet (elevation)	
	bath (elevation)	
	water closet (WC) (elevation)	
	urinal bowl (elevation)	

Symbol	Description	Application
CWSC	cold water storage cistern (storage and feed cistern) (feed cistern)	
F&ExC	feed and expansion cistern	
HWC	hot water storage cylinder or tank (plan)	
HWC	hot water storage cylinder or hot store vessel (direct types) (elevation)	
HWC	hot water storage cylinder or hot store vessel (indirect types) (elevation)	
	boiler (elevation)	
	temperature relief valve	
	tundish	

Figure 4.12 continued

124

Identification of pipelines

According to the complexity of an installation and to the variety of fluids conveyed, pipes should be identified by either:

- basic identification colours only for installations where the determination of merely the basic nature of the contents is sufficient or
- basic identification colours and code indications for installations where the precise determination of the contents is of importance.

Basic identification colours

These are listed in Table 23. The basic identification colour may be applied:

a) over the whole length or
b) as a band over a length of about 150 mm, depending on the diameter of the pipe.

Table 23   Basic identification colours

Pipe contents	Basic identification colour	BS colour references BS 4800
Water	Green	12 D 45
Steam	Silver-grey	10 A 03
Mineral, animal and vegetable oils; combustible liquids	Brown	06 C 39
Gases in gaseous or liquified condition (except air)	Yellow ochre	08 C 35
Acids and alkalis	Violet	22 C 37
Air	Light blue	20 E 51
Other fluids	Black	Black
Electrical services	Orange	06 E 51

Where banding is adopted, any decorative or protective colour of the pipe shall not be any of the other basic identification colours.

The basic identification colour shall be placed at all junctions, at both sides of valves, bulkheads, wall penetrations and at any other place where identification is necessary. Valves may be painted with the identification colour except where the pipeline has been coded with the safety colour for fire fighting, when the valves should be painted red.

Code indications

Code indications are:

1) the safety colours (see Table 24), viz:
   - red for fire fighting;
   - yellow, with black diagonal stripes, for warning of danger;
   - yellow, with black trefoil symbol for ionizing radiation;
   - auxiliary blue in conjunction with green basic colour, to denote pipes carrying fresh water, either potable or non-potable.
2) information regarding the nature of the contents.

Table 24   Safety colour references

Safety colour	BS colour reference BS 4800
Red	04 E 53
Yellow	08 E 51
Auxiliary blue	18 E 53

Where code indications are used, they should be placed at all junctions, at both sides of valves, service appliances, bulkheads, wall penetrations and at any other place where identification is necessary.

Figure 4.13 shows the application of safety colours and code indication colours.

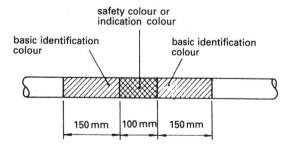

Figure 4.13

Table 25 shows the optional colour code indications for general building services.

Table 25 Optional colour code indications for general building services

Pipe contents	Basic colour (approx. 150 mm)	Colour code indication (approx. 100 mm)			Basic colour (approx. 150 mm)
Water					
Drinking	Green		Blue		Green
Cooling (primary)	Green		White		Green
Boiler feed	Green	Crimson	White	Crimson	Green
Condensate	Green	Crimson	Em. green	White	Green
Chilled	Green	White	Em. green	White	Green
Central htg <100°C	Green	Blue	Crimson	Blue	Green
Central htg >100°C	Green	Crimson	Blue	Crimson	Green
Cold down service	Green	White	Blue	White	Green
Hot water supply	Green	White	Crimson	White	Green
Hydraulic power	Green		Salmon pink		Green
Sea, river, untreated			Green		
Fire extinguishing	Green		Safety red		Green
Compressed air			Light blue		
Vacuum	Light blue		White		Light blue
Steam			Silver grey		
Steam			Silver grey		
Drainage			Black		
Electric conduits and ducts			Orange		
Town Gas					
Manufactured gas	Yellow ochre		Emerald green		Yellow ochre
Natural gas	Yellow ochre		Yellow		Yellow ochre

Bending of pipes

Ideally for maximum flow through a pipe, the bore should be smooth, of uniform diameter and with no joints or bends. In practice, this of course is impossible. Therefore every effort must be made to create conditions as close as possible to perfection. Changes in direction are unavoidable, and purpose-made bends or elbows are generally fitted to accommodate for this. The bends used wherever possible should be purpose-made and be of large radius to minimize the frictional resistance to the flow through the system. In some instances it may be necessary for one pipe to pass over another pipe or obstruction, necessitating the use of offsets (double bends) or passovers. These could be made up from purpose-made fittings or the pipe can be bent to give a very effective result.

The methods of bending vary according both to the material from which the pipe is manufactured and to the size of pipe and the thickness of the pipe wall.

When pipes are subjected to the process of bending, particularly with small radius bends, tremendous stresses are set up in the material. The stresses will be either compression or tension, depending upon where the stress reading is taken.

Figure 4.14 illustrates the possible effect of bending a pipe, showing the thinning of the material

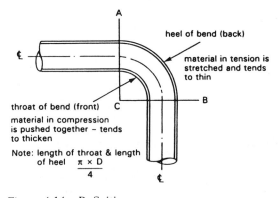

Figure 4.14 Definitions

at the heel and the thickening at the throat. In the case of small-diameter pipes, if these are of a heavy-gauge material, little or no adverse effect should be experienced with bends of normal radii. As a guide this could be taken as four times the diameter of the pipe (4 × dia.).

The generally accepted methods of bending are classified as:

- loaded
- mechanical

126

Loaded

This could be by using a steel or rubber insert or loose fill material. It is also possible to a limited extent to use air pressure on certain pipes.

Mechanical

The use of various types of bending machine is perhaps the most commonly accepted method. They are either manual (for the smaller diameter pipes) or hydraulic (for the large diameter pipes).

Note It must be remembered that it is not always the correct procedure to bend the pipe. As in the case of thin-walled copper tube (Table Z of BS 2871) and for certain plastic pipes, the change of direction must be performed by the use of purpose-made bends or elbows.

Copper tube

One of the main advantages in the use of copper tubes is the ease with which they can be bent, either by the loading method or with the aid of bending machines.

Methods of loading

1) *Springs*
   (a) internal
   (b) external
2) *Loose fill*
   (a) dry sharp sand
   (b) resin
   (c) low melting point alloy } little used today
3) *Machines*
   (a) former and guide
   (b) internal mandrel

Template

Where bends have to be made to a given radius and accuracy and shape is important, the required bend/bends should be set out full-size in the form of a working drawing. A 4–6 mm steel *template* rod is then bent to fit the centre line, or alternatively the template could be a piece of sheet steel cut accurately to fit the inside line of the bend.

The British Standard for copper tubes is detailed in **BS 2871: 1971. Part 1** states the metric dimensions. These tubes are suitable for connection by capillary or compression fittings (metric sizes) or other appropriate methods such as silver soldering (brazing) and bronze welding.

The tubes are standardized on the basis of the outside diameters. The dimensions and wall thicknesses of four varieties of tube are given in Tables W, X, Y and Z of BS 2871. Within these ranges of tube there are three different tempers:

- H = hard (as drawn),
- $\frac{1}{2}$H = half hard,
- O = annealed.

BS 2871: Part 1 Tubes for water, gas and sanitation

Table W annealed copper tube – O
Table X half hard light gauge copper tube – $\frac{1}{2}$H
Table Y half hard and annealed copper tube – $\frac{1}{2}$HO
Table Z hard drawn thin walled copper tube – H

Bending springs

These are available in both internal and external types. Spring bending is by far the most commonly used method and is perhaps the easiest. The main advantage of spring bending is that the bend can with care be moved slightly should it be wrongly positioned.

Copper tube can be bent using internal springs up to 28 mm diameter, although at this size it requires strength, a fairly large radius and annealing after each pull or throw.

External springs

These are used only on the smaller diameter size tubes up to 22 mm maximum. Their main advantage is that it is an easy operation to place and remove the spring in cases where the bend is required mid-way along the pipe.

Note Small diameter copper tubes can be bent satisfactorily without being annealed.

Internal spring bending of copper tube

Care must be taken to ensure that you have selected the correct type of spring and to check whether the tightening effect is in a clockwise or anti-clockwise direction to assist in the removal of the spring after bending.

The bending of light gauge copper pipe up to 28 mm diameter can be performed fairly easily with the aid of bending springs (particularly 15 and 22 mm tube). The bends should be of an easy radius from 3 × dia. for the smaller size pipes up to 6 × dia. for the sizes up to 54 mm.

Before commencing to bend the pipe, first ensure that the bending spring passes easily down the pipe until the centre of the spring is positioned at the centre point of the bend. If satisfactorily withdraw the spring.

Method

1) Set out the bend and make a template to fit the centre line of the bend.
2) Ensure uniformity of pipe and mark length of bend.
3) Anneal pipe (heat until red hot) from the *beginning* to the end of the bend. It is important not to heat either short of or outside the marks of the bend as this will affect the finished length of the bend making it either short or too long.
4) Insert the spring and pull the bend round the knee until it fits the template.
5) Bend slightly more than the required angle, then open the bend (this releases the pipe grip on the spring).
6) Turn the spring to tighten the coil and withdraw.

It is advisable to lubricate the spring with a smear of grease or thin oil. The pipe can be bent while still hot or alternatively the pipe may be cooled, then bent. The softening is done by the heating until red hot and is equally annealed irrespective of the cooling.

Loose fill loading

Sharp sand is by far the easiest and safest loose fill loading material for pipe bending (provided the sand is *dry*) and can be satisfactorily used for all the types of pipes mentioned and for all sizes (see Figure 4.15). It is possible to bend the pipes to much smaller radii and to more complex shapes. The removal of the sand is a simple operation of removing the bungs and tapping the sides of the bend, the sand being returned to a receptacle for further use.

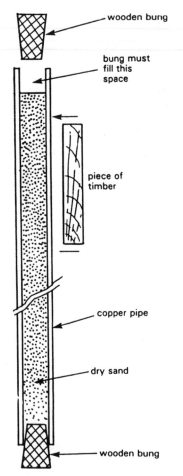

Figure 4.15   Loose fill loading

Method

1) Set out the bend and make a template to fit the throat of the bend.
2) Seal one end of the pipe, then fill with dry sharp sand.

3) Compact the sand by tapping the side of the pipe, and gently bumping the sealed end of the pipe on the floor (this compacting is perhaps the most important point).
4) Seal the open end with a wooden bung.
5) Mark the beginning and end of the bend, heat until red hot the portion between the marks, allowing the heat to soak through the pipe into the sand (annealing process).
6) The bend can be formed while the pipe is hot or it can be allowed to cool (safer to handle).

Note It is advisable to start the bending from the sealed end; the pipe may be held in a vice by means of purpose-made vice protectors.

7) When the bends are completed, remove the bungs and empty the sand back into the receptable for re-use.

Note Care must be exercised in handling the completed work as the annealed work remains soft and can only be hardened by work hardening, which is explained under that heading.

Loading method

It is advisable to have purpose-made hardwood plugs (bungs) with a fairly long taper to ensure maximum surface contact with the inside of the pipe. Figure 4.16 illustrates methods of sealing the pipe ends before the dry sharp sand is compacted by gently bumping the pipe on the floor and at the same time tapping the side of the pipe with a piece of wood. When the sand will not compress any more, remove sufficient sand to leave a void of approximately 30–40 mm. Drive in the wooden bung to seal the pipe, ensuring that there is no cavity under the bung. An alternative method is to use sand compressors as shown in Figure 4.17.

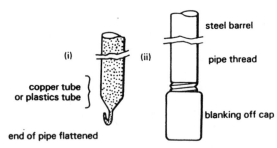

Figure 4.16   Sealing on pipe

Vice holding method

When holding a pipe in a vice some form of protection is essential or the pipe will become either marked or even damaged. Purpose-made clamps of cast lead are made which accurately fit the various sizes of pipe (see Figure 4.18). An alternative method is to make them from wood, but a much better method is to cut an old bending machine guide (slide) into pieces as shown in Figure 4.18.

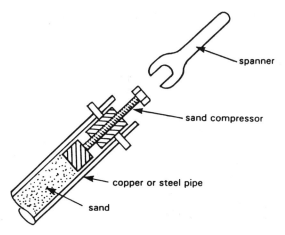

Figure 4.17   Sand compressor

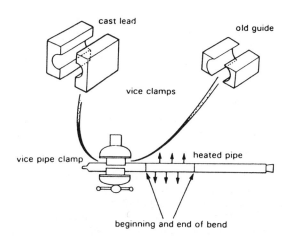

Figure 4.18   Method of holding pipe while bending

Forming bend to a template

As stated earlier a template could be made from a 4–6 mm diameter wire or it could be made from a piece of sheet metal. The type shown in Figure 4.19 is perhaps the easiest to make. It also gives the most accurate check on the finished bend. The required bend is set out on the sheet material which is then cut out accurately to fit the internal size of the bend. The pipe is then pulled to form the bend, the template being held in position as shown.

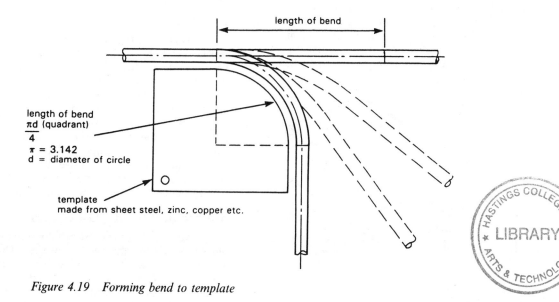

Figure 4.19   Forming bend to template

Plastic pipe bending

There are many different types of plastics on the market, some of which are not suitable for bending. Care must be exercised and consultation made with the manufacturers' literature if there is any doubt concerning the bending of a specific type of plastic. Where a particular plastic pipe is used which should not be bent the manufacturers have provided a comprehensive range of purpose-made fittings to enable all or most problems to be overcome.

There are several methods of heating and bending polythene and polyvinyl-chloride pipes. Perhaps the most commonly used method is that of dry sharp sand loading which is carried out in the manner described as for the loaded bending of steel and copper. The main difference is that plastic pipe does not change colour when heated and, because plastic material is a very poor conductor of heat, it is very easy to char or destroy the material completely.

Plastic memory

This is a term given to plastic material and can best be explained by using a straight length of plastic pipe as the subject. The plastic pipe when manufactured is in a straight length. It is then heated, softened and can be bent into the required position; it is held in this position until cold, whereupon it will remain in the new position so long as it remains below the temperature at which it was worked. Should the pipe be reheated the bend will tend to open and the pipe return to the original straight position. This is known as its memory, hence the term 'plastic memory'.

The accepted methods of heating plastic pipes prior to bending are:

1) Immersing in boiling water,
2) Heated air,
3) Radiated heat,
4) Direct heat.

Immersion in boiling water

Although satisfactory from the softening point of view, it has its limitations in practical use: the availability of boiling water and the difficulty of manoeuvring, filling and emptying a large container of water (Figure 4.20) being the main problems. It is also very difficult to cater for long lengths of pipe so that this method tends to be restricted to bending short lengths.

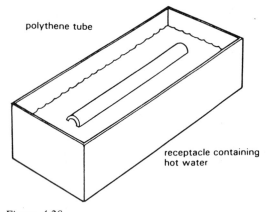

Figure 4.20

Heated air

This is one of the better methods of heating plastic pipe prior to bending. It is possible to devise several different types of heating apparatus to be used with heating appliances which give greater flexibility to their use. With the use of the equipment illustrated (Figure 4.21) and a little care it is possible to heat the plastics pipe fairly quickly, yet at the same time avoid the risk of overheating and charring it.

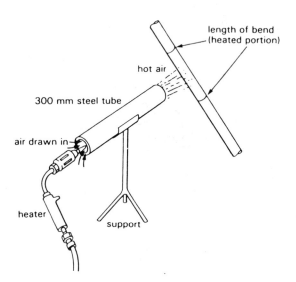

Figure 4.21　Heated air method

Radiated heat

This form of heating is the safest method, but because of this it is very slow. It is also difficult to control the area being heated. It is therefore seldom used.

Direct heat

This is perhaps the most commonly used method. It is fast and effective but it must be stressed that it is very easy to destroy the nature of the plastic by overheating or charring it. As already stated, plastics are poor conductors of heat and this means that if a direct flame is played on to one point, even for a very short time, the result will be charring and irretrievable damage to the pipe. It cannot be overemphasized how important it is to keep the flame continually on the move, at the same time revolving the pipe to ensure a slow heating of the pipe throughout its thickness and the length of bend.

Method of bending plastic pipes

The walls of the pipe must be fully supported both during the heating and bending process. This can be achieved by the use of a rubber insert which performs the function of a traditional steel-bending spring used for the bending of copper pipes. An alternative method is to support the walls of the pipe with a dry loose in-fill such as dry sharp sand.

Bending operation

1–4) As for copper tube (see pp. 128 and 129).
5) Heat the pipe very slowly, revolving it continuously, and constantly moving the torch flame backwards and forwards along the length of the bend.

Note This is a slow procedure and must not be rushed. Plastics have a very low conductivity and will very easily char. The pipe is ready for bending when it becomes pliable and floppy. A slight change in surface appearance may be detected: it takes on a more shiny look.

6) To form the bend place the heated pipe into a purpose-made jig (see Figure 4.22) or simply bend by hand. No force is required.
7) Cool the bend by applying cold water. This will set the bend in the required position.
8) Remove the bung and return the sand to its receptacle for reuse.

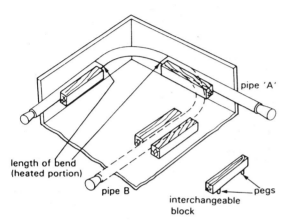

Figure 4.22   Purpose-made jigs

Polythene pipe

This is a plastic material used for conveying cold or at least cool liquids. It is a clean, lightweight, smooth bore pipe, unaffected by corrosion. It has a low conductivity which means it is a poor conductor of heat. Plastics have a high rate of thermal expansion which must always be taken into account when jointing and fixing plastic pipes. They also have considerable elasticity, particularly when warmed above a temperature of 60 °C.

Bending polythene pipe

Polythene can be bent cold as long as the bend has an easy radius of approximately 12 × dia. of pipe. A bend with a large radius is not usually acceptable. It is therefore necessary to heat the tube so as to produce neat bends with smaller radii of approximately 4 × dia. of pipe.

Polyvinyl chloride tube

This type of tube is known simply as PVC. It is light in weight, smooth of bore, resistant to corrosion, all of which make it a very useful conduit for the conveying of cold or hot water.

Unplasticized polyvinyl chloride

This is PVC without additives. In this form it is more rigid and can be fractured if subjected to a severe blow. It is more rigid than plasticised

polyvinyl chloride but when fixed, supported and used in the correct manner, should give trouble-free service. It is used for above-and below-ground drainage discharge systems. This type of plastic should not be bent, any change of direction being accommodated by purpose-made bends.

Plasticized polyvinyl chloride

This is the same plastic, manufactured with the addition of rubber and thus changing the rigid PVC into a more flexible material which makes it suitable for bending and more resistant to impact.

Machine bending

Bending machines are supplied in various forms suitable for bending all types of metal pipes both ferrous and non-ferrous, thin-and thick-walled varieties. They come under one of the following headings:

1) Compression bending,
2) Draw bending,
3) Push bending.

Compression bending

This method is used when bending thin-walled pipes as it gives the greatest support to the pipe at the point of bending. In this type of machine the centre former is fixed; the pipe is fitted into the groove of the former, and is surrounded and held in position by the guide. The former and guide together support the walls of the pipe and prevent it from collapsing, during the bending operation (see Figure 4.23).

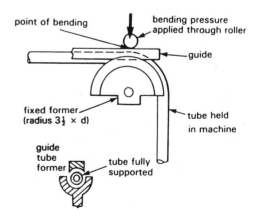

Figure 4.23   Compression bending

The pressure for bending is transmitted by a rotating lever arm and roller, positioned adjacent to the guide. The position of the roller is vital to the quality of the bend: too little pressure will result in a wrinkled bend; too much pressure will give a bend with excessive throating.

Draw bending

Although very effective, the type of machine used for draw bending is of a more specialist nature (see Figure 4.24). It can produce bends to a much smaller radius than those required in normal domestic work. This type of machine is not commonly used on site work. Due to the accuracy and perfection of the bending and the necessary tooling provided, these bending machines are also expensive to purchase.

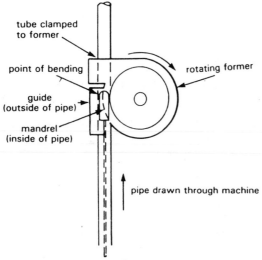

Figure 4.24   Draw bending

In this type of machine the pipe is clamped to a centre-rotating former which when operated pulls the pipe forward, so forming the bend. The pipe is again fully supported by means of an internal mandrel and an external guide, the adjustment and position of the mandrel being very critical.

Push bending

This type of bending is the simplest and requires the least skill or knowledge of pipe bending on the part of the operator. It is sometimes called centre point bending because the bending pressure is applied at a single point in the centre of the bend.

This type of machine (see Figure 4.25) is also known as the three point bender because of its two support points in addition to the centre bending point. It is very satisfactory for bending heavy gauge

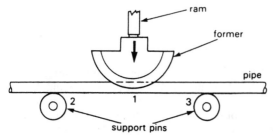

Figure 4.25   Push bending

(thick-walled) steel pipe, but unsuitable for light gauge (thin-walled) pipe, unless the walls of the pipe are again supported by the use of a suitable loose fill material.

Types of bender

Light gauge copper tube can be easily bent by machines of which there are several different types to choose from.

Bending machines Benders (a) and (b) in Figure 4.26 are by far the most commonly used, and are similar in their set-up and use. They can be used in either vertical or horizontal positions. Proficiency in their use is a must for all practising plumbers. Figure 4.27 shows an exploded view of a bending machine, detailing its component parts.

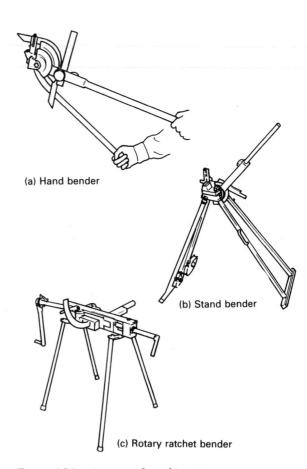

(a) Hand bender

(b) Stand bender

(c) Rotary ratchet bender

Figure 4.26   A range of machines in common use

Note When bending, the pipe is completely encircled by former and guide, thereby supporting the pipe wall and preventing deformation.

Setting the pressure indicator Some of the smaller types of machines have fixed formers and guides with no pressure adjustment yet still give satisfactory performance, particularly when new. The better

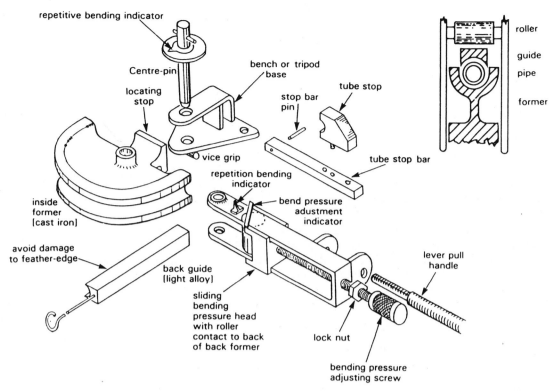

Figure 4.27   Bending machine components

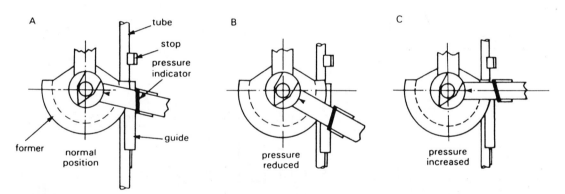

Figure 4.28   Pressure adjustment

machines have incorporated in their design an adjustable pressure indicator and the correct positioning of this is very important if perfect bends are to be produced. Figure 4.28 indicates the correct position and also the reduced and increased pressure position.

The information given forms the basic guidelines about where to commence pipe bending, although with slightly worn machine parts and various grades of pipe it is always advisable to make a test bend first as slight adjustments may be required.

Figure 4.28(A) indicates the correct setting. This setting should give a perfect bend on light gauge copper pipe. Pressure indicator should be parallel with pipe.

Faults in bends

1) *Throat of bend rippled, heel flattens* This is caused by a reduced pressure setting as shown in Figure 4.28(B).
2) *Excessive throating* This is caused by increased pressure as shown in Figure 4.28(C).

Making a square bend on light gauge copper pipe

This example deals with setting the bend to the outside of the former.

Method

1) Mark off pipe to the required distance.

133

2) Insert measured distance in the backside of the machine.
3) Ensure that the pipe fits right into the former and on to the stop.
4) Place alloy guide around the pipe, tighten pressure slightly to hold pipe in position.
5) Place square against mark on pipe, adjust pipe until the square touches the outside of the former.
6) Adjust pressure to the correct bending position (if of the adjustable pattern).
7) The lever arm is then pulled around and the pipe bent to the required 90° angle.
8) The bend will need to be very slightly over-pulled to counteract the spring back in the bend.

In the example shown in Figure 4.30 the procedure is almost identical to that explained previously and shown in Figure 4.29 except that in this case we work to the inside of the bend and the inside of the former. Both methods are equally correct and will produce identical bends.

Method

1–4) As for previous bend.
5) Adjust pipe until the square touches the inside of the former.
6–7) As for previous bend.

Note It must always be remembered that all bends *must* be placed at the *back* of the machine or errors in distances will occur.

Making an offset

An offset (Figure 4.31) is also known as a double set, an ordinary single bend being known as a set. The method of setting up and operating the machine is as previously described.

Method

1) The first bend or set on the pipe is made at the required position. The angle of the bend is not critical but 45° is usually recommended as satisfactory.

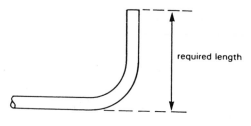

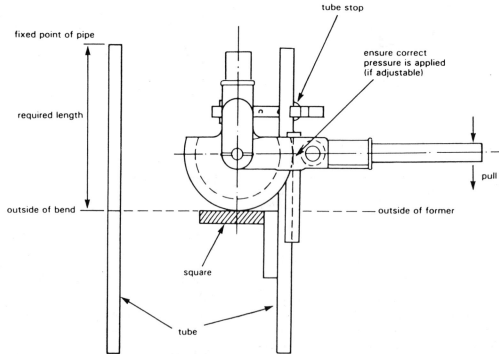

Figure 4.29   Making a square bend

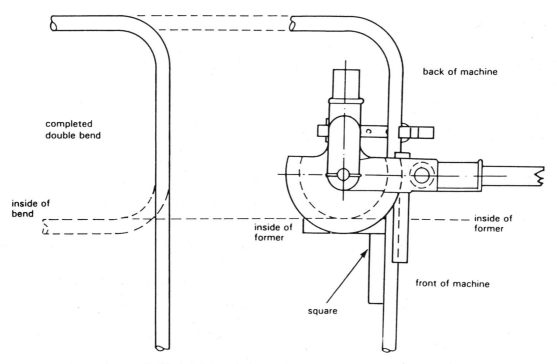

Figure 4.30   Making a double bend (using the inside of the former)

X = SIZE OF OFFSET

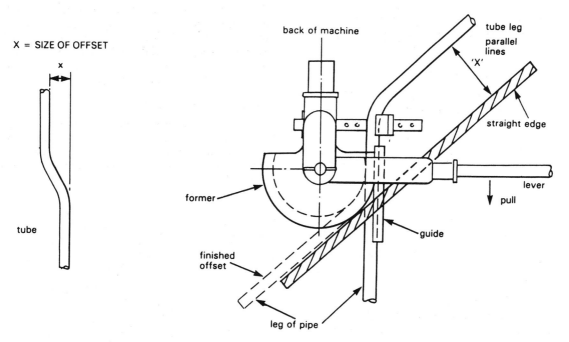

Figure 4.31   Making an offset

2) As stated previously all the bends must be placed at the back of the machine. Adjust the pipe in the machine, holding a slight pressure on the lever handle to hold the pipe in place.
3) Place straight edge against the outside of the former and parallel with the pipe.
4) Adjust the pipe in the machine until the required

measurement is obtained.

Note To increase the size of the offset, push the pipe further through the machine. To decrease the size pull the pipe towards the front of the machine.

5) Apply pressure to lever arm and bend pipe until the legs are parallel.

Left-hand bending

It is sometimes necessary to form left-hand bends, such as when a number of bends are required on one length of pipe or it may be impossible to locate the pipe in the machine due to the length of the pipe fouling the bench or the floor. In these cases the machine stop bar and lever arm are changed to operate from the reverse side as shown in Figure 4.32. The long length of the pipe is now situated in a vertical position. In the case of a vertical positioned bender on tripods the problem is solved by reversing the stop and placing the pipe in the bottom of the former and pulling upwards instead of downwards in the normal way.

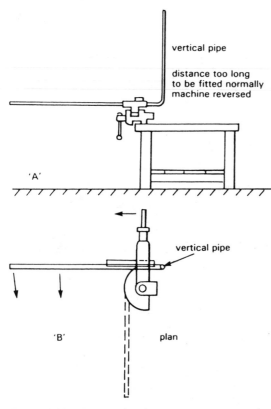

Figure 4.32   Reverse bending

Repetition bends

On some of the better types of machine there are attachments which enable bends to be accurately repeated such as:

1) Indicators,
2) Stops,
3) Graduated protractors.

Indicator method

This is as shown in Figure 4.33 where both fixed and adjustable indicators are an integral part of the bending machine. First, it is always necessary to make a trial bend, allowing for the spring back

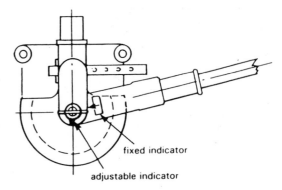

Figure 4.33   Repetition bending

which will differ for different diameter pipes and machines.

1) Set and bend the pipe to the required angle.
2) Adjust the bend indicator to coincide with the fixed indicator on the handle mechanism.
3) Remove the pipe, ensuring the indicator is not altered. The machine is now set for repeat bends.

Stop method

An adjustable locking stop, which is situated in the bending quadrant of certain machines, is an alternative method of making repeat bends. The method of bending is as described in the indicator method. When the trial bend is correct the stop is then locked in that position; all repeat bends will now be bent to the same degree.

Protractor method

On some machines of the larger type the angles are shown on a protractor. On the top of the former in this instance the pipe is bent until the bending arm indicates the required angle on the protractor, as in Figure 4.34.

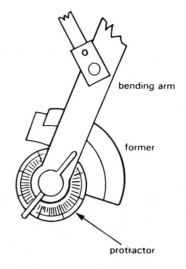

Figure 4.34   Repetition bending

Passover bend

This is a double bend and another variation of the offset. This type of bend is used where a branch pipe is required to pass over another parallel pipe as shown in Figure 4.35. The method of making a *'passover'* is the same as for an ordinary offset as shown by the dotted lines in the sketch. The size of the offset (C–C) is indicated by distance 'X'.

1) Set out passover bend to required dimensions.
2) Bend first bend to approximately 45°.
3) Place pipe in machine as previously shown to obtain second bend.
4) This second bend is over-pulled to give the required angled bend.

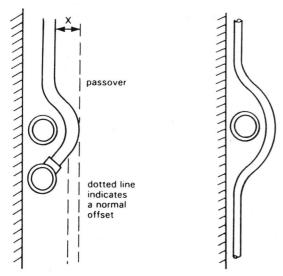

Figure 4.35 Passover bend

Figure 4.36
Passover crank

Crank

Another variation of the passover bend is shown in Figure 4.36 and is known as a *'crank'*. This type of bend requires both skill and practice to ensure that it fits evenly to wall and passes uniformly over the obstruction (pipe). The size of the former of the bending machine will govern the length of the 'crank'.

Method

1) Bend the pipe to form the first bend to an angle of approximately 90° (this angle is governed by the size of the obstacle) (see Figure 4.37).
2) Mark the two points for the second and third bends (make allowance for space between pipe and obstacle).
3) Line up mark with outside of former and pull the bend to the required angle (use template).
4) Reverse the pipe and repeat operation for the third bend; check alignment of pipe and clearance of obstacle by the use of a straight edge (see Figure 4.38).

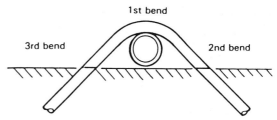

Figure 4.37 Forming a crank

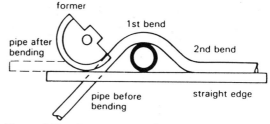

Figure 4.38 Forming a crank

Bending of steel pipe by machine

Steel pipe is manufactured in several grades and thicknesses depending on its use. Regardless of thickness there are machines available to bend the pipes used in any domestic situation satisfactorily. In the case of thin-walled pipes the machine shown for bending copper pipe (see Figure 4.27 on p. 133) is equally suitable; for the thicker-walled pipes the machine commonly used is the centre point push bender (see Figure 4.39). Although the actual working of the hydraulic bender is very simple there are one or two points which the operator must observe.

1) Select the correct former for the pipe to be bent. (Different formers are used when bending copper pipe with the same bender.)
2) Locate the pins in the correct holes. (This is most important or serious damage may result.)
3) The vent or breather valve is in the open position for most machines during the operation.

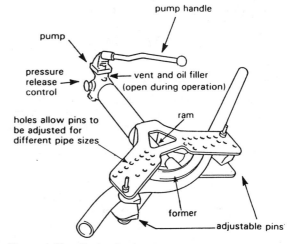

Figure 4.39 Hydraulic bender

4) Should the ram fail to operate, check the oil level. If it is low, replenish, using only the correct type of oil. Do not overfill.

5) If the pipe is over-pulled replace the former with a flattener (supplied with most benders, see Figure 4.40); reverse the pipe, relocate pins in the flattening position, then apply pressure in the normal manner.

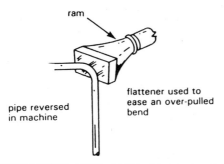

Figure 4.40   Easing a bend

6) The use of a 4 mm steel template rod is strongly recommended.

7) During the bending operation the pipe often becomes wedged in the former; do *not* hammer the former to remove it. Completely remove the pipe and the former from the machine and strike the end of the pipe sharply on a wooden block. Hold the former if possible to prevent damage when it is released from the pipe (see Figure 4.41).

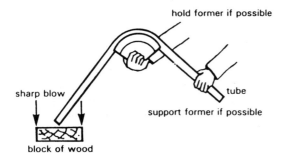

Figure 4.41   Method of removing former

Making a square bend

The method of making a square bend with a centre point bender will present no problem except when working from a fixed end of pipe. Even this is relatively simple once you appreciate that there will be an increase in length when the bend is pulled. This increase in length is equal in length to the diameter of the pipe being bent (see Figure 4.42).

As previously indicated the bend must be slightly over-pulled to allow for spring back when the pressure is released on the ram. Check the bend with the aid of a square or a steel template before removing the pipe from the machine.

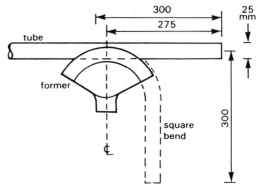

Figure 4.42   Making a square bend

Offsets, passovers and cranks

Making an offset

1) Set out full size the required bends (angles approximately 45°).
2) Bend the 4 mm steel template rod to fit the centre line accurately.
3) Mark the centre of the first bend on the pipe and place it centrally in the machine.
4) Bend the pipe to fit the template.
5) Mark the centre of the second bend on the pipe (either from the template or from the drawing).
6) Replace the pipe in the bender with the mark coinciding with the centre of the former; check with the template that the bend is being made in the correct direction and that the pipe is level.
7) Bend the pipe to fit the template.
8) Check accuracy of the bend with the tmplate before removing the pipe from the machine; if satisfactory remove and give final check with the drawing, straight edge and rule.

Passover

It will easily be recognized that the passover bend (see Figure 4.44) is very similar to that of the offset shown in Figure 4.43 the difference being that the second bend is continued past the 45° angle until the required passover is obtained.

The method of setting out and bending is as already described for the offset.

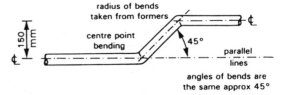

Figure 4.43   Offset

Figure 4.44   Passover

Crank/passover

Differences in terminology have already been pointed out and here again we find two different names given to an object.

Figure 4.45 is a further progression from the passover shown in Figure 4.44. Once again the actual bending procedure is as described for Figures 4.43 and 4.44 the centres of the bends being marked, then lined up with the centre of the former.

Figure 4.45   Crank

Emphasis on the use of templates cannot be over-stressed particularly when the bending becomes a little involved, i.e. in two planes or when the bending operation is to be performed some distance from the fixing location.

The GF dimensioning system

Malleable iron fittings

Screwed malleable iron fittings are manufactured in accordance with BS 1256, with threads conforming to BS 21.

The specifying of the fittings is covered by BS 143 and 1256 which state:

1) *Equal sized fittings* Specify by reference to size, irrespective of the number of outlets, i.e. $(\frac{1}{2})$ 15 mm tee.
2) *Unequal fittings with two outlets* Specify the larger outlet size first, i.e. $(\frac{3}{4} \times \frac{1}{2})$ 20 × 15 mm elbow.
3) *Unequal fittings with more than two outlets* Specify outlet sizes in the following sequence (see Figure 4.46):

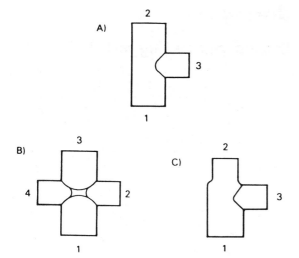

Figure 4.46

Note Where outlets 1 and 2 are equal, both are described by a single reference to size, i.e.

(A) 22 × 15 mm tee $(\frac{3}{4} \times \frac{1}{2})$
(B) 22 × 15 mm cross $(\frac{3}{4} \times \frac{1}{2})$
(C) 22 × 15 × 15 mm tee $(\frac{3}{4} \times \frac{1}{2} \times \frac{1}{2})$.

Sizes and dimensions

Malleable iron fittings are manufactured for use with steel pipe and are identified by reference to the nominal size expressed in imperial terms. This is common in both the United Kingdom and in Europe, and the use of the term 'inches' will eventually disappear. The dimensions of fittings – as distinct from the nominal sizes – are expressed in millimetres in accordance with current metric practice. All the pipes and fittings are available in black or hot dipped galvanizing.

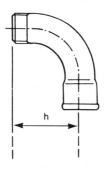

Figure 4.47

h   is the centre-to-face dimension of the fitting with an external thread (see Figure 4.47).

Z   is the dimension which remains after subtraction of the length of engagement of the thread from the centre-to-face or face-to-face dimension of a fitting (see Figure 4.48).

M   is the centre-to-centre dimension of a pipe combination (see Figure 4.48). It is equal to the h and Z dimensions added together. M may also include the length of pipe between the two fittings (see Figure 4.50);

L   is the cutting length of the pipe.

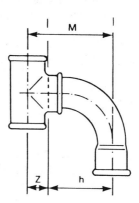

Figure 4.48

Note To determine the Z dimension of ancillary equipment, e.g. valves, take half the face-to-face dimension less one-third thread engagement length.

Allowance for threads and fittings

One accepted method is the GF dimensioning system known as the Z dimension. The Z dimension is the distance from the centre of the fitting to the point reached by the end of the pipe when screwed the standard distance into the fitting (see Figure 4.49). This is a simple and reliable means of calculating the *actual length* of pipe when centre-to-centre measurements are known.

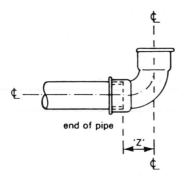

Figure 4.49

To obtain the length of pipe L subtract the two Z dimensions from the centre-to-centre dimension M. The length obtained will be the actual length of pipe required to be threaded to produce the assembly (see Figure 4.50).

Note Z measurements are read from the GF Tables (book of fittings).

The lengths of thread given in Table 26 are the standard engagement length of thread screwed into a fitting.

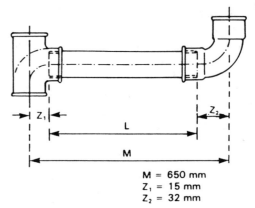

M = 650 mm
Z_1 = 15 mm
Z_2 = 32 mm

Figure 4.50

Table 26 Standard lengths of pipe threads

Nominal pipe size	Length of thread	Nominal pipe size	Length of thread
8 mm	10 mm	32 mm	19 mm
10 mm	10 mm	40 mm	19 mm
15 mm	13 mm	50 mm	24 mm
20 mm	15 mm		
25 mm	17 mm		

Example 6

Calculate the length of 15 mm pipe required for Figure 4.50.

$L = M - (Z_1 + Z_2)$
$L = 650 - (15 + 32)$
$L = 650 - 47$
$L = 603$ mm (actual length of pipe)

Note For more detailed reading of this subject see GF literature.

Drills and drilling

During the course of installation work a plumber will be required to drill holes in a wide range of materials e.g. metal, wood and masonry, and will need to use a variety of drills and drill bits.

Perhaps the most common tool in use is the hand-held portable electric drill used with carbon steel or high-speed bits (twist drills) for drilling small holes into metal, wood and partition materials, and with Durium tipped drill bits for use when drilling into brick or stone. Where no electric power in conveniently available, a wheel brace or breast drill is used.

Rotary/impact or hammer drills are often available on building sites and are particularly useful for drilling holes into hard masonry. They are used with toughened steel bits having specially hard carbide tips, designed to withstand rapid percussion.

Drilling and cutting metal

Twist drills come in two grades: carbon steel, which tends to lose its temper when overheated, and the more expensive high-speed steel, which is a better buy. High-speed steel drills are essential for drilling hard steel (Figure 4.51).

Twist drills are not so good for sheet metal – the holes are often out of true, the drill tends to catch and screw into the metal, and the undersides of the holes are heavily burred.

It is usually easier to punch holes in sheet metal, though a standard twist drill can be modified for sheet metal by grinding the edge to 140°. Positioning the modified point in a centre punch mark will be more difficult.

Large holes in sheet metal, such as those required

Body. Portion of drill from commencement of shank to point.

Shank. The portion of the drill by which it is held and driven, two types being in general use – straight and morse taper.

Tang. Flattened portion at the end of the morse taper shank for ejecting the drill from the socket.

Flutes. Grooves in the body of a drill which provide lips at the cutting edge, permit removal of swarf and allow cutting oil to reach the cutting edge.

Web (core). The central portion of the drill, which at the cutting end forms the chisel edge.

Lands. Leading edges of the flutes.

Body clearance. Part of the body surface reduced in diameter to provide clearance, thus forming lands.

Lip (cutting edge). Formed by grinding the flutes to give a cutting angle.

Diameter. The measurement across the cylindrical lands at the outer corners of the drill.

Chisel edge. The edge formed by the cross-section of the webb.

Point angle. The included angle of the cutting lips; general use 118°.

Lip clearance. Necessary for the drill to penetrate into the work.

Angle. Angle for general use 10° to 12°.

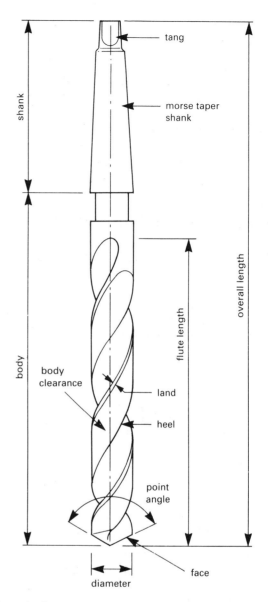

Figure 4.51   Twist drill terminology

for the pipe connections to steel cisterns and tanks, are best cut with an expanding tank cutter (Figure 4.52), a hole saw (Figure 4.53) or a 'Cooks' type cutter (Figure 4.54).

When drilling metal, it is necessary to accurately mark the point where the hole is to be cut: this is done by drawing two lines at 90° to each other with the hole position at the intersection of the lines. With the aid of a centre punch, make an indentation into the metal at the intersection point and commence drilling (Figure 4.55). If a large hole is to be drilled, it is easier to drill a small pilot hole first and increase the hole size with larger hole drillings until the required size is obtained.

Always clamp metal down while you are drilling it – if you do not, it may suddenly catch in the drill and

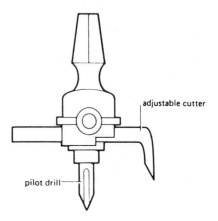

Figure 4.52   Tank cutter

start to revolve dangerously at high speed. A gripping plate (Figure 4.56) can be used to secure the metal. The spacer must be the same thickness as the metal, and the bolt close to the work for maximum grip.

If using a hand-held power drill, ease up the pressure as the drill breaks through the metal (Figure 4.57).

Do not hold small pieces of metal in the hand while they are being drilled – use pliers padded with paper if you do not want to mark the work, or hold it in a vice with a piece of wood backing.

Essentials for accurate drilling

Efficient and accurate drilling depends on a number of factors. The main ones are:

(a) the twist drill
(b) correct positioning
(c) correct speed
(d) correct feed
(e) correct cutting oil, if required
(f) rigidity.

(a) The twist drill must be in good condition and correctly ground, and be the correct type of drill for the material to be drilled.

(b) The hole must be correctly positioned, usually by a centre punch mark. For large diameter drilled holes it is usual practice to scribe a circle

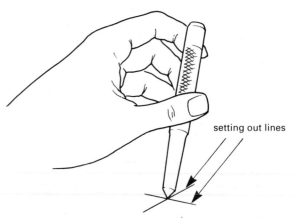

setting out lines

1. When setting the punch to the work, it should be held at an inclined angle in order that the point can be accurately located.

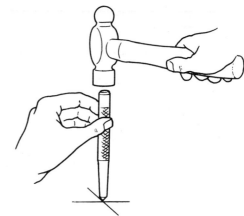

2. When the punch has been set, bring it upright to the face of the work before striking it with a hammer.

Figure 4.55   Use of a centre punch

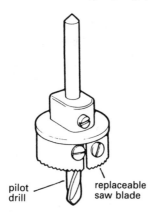

pilot drill

replaceable saw blade

Figure 4.53   Hole saw

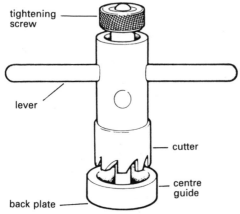

tightening screw

lever

cutter

centre guide

back plate

Figure 4.54   'Cooks' type cutter

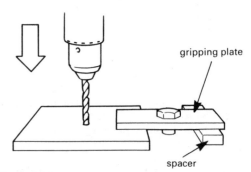

gripping plate

spacer

Figure 4.56

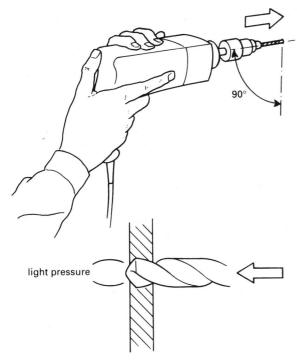

90°

light pressure

Figure 4.57 Drilling technique

1. Hold the butt of the drill firmly in one hand, and with the forefinger and thumb of the other hand grasp the drill as high up on its body as possible.
2. Operate the trigger switch with the second finger and make sure that the drill is square to the surface of the work.
3. As the cut deepens towards the break-through point, apply a reduced pressure to make sure that the break-through is clean, and that the drill does not stall or pick up the work.

around the centre punch mark. If drilling large holes, it is often best to drill a pilot hole with a smaller diameter drill first: this will guide the larger drill and at the same time remove the material that would be under the chisel point of the drill.

(c) Always use the correct speed, quoted by the drill manufacturer. If in doubt, use the slowest of the speeds quoted and gradually increase, keeping a check on drill wear until you find the most satisfactory speed for drilling without undue wear on the drill.

(d) Care should be taken to apply a continuous and even pressure. If drilling deep holes, it is advisable to frequently withdraw the drill so that swarf will not clog the flutes.

(e) Correct cutting oil – always use a cutting oil if the material calls for one. It is important that the cutting oil does reach the cutting edges.

(f) Rigidity is necessary for all drilling operations. Work should either be clamped directly to the

drill table or held in a vice which in turn should be clamped to the table. Never hold a job by hand. It is very easy to cause personal injury, quite apart from possible damage to the drill and the machine by loose work.

If packing is placed under the work to support it, make sure that it is as near as possible to the intended hole.

Drilling into wood

For small holes, especially into softwood, a bradawl will be adequate. On hardwoods, spiral ratchet screwdrivers can be fitted with a drill bit, capable of making holes large enough to accept screw fixings. A hand drill with a range of drill bits from 2 mm to 7 mm will be found adequate for many plumbing installation purposes.

A carpenter's brace and bit is invaluable when making screw fixings into wood. Screw auger bits are available which correspond in size with the usual range of pipe sizes (Figure 4.58). The centrally located screw tip literally screws itself into the wood with each clockwise turn of the brace, while the cutting edges cut around and lift layers of wood which are ejected by the spiralling action of the bit. Holes can be drilled through thick wood by using the larger sizes of auger bits. Screwdriver bits and countersink bits can also be fitted. A ratchet brace is useful for drilling in awkward corners or in confined places where movement is restricted.

Figure 4.58 Auger bit

Electric tools can also be used with twist drills or with round-shanked power drilling bits designed for making deep holes into wood. Power tools will make drilling into awkward corners a lot easier and speed up the drilling process.

A power drill can be used with twist drills for all screw fixings into wood, metal or plastic materials; and with high-speed wood drill bits to drill large diameter holes into wood.

When using power drills, locate the tip of the drill over the centre point before pressing the trigger switch to commence drilling. The tool must be held at right angles to the surface and the minimum pressure should be used to maintain accuracy.

Safety

Note: Great care must be exercised when using power drills. Keep sleeves, ties and other clothing away from revolving parts. Use gloves to avoid injury from splinters. Switch off the drill and make sure the drill has stopped revolving before putting it down (Figure 4.59).

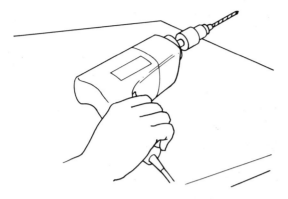

Figure 4.59   Safety after drilling

Drilling plastic laminates

Plastic laminates are now much used in the building industry; perhaps most commonly as 'wipe clean' surfaces in kitchens and bathrooms or as decorative wall surfaces in shops, offices and public buildings.

Several types of laminate comprise hard plastic surfaces bonded to a thin metal sheet. High speed or carbon steel twist drills should be used for drilling into these materials, and care taken to give the drill bit a 'good start' otherwise the point may slip causing damage to the decorative surface. It is usual to mark the position of the hole with a centre punch; this gives sufficient stability to the drill bit to ensure a good start. It is often best to drill a small pilot hole first before attempting to use a larger drill bit.

Care should be taken when drilling or cutting large holes in plastic laminates. Some surfaces are very brittle, and have a tendency to chip and flake away at the edge of the hole. Where possible a hole saw should be used in preference to a carpenter's brace and auger; these are too coarse to make a clean cut.

Some laminates are more easily marked than others, and it is wise to protect the decorative surface where possible from accidental damage from tools and equipment. Newspaper, cardboard or hardboard should be used to cover surfaces adjacent to the work, before work begins and all debris cleared away afterwards.

Hole drilling in masonry

Plumbing operatives often have to drill or cut holes in masonry to enable pipes to pass through walls and floors. Masonry drilling is a pulverizing, or scraping process, rather than a cutting one, involving considerable abrasion at the drilling point.

To combat this, drills used in drilling machines have cutting faces formed in hard carbide. Even so, wear does occur on drill diameters, the degree of wear depending on the drill method used.

Four methods are currently used by plumbing contractors.

1) Percussion, using hand tools (rawldrills). This method can produce accurate holes, but is labour intensive and slow.
2) Rotary, by electric or hand tools (durium drills). Rotary masonry drills produce the most accurate holes, but the masonry hardness can influence the tool's effectiveness above 16 mm diameter.
3) Rotary impact, by electric tools (vibroto drills). Rotary impact methods give accurate holes in hard masonry, but again, the masonry hardness can influence their effectiveness above 16 mm diameter.
4) Hammer drilling, by electric tools (hammer drills). Hammer drilling is quicker, provides a reasonable degree of accuracy and is favoured for holes up to 24 mm diameter.

Hammer drilling is recommended for all hard masonries. For less hard types, such as common brickwork and lightweight concrete, rotary, or rotary impact drilling is satisfactory.

Masonry drills give their best performance when used at medium to low drilling speeds, when the heat generated at the drill point can be absorbed into the drill shank. High speeds tend to produce overheating and can result in premature drill wear and loss of the carbide insert.

Whatever method of drilling is adopted, the recommended drill type and size for the particular fixing should be used.

Eye protection must be worn for all types of drilling operation.

Rawldrills

The rawldrill is a percussion hole boring tool used with a hammer. It is fluted to allow maximum debris clearance and ensure fast penetration.

Its shank is tapered to fit into the toolholder (Figure 4.60) which is shaped to ensure a comfortable grip in use and is hardened to withstand hammering.

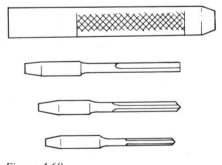

Figure 4.60

Method of use

Figure 4.61 illustrates the following steps.

1) Insert the shank of the rawldrill into the toolholder.

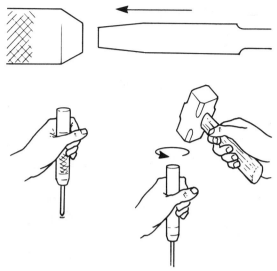

Figure 4.61   Percussion, using hand tools

2) Holding the tool in position commence drilling, lightly striking the toolholder with a hammer, and turning it between blows.
3) Continue until the hole has reached the required depth.

Rotary masonry drills

Rotary masonry drills may be tipped with durium, a specially hard abrasion resistant carbide, or with tungsten carbide (Figure 4.62). The fluting design ensures quick spoil removal resulting in greater drilling accuracy and longer drilling life.

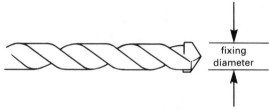

fixing diameter

Figure 4.62   Rotary masonry drill

Tipped masonry drills will penetrate easily into brickwork and marble, as well as glazed tiles, slate, hollow building blocks, and concrete. The longer drills are ideal for penetrating thick walls for tubes and pipes.

Method of use

1) For best results use at low speed in a rotary drill or a wheelbrace.
2) Exert a firm pressure behind the drill for fast accurate penetration.

Rotary impact masonry drills

These drills are specially manufactured for use in rotary impact drilling machines, and have a hard carbide tip, designed to withstand rapid percussion.

The tip is supported by a high quality tough steel shank (Figure 4.63)

Figure 4.63   Rotary impact drill

The standard series of drills includes drills ranging in cutting diameter from 4 mm to 25 mm. Longer drills are available to deal with the problem of extra deep hole cutting.

These drills will bore rapidly and accurately into structural concrete, engineering brick and other hard masonry.

Method of use

1) Use in a rotary impact drilling machine.
2) Exert a firm pressure behind the drill for fast accurate penetration.

Hammer drills

Hammer drills (Figure 4.64) are designed for use with the wide range of rotary hammers available. These machines have a more powerful hammer action than rotary impact drilling machines.

Hammer drills have a taper shank and are suitable for use with rotary hammers for drilling into structural concrete, stone and engineering brick.

These drills have a toughened shank and are tipped with tungsten carbide. The combined performance of the rotary hammer and the hammer drill provides a greater number of holes more quickly than rotary impact methods.

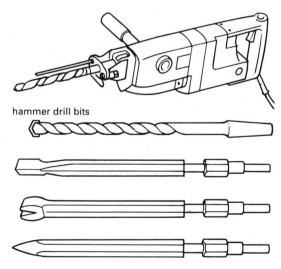

hammer drill bits

Figure 4.64   Hammer drill

Basic fixing techniques

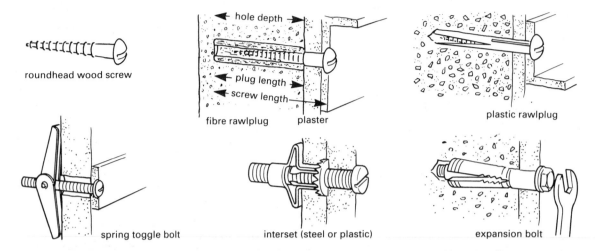

Figure 4.65 Basic fixing devices

There are many devices available for making fixings into building materials. Figure 4.65 shows a selection of these.

Loading

Fixings can be subjected to various loading conditions. These include combined tensile and sheer or cantilever loads and also shock loads, in addition to normal steady loading. Fixings need to resist both tensile and sheer loads.

Tensile loads

Tensile loads are those tending to pull the fixing out of the masonry. They result from the applied load of the fixture and that generated in tightening the fixing.

Sheer loads

Sheer loads are those applied across the axis of the fixing, such as that imposed by a fixture hanging on a fixing projecting from the wall.

Fixing devices

Gravity toggle

The gravity toggle comprises a plated steel toggle bar pivoted off-centre on a swivel nut. When run on to the end of a screw, the toggle can be passed through a fixing hole into a cavity where upon the heavier end of the toggle drops down and is then pulled back against the material to tighten the screw (Figure 4.66).

Typical applications

The gravity toggle is designed to provide fixings

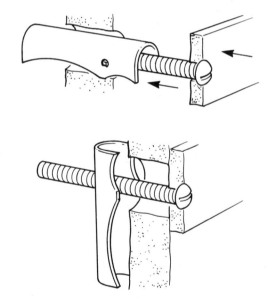

Figure 4.66 Gravity toggle bolt

into vertically mounted plasterboard and similar materials used in the construction of cavity walls, partitions, etc.

Method of use

1) Drill hole of recommended diameter into cavity.
2) Pass the fixing screw through the fixture into the toggle.
3) Pass toggle through hole into cavity allowing it to drop and rest against the reverse face of the material.
4) Tighten the screw until the fixing is firm.

Spring toggle

The spring toggle consists of a plated steel, spring actuated toggle bar pivoted on a swivel nut. When the nut has been run on to the end of a screw, the toggle is pushed through the fixing hole into a cavity whereupon it springs open and is then pulled back against the material to tighten the screw. The design of this fixing causes the load to be spread over a wide area. (Figure 4.67).

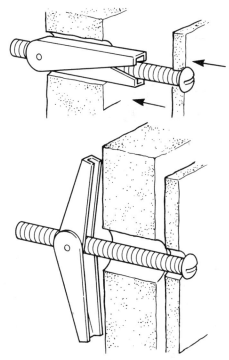

Figure 4.67   Spring toggle bolt

Typical applications

The spring toggle is ideal for making fixings to cavity walls and ceilings where only one side of the material is accessible. It is especially effective when making fixings into plasterboard, lath and plaster, fibre board and similar materials of low structural strength where it allows reasonable loads to be supported.

Methods of use

1) Drill hole of recommended diameter into cavity.
2) Pass fixing screw through fixture and into toggle.
3) Pass toggle through hole and allow toggle wings to spring apart and rest on reverse face of the material.
4) Tighten screw until the fixing is firm.

Fixing using wood screws

In order to identify the different types of screws in use it is essential first to be able to recognize the different types of threads and points.

Woodscrews

Conventional woodscrews have a single spiral of thread running from the point, clockwise for about two thirds of the length. The unthreaded part is called the shank and gives the 'screw gauge'.

Twinfast woodscrews

These have twin spirals, parallel to each other and can be recognised by the twin 'starts' at the point. They are particularly suited for use on softer timbers and in chipboard because of their increased holding power.

Twinfast screws are usually threaded up to the head on the shorter lengths up to 19 mm and their shanks unlike those on conventional woodscrews are 'relieved', minimizing the danger of splitting the wood.

Screw heads

Most screws have a head designed to suit a specific use or application.

Flat heads

These are used where the head has to be flush with the adjacent surface. This will normally require a 'countersunk' head.

Round heads

'Raised countersunk' are usually used with screw caps to improve the appearance when fixing glass or panelling.

Several variations of the standard 'round head' are in common use, ranging from 'pan', 'mushroom' and 'flanged' to the 'square' head used on coach screws and bolts.

Types of woodscrews

The main types of woodscrews are shown in Figure 4.68.

Countersunk (flat-head)

For general woodwork, fitting miscellaneous hardware: drive until head is flush with work or slightly below surface.

Posidrive head

Used with special screwdrivers which will not slip from cross-slots.

Posidrive twinfast

For use in low density chipboards, blockboard and softwood; they can be driven home in half the time of conventional screws.

Raised head

Used to fix decorative hardware; must be countersunk to rim. Usually nickel or chromium-plated.

Round head

Used for surface work, installing fittings and pipe clips.

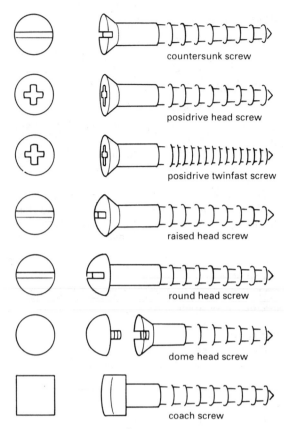

Figure 4.68   Types of screw

Dome head

A 'hidden' screw for fixing mirrors, bath panels and splashbacks; chromed cap threads into screw head.

Coach screw

Provides strong fixing in heavy construction and framework. Turn into work with a spanner.

Thread cutting

Cutting threads by hand falls naturally into two processes: internal threads and external threads.

- An internal thread (the thread in a nut) is cut with a *tap*. The process is called *tapping*.
- An external thread (the thread on a pipe) is cut with a *die*. The process is called *threading*.

Cutting internal threads

Taps are supplied in sets of three consisting of:

Taper tap: this is tapered for two-thirds of its length and is used to start a thread. When tapping in thin plate, no other tap is necessary since the upper third of the tap will cut a full thread.

Second or intermediate tap: this tap is tapered for only one-third of its length and is used, after the taper tap, to extend the started thread.

Bottoming or plug tap: this tap is straight throughout its length except for a small chamfer lead. It is used last in the set, and must always be used when threading a blind hole.

Tap wrenches: there are several types of wrenches used to hold the taps for cutting; they are all designed to grip the square shank of the tap (see Figure 4.69).

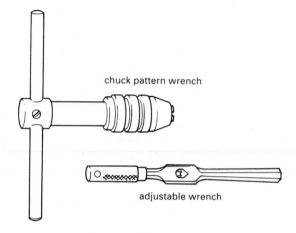

chuck pattern wrench

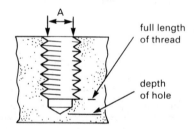

adjustable wrench

Figure 4.69   Tap wrenches

Procedure

1) Mark and punch the position of the hole accurately; select taps of the same diameter and thread as the bolt.
2) Drill the correct size hole. The correct drill will have a diameter equal to the distance A on the diagram (Figure 4.70) or very slightly larger.

Figure 4.70   Drill the correct diameter and depth of hole

3) Drill blind holes (i.e. holes that do not go right through the metal) deeper than the required thread to prevent the taps from binding on the bottom of the hole.
4) Set the taper tap firmly and squarely in the tap wrench.
5) Put the taper tap squarely into the hole and, with slight downward pressure on the tap, turn it in a clockwise direction (for a right-hand thread). As soon as the tap starts to cut, stop pressing down and let the tap screw itself into the hole, cutting a thread as it goes. Clear the chippings by turning

the tap back a quarter of a turn at frequent intervals.

6) After the taper tap has been used fully, work the intermediate tap in the same way.

7) Complete the hole with the plug tap. When tapping a blind hole, occasionally withdraw the tap completely to clear chippings. Take care near the bottom of the hole – just a fraction of a turn after the tap has reached the bottom will break the tap.

No lubricant is required for tapping in brass and cast iron. Lubricate the tap and hole with paraffin in aluminium, and with light oil in steel, copper or bronze.

Extracting broken taps

If sufficient tap projects, it may be possible to unscrew the tap with pliers. Larger taps can be unscrewed with a special three-pronged tool which engages in the flutes of the tap.

If neither of the above methods work, heat both tap and workpiece and then drill the tap out. Retap the hole afterwards. This method is not possible in metals such as brass, which has a lower melting point than the annealing temperature of the tap.

As a last resort, large taps can sometimes be broken up using a suitable punch, but you are likely to badly damage the work.

Easy-out

This is a tool for removing bolts or screws that have broken off in the work. Drill the end of the broken bolt and screw the easy-out into the hole.

The thread on the easy-out turns in the opposite direction to the bolt thread which can therefore be removed.

Easy-outs are available in three sizes – large, medium and small (Figure 4.71).

Figure 4.71   Easy-out tool

Cutting external threads

Dies for cutting external threads are of several types.

Circular split dies: these are one-piece dies with a limited adjustment, usually used in sizes below 12 mm diameter. Care is required in starting the die, to ensure that it is square to the pipe or rod.

Die nuts: these are solid dies having no adjustment, and are not intended for cutting threads from scratch. Use them for running an existing thread down to size, or rectifying damaged threads.

Pipe thread dies: these circular dies are fitted with a guide bush which enables the die to cut squarely. Ideal for cutting accurate, fine threads on tubing.

The smaller sizes of low carbon steel tubes used in plumbing are usually jointed by cutting and threading British Standard Pipe Threads to BS 21. Pipes are usually threaded by using hand-operated pipe thread dies or powered machines which complete the threading mechanically.

The cutting dies on powered machines and some types of hand-operated dies are adjustable and usually designed to cut two or more thread sizes. The cutting dies are numbered 1 to 4 and must be correctly located in the die stock. One-piece dies used for threading smaller diameter tubes are only suitable for one particular size of pipe.

During the threading procedure, relatively large amounts of steel are cut from the tube and, to avoid overheating and assist cutting, cutting oil or lubricant must be applied direct to the cutting area.

The dies used for cutting threads for pipe jointing are designed to cut a tapered thread which, when screwed into a fitting which has a parallel thread, will expand the fitting slightly, ensuring that both thread surfaces (external and internal) are in close contact and make a water tight joint. If good threads have been cut, and new fittings are being used, it may not be necessary to use any joint sealing compound, although the majority of plumbers prefer to seal these joints using PTFE tape or an approved proprietary sealant.

Jointing and installation of pipework

Jointing of pipework for potable water supplies

The jointing of pipework for potable water supplies is an essential part of a plumber's installation skills. Research has shown that some of the traditional materials promote or harbour the growth of bacteria: as a result of this, Water Authorities

have banned the use of these materials. Primarily lead-based solders must not be used for jointing purposes as lead can be leached into solution by certain types of water and consumed. Linseed oil based jointing compounds support and encourage bacterial growth under certain conditions. Table 27 (from BS 6700) lists permitted jointing materials and gives guidance on their use.

Table 27 Jointing of potable water pipework

Type of joint	Method of connection	Jointing material	Precautions/limitations
Copper to copper pipe (pipe to pipe or fitting, or fitting to fitting)	Capillary-ring or end feed, soldered joint	Flux	No solder containing lead to be used See note
Copper to copper (pipe to fitting or fitting to fitting)	Non-manipulative compression fittings	—	Above ground only
	Manipulative compression fittings	Lubricant on pipe end when required	
Copper to copper (pipe to fitting or fitting to fitting)	Bronze welding or hard solder	Flux	See note
Galvanized steel (pipe to pipe or fitting), including copper alloy fittings	Screwed joint, where seal is made on the threads	PTFE tape or proprietary sealants	PTFE tape only up to 40 mm ($1\frac{1}{2}$) diameter See note
Galvanized or copper (pipe to pipe or fitting)	Flanges	Elastomeric joint rings complying with BS 2494, or corrugated metal. Vulcanized fibre rings complying with BS 216 or BS 5292	See note
Long screw connector	Screwed pipework with BS 2779 thread	Grummet made of linseed oil-based paste and hemp	See note
Shouldered screw connector	Seal made on shoulder with BS 2779 thread	Elastomeric joint rings complying with BS 2494 and plastics materials	—
Unplasticized PVC (pipe to fitting)	Solvent welded in sockets	Solvent cement complying with BS 4346: Part 3	—
	Spigot and socket with ring seal. Flangers. Union connectors	Elastomeric seal complying with BS 2494. Lubricants	Lubricant should be compatible with the unplasticized PVC and elastomeric seal
Cast iron (pipe to fitting)	Caulked lead	Sterilized gaskin yarn/blue lead	See note
	Bolted or screwed gland joints	Elastomeric ring complying with BS 2494	—
	Spigot and socket with ring seal	Elastomeric seal and lubricant	—
Copper or plastic (pipe to tap or float-operated valve)	Union connector	Elastomeric or fibre washer	—
Stainless steel (pipe to pipe or fitting, including copper alloy fittings)	Soldered socket and spigot	Flux (phosphoric acid based) complying with BS 5245	No solder containing lead to be used See note
Stainless steel (pipe to fitting, including copper alloy fittings)	Non-manipulative compression fittings	Lubricant when required	See note
	Manipulative fittings	Elastomeric seals when required	—

Table 27 *Continued*

Type of joint	Method of connection	Jointing material	Precautions/limitations
Pipework connections to storage cisterns (galvanized steel, reinforced plastics, polypropylene, polyethylene)	Tank connector/union with flange backnut	Washer: elastomeric, polyethylene, fibre	—
Polyethylene (pipe to fitting)	Non-manipulative fittings	—	Do not use lubricant
	Thermal fusion fittings	—	—
Polybutylene (pipe to pipe or fitting)	Non-manipulative fittings	Lubricant on pipe end when required	Lubricant if used should be listed and compatible with plastics
	Thermal fusion fittings	—	—
Polypropylene (pipe to pipe)	Non-manipulative fittings	Lubricant on pipe end when required	Lubricant if used should be listed and compatible with plastics
	Thermal fusion fittings	—	—
Cross-linked polyethylene (pipe to fitting)	Non-manipulative fittings	Lubricant on pipe end when required	Lubricant if used should be listed and compatible with plastics
Chlorinated PVC (pipe to fitting)	Solvent welded in sockets	Solvent cement	—

Note Where non-listed materials are to be used, due to there being no alternative, the procedure used should be consistent with the manufactuer's instructions taking particular note of the following precautions:
(1) use the least quantity of material necessary to produce good quality joints;
(2) keep jointing materials clean and free from contamination;
(3) remove cutting oils and protective coating, and clean surfaces;
(4) prevent entry of surplus materials to waterways.

Installation of pipework

Pipes and fittings need to be selected and installed to suit the job they have to do and the conditions in which they are located.

Pipes should be fitted and jointed:

(a) so that they do not leak or permit any contamination of the water contained in them
(b) so that they do not cause vibration or noise
(c) to avoid mechanical damage, corrosion or fracture by frost attack
(d) to comply with the requirements of the Water Byelaws or relevant British Standards.

When installing pipes in buildings, it is necessary to make provision for expansion and contraction of the pipeline and its fittings; this is particularly important where pipe runs are long and where the temperature changes are considerable, such as with central heating and hot water distribution systems.

Where pipes pass through walls, they should always be sleeved (Figure 4.72) so that movement in the pipeline does not cause damage or noise.

Sleeves should:
• permit ready removal and replacement of pipes;
• be strong enough to resist any external loading exerted by the wall or floor;
• be sealed with fire resistant material that will accommodate thermal movement.

Sleeves passing through cavity walls must pass right through the cavity and the pipe must be insulated. Other than this arrangement, no pipes should be in a cavity.

In larger installations, it is usual practice to include an expansion horseshoe or loop, or specialist fittings to accommodate pipe movement (Figures 4.73 and 4.74). All clip or bracket fixings must be capable of allowing for lateral movement.

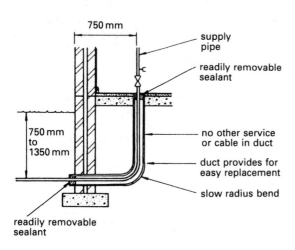

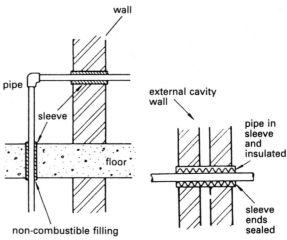

(a)   Access to pipes entering buildings

(b)   Pipe sleeved through wall and floor

(c)   Pipes passing through external walls

Figure 4.72   Ducting and sleeving of pipes

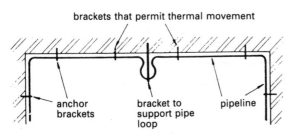

(a)   Use of horseshoe expansion loop (plan view)

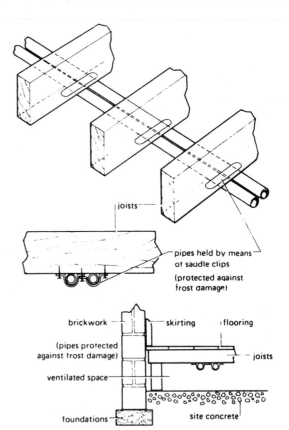

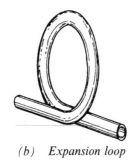

(b)   Expansion loop

Figure 4.73 Expansion loops

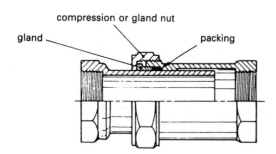

Figure 4.74   Gland type expansion joint

Figure 4.75   Pipe fixing under the ground floor

Pipes under suspended floors should be avoided, but, when this is not possible, they must be fully insulated and supported (Figure 4.75), and access panels formed in the flooring for inspection, maintenance and repair. Structural timbers such as joists must not be unduly weakened by drilling or cutting, and all holes must be as small as practicable

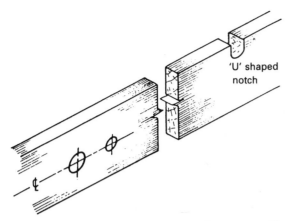

'U' shaped notch

(a) Holes and notches to be as small as practicable but large enough to permit pipes to expand and contract

(Figure 4.76), but large enough to allow pipes to expand and contract. The positions of notches or holes are important to the strength of a structural timber and should be made close to supporting members.

Concealed pipes, such as those in walls, solid floors and ceilings, must be correctly accommodated and protected as shown in Figures 4.77 and 4.78, and access should be provided at joint positions. Pipes that run on the surface of walls, etc. must be adequately clipped and supported as determined by the pipe use, material and size, as described earlier.

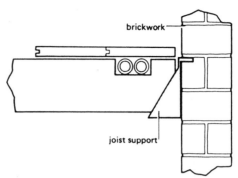

brickwork

joist support

(b) Joist cut near the wall

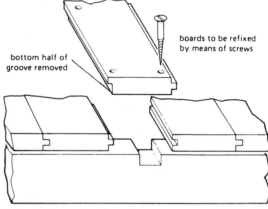

boards to be refixed by means of screws

bottom half of groove removed

(c) Refixing floorboards

Figure 4.76 Pipes passing through structural timbers

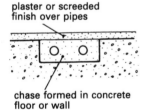

plaster or screeded finish over pipes

chase formed in concrete floor or wall

Closed circuit pipes may be screeded or plastered over provided they are in a proper chase, and can be readily exposed for repair or replacement.

(a) Pipes plastered or screeded over

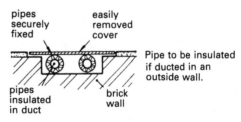

pipes securely fixed

easily removed cover

pipes insulated in duct

brick wall

Pipe to be insulated if ducted in an outside wall.

(c) Pipes in external walls

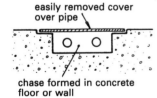

easily removed cover over pipe

chase formed in concrete floor or wall

Pipes other than closed circuits must be in a duct that is reasonably easy to expose for examination, repair or replacement, without causing any structural damage.

(b) Pipes under removable cover

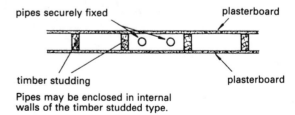

pipes securely fixed

plasterboard

timber studding

plasterboard

Pipes may be enclosed in internal walls of the timber studded type.

(d) Pipes in internal studded partition

Figure 4.77 Pipes in ducts, chases and partitions

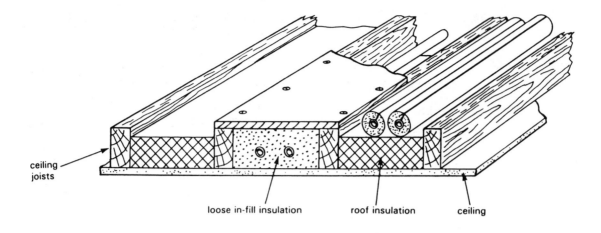

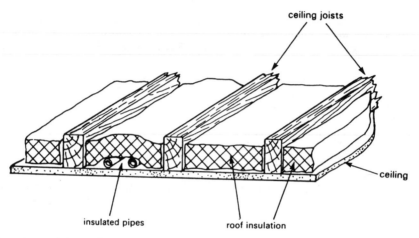

(a) Insulating pipework in roof space

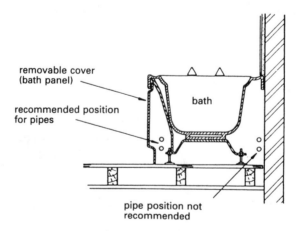

(b) Locating pipes behind a bath panel

Figure 4.78 Concealed pipes

Lifting and replacing flooring

Some plumbing pipework systems are run horizontally in the floor void and there may be occasions when floorboards will need to be lifted. This work must be undertaken with precision and care, without damage to the floor.

Basic preparations

1) Find out what it is you have to do. This will help you decide whether or not floorboards will need to be lifted, and their location.
2) Obtain the right tools and equipment for the job. These will include a bolster chisel, a carpenter's claw hammer, a flooring saw or a tenon saw, a nail punch and a short length of 20 mm thick batten or pipe.
3) Find the work area. In addition to knowing what it is you have to install, it is important to know exactly where you are required to install it. Check this with your client or supervisor, or consult working drawings or specification.
4) Safety precautions: make sure that you know where the isolating points for gas, water and electricity are.
5) It is usual to try to trace back from sanitary appliances, radiators, or components to establish the direction of the pipe run, so that where possible only a single floor board need be lifted.
6) Examine the floor boards. Where there are no visible spaces between boards it can be assumed that tongue and grooved floorboards have been used (some floors are not tongue and grooved and may be plain edge boarding).
7) If possible, find a section of board which has been butt-jointed and work from that. Joints are usually obvious, the ends of the boards being nailed to the supporting joists.
8) Think the job through before you begin cutting and lifting the floor. Some time spent planning the job will usually save work and avoid unnecessary damage to the floor.

Lifting tongue and groove floorboards

It will be much easier to work if the room can be cleared of furnishings (i.e. carpets, lino, furniture, etc.); where this is not possible clear items to one side of the room.

Examine the floorboards and determine whether or not they are running in the same direction as the proposed installation. Check for visible spaces between floorboards, using a knife or small screwdriver to confirm tongue and groove boards.

Lifting method

1) Find a floorboard with a butt-joint as near to the point of installation as possible.

2) Start at the join and use a flooring saw to cut away the tongue on one side of the floorboard using the convex part of the saw to start the cut (Figure 4.79)

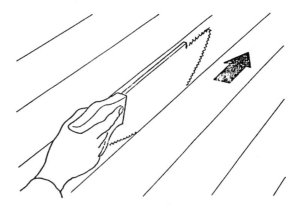

Figure 4.79

3) The tongue is situated at the edge of the floorboard and is usually (6–10 mm) thick.
4) Continue sawing, holding the saw upright and level, allowing the saw to move forward with each stroke. Avoid cutting down through the board. Keep the saw moving forward in a straight line as the tongue is cut through (Figure 4.80).

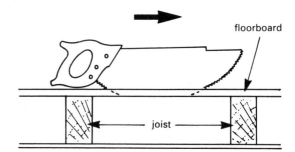

Figure 4.80

5) Repeat the sawing process on the other side of the floorboard.
6) With the tongue cut through on both sides of the floorboard, position the point of the punch on the head of the nails and hammer them down through into the joists (Figure 4.81).
7) Insert a bolster chisel into the gap between boards about 100 mm from the end and pull back to lever up the floorboards clear of the nail heads (Figure 4.82)
8) Move the bolster chisel 300–450 mm away from the join and lever the floorboards up sufficiently to allow a batten to be slid under the loosened

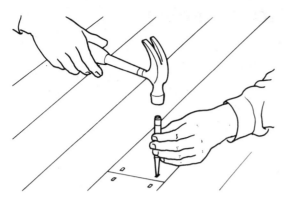

Figure 4.81

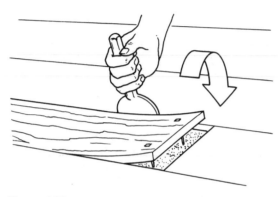

Figure 4.82

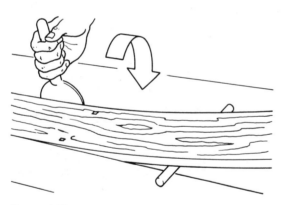

Figure 4.83

floorboard to prevent it from falling back into place.

9) With the batten in this position continue cutting away more of the tongue on both sides of the board, sliding the rod or batten along towards the saw after each stage.

10) Use the bolster to prise the floorboard at points where it has been nailed to the joists. Position the chisel alongside the joist and push it into the gap as far as it will go before commencing to lever (Figure 4.83).

Lifting one length floorboards (tongue and groove flooring)

One length floorboards are boards which span the room in one unbroken length.

1) Starting in the centre of the room cut the tongues on both sides of the floorboard.
2) Punch nails through floorboard into joists.
3) Use a bolster chisel to prise up the floorboard as far as it will go, as shown previously.
4) Now use a scrap piece of wood to increase the leverage and widen the gap to enable a batten to be slid underneath the partly raised floorboard (Figure 4.84).

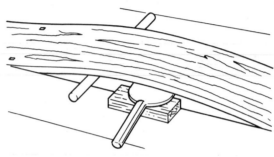

Figure 4.84

5) Shift the batten to rest over a joist and use the tenon saw to cut the floorboard squarely so that the cut lies centrally along the line of the joist (Figure 4.85). This will only be possible if the nails have been driven in or removed.

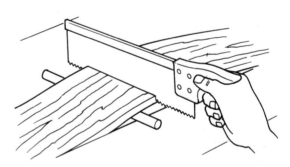

Figure 4.85

The alternative is to cut along the edge of the joist in which case a 25 × 50 mm batten must be nailed to the joist to support the floorboard when it is replaced.

6) Slide the batten under the part to be lifted and use a bolster chisel to prise up the floorboard.
7) Move the batten along towards the wall at each step until the floorboard is completely free for lifting out.

Jig saws

Jig saws (Figure 4.86) provide an alternative method for cutting into floorboards. These are available in the form of attachments for power drills or purpose designed power tools.

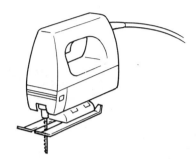

Figure 4.86   Jig saw

The important safety precaution is to turn off all gas and water at the mains and to ensure that the length of saw blade under the guide plate is equal to the thickness of the floorboard.

The saw blades can easily be ground down or broken off in a vice or cut with pliers, to the length required. Make certain that the saw blade is at the bottom of its cutting stroke when checking the blade length with the board.

Method of use

1) First drill a small hole to accept the saw blade (Figure 4.87).

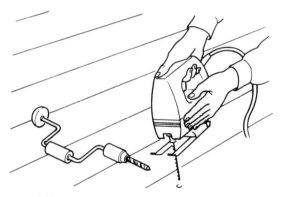

Figure 4.87

2) Alternatively holding the jig saw in this way, start the saw and allow it to cut its way into the floorboard until the guide plate is flush with the floorboard (Figure 4.88).
3) The jig saw is now correctly positioned to make the forward cut. While it is possible to make a reasonably straight cut freehand, it is advisable to use a piece of timber as a guide (Figure 4.89).

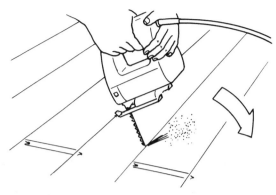

Figure 4.88

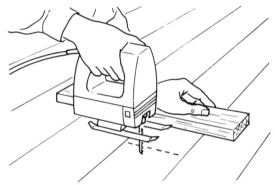

Figure 4.89

When making this cut across the board, even though you have taken the precaution of shortening the blade, listen out for obstructions which are usually indicated by marked changes in the tone of the motor.

4) Cutting into the tongue of the floorboard is a lot easier than cutting across the board. A straight edge will ensure that the jig saw is cutting straight along the side of the floorboard.
5) Start the cut as already described at each corner before sawing forward using the straight edge as a guide until the floorboard is ready for lifting.
6) Use a bolster chisel to lever the floorboard up from where it has been nailed to the joists.
7) Remove all nails before laying the floorboard aside.
8) Where larger floor areas have to be lifted to permit access the same cutting methods are used to cut into the floorboards, except that it will only be necessary to cut through the tongues along two sides of the area chosen, and not both sides of each board.

Replacing floorboards

Where possible floorboards should be replaced exactly in the same positions they occupied before they were lifted. Where single floorboards have been lifted, distinguishing features such as nail marks, saw cuts and discolouration, etc. will help identify which end is to go where when replacing the floorboards.

Where more than one floorboard has been lifted it is worthwhile numbering the boards to show their relationship to each other and to other fixed boards. This will ensure they are returned to their former positions.

Additional supports

Where more than one floorboard has been lifted, and especially where the boards have been left unsupported or too near the edge of the joist, it is advisable to nail battens along the joists to ensure the floor surface remains even and stable under foot (Figure 4.90). The 50 × 25 mm supports are cut 100 mm longer than the width of the trap and fixed with 63 mm wire nails suitably spaced. Hold the batten flush with the floorboards and against the joist when completing the nailing operation.

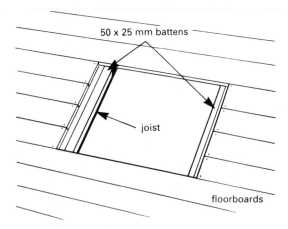

Figure 4.90

Securing the floorboards

It is better to screw lifted floorboards back into place after completing any installation. Stagger the screw positions using two screws at both ends and one screw on intermediate joists making certain the screwheads are properly countersunk.

Chipboard flooring

Chipboard is made from wood particles bonded with a synthetic or organic agent. High density boards are often used on floors and these are usually 18 or 22 mm thick. The boards are 2440–2745 mm long and come in widths of 400, 600, 1200 or 1220 mm. Chipboard has a limited resistance to moisture and it is known to become permanently deformed when subjected to heavy loads over long periods.

Flooring grade chipboards are often used in place of softwood floorboards on standard joists which are 380 mm between centres. They are butt-joined at the

joists with the joints staggered. It is possible to find them grooved along both sides in which case a timber fillet (20 × 10 mm) is used as the tongue.

Lifting chipboard flooring

Because these boards can be anything between 400 and 1200 mm wide the room should be cleared of all furnishings to make the task of lifting easier.

Floorboards usually run at right angles to their supports and depending on what is to be installed and where it is to be positioned, a decision will need to be made as to which floorboard needs to be lifted. In practice instead of lifting up the whole floorboard, inspection traps are usually cut at convenient locations between joists.

Lifting method

1) Use a knife or small screwdriver to test if there is a tongue between the boards. The tongues will offer solid resistance to the knife or screwdriver at a depth of between 6–10 mm and will need to be cut through.
2) Using the convex part of a flooring saw start, cutting into the tongue at the mid-point between any two joists. The forward part of the saw can later be used to complete the cut at the corners.
3) The tongue is situated in the centre of the floorboard and is usually 6–10 mm thick (Figure 4.91).

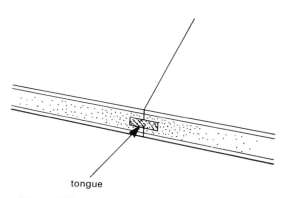

tongue

Figure 4.91

4) Saw cuts will often extend beyond the corners particularly where these happen to lie over the joists.
5) Avoid cutting down through the floorboard. Keep the saw moving forward in a straight line as the board is cut through.
6) After completing the first cut (A on Figure 4.92) it is necessary to mark out the other cuts using a try square. Cut B should run along the edge of the joist and be at least as long as cut A.
7) Where 400 mm or 600 mm wide chipboards have been used, cut B will extend to the full width of these boards.

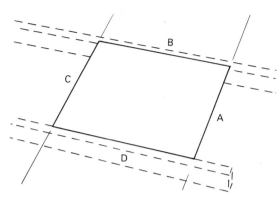

Figure 4.92

8) Start the cut in the centre using the convex part of the flooring saw until the board is sufficiently cut through. The saw can now be used at an angle to complete cutting to the corners of the trap.

   Remember when sawing blind that there may be hidden hazards – cables, pipes, etc. under the floorboard.

9) Use the same technique, starting at the middle and working outwards to the corners.
10) Where there is a join in the floorboards located over a joist, raise the flap which has now been cut through on three sides and prise the nails clear of the joist, using the bolster chisel to lever with (Figure 4.93).

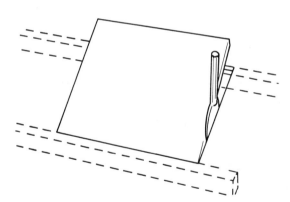

Figure 4.93

11) Where the trap is being cut in the centre of the board, it will be necessary to make a fourth cut along the edge of a joist.

Replacing traps

Whenever traps are cut in chipboard floors it is always necessary to put in some timber framework to support the piece which has been cut out. As a general rule, support for most traps should be provided on all sides.

Butt-joined frames

1) Cut two timbers 50 mm longer than the size of the opening (Figure 4.94).

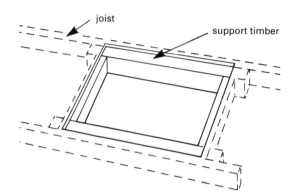

joist

support timber

Figure 4.94

2) Drive two 80 mm oval nails partly through the timbers ready for nailing to the joists. Locate each centrally and level with the top of the joist and complete the nailing operation.
3) With both timbers fixed in position, measure the distance between these and cut timbers to fit these gaps.
4) Drive a single 80 mm oval nail at an angle into each end. The object is to nail these pieces to the timbers which have been securely fixed to the joist.
5) Hold the pieces in squarely making sure that a 25 mm lip is left for the trap cover to rest on.

   Complete nailing operations at both ends of each timber.
   Screw down the trap cover.

Questions for you

1. State the scales used on the following types of drawing:
   (a) assembly _____
   (b) component _____
   (c) location _____
   (d) block plan. _____

2. What are graphical symbols and abbreviations used for?
   _____
   _____
   _____

3. What is the function of the 'guide' on compression-type bending machines?
   _____
   _____
   _____

4. Name *three* methods used for bending copper tube:
   (a) _____
   (b) _____
   (c) _____

5. Draw the graphical symbols for the following plumbing components:
   (a) double check valve assembly
   (b) filter or screen
   (c) servicing valve
   (d) draining valve.

6. State the colour code identification for pipelines conveying:
   (a) natural gas _____
   (b) drinking water _____
   (c) electrical services. _____

7. Describe what is meant by each of the following terms:
   (a) throat of a bend _____
   _____
   (b) heel of a bend _____
   _____
   (c) template _____
   _____
   (d) plastic memory. _____
   _____

8. Why are pipes 'sleeved' when they pass through a wall?
   _____
   _____
   _____

9. List the tools that may be used when cutting and lifting floorboards:

_____

_____

_____

10. Name *three* types of fixing suitable for securing a pipe clip to a plasterboard partition:
    (a) _____
    (b) _____
    (c) _____

11. When removing a bending spring from a bend in copper pipe, the correct procedure is to:
    (a) twist to tighten the coil of the spring
    (b) twist to loosen the coil of the spring
    (c) straighten the copper as far as possible
    (d) pull it straight out.

12. Copper pipe bending machines are designed to produce good quality bends with minimum distortion of the bore. This is achieved by:
    (a) supporting the pipe wall
    (b) increasing the throat thickness
    (c) stretching the back of the bend
    (d) maintaining an even pull.

13. When using sand as a filler material for the hot bending of pipes, it is essential that the sand is dry to prevent the:
    (a) generation of steam
    (b) pipe from burning
    (c) collapse of the pipe
    (d) pipe distorting.

14. To avoid undue weakening of joists when notching for pipe runs, the notches should be:
    (a) on the underside in the centre of the span
    (b) on the underside at a point one-third of the span from the support
    (c) on the top close to a supported end
    (d) on the top in the centre of the span.

15. An electrically powered hammer drill in conjunction with a tungsten tipped bit is specifically designed for drilling into:
    (a) plastic sheets
    (b) laminated sheets
    (c) steel joists
    (d) brick and stone.

16. When pipes are installed under floor boards, the board should be re-fixed using:
    (a) nails
    (b) glue
    (c) screws
    (d) bolts.

17. The tool allowing small adjustments used for threading small diameter round bars is known as a:
    (a) solid die
    (b) split stock
    (c) solid stock
    (d) circular split die.

18. If a large tap wrench was being used with a small tap to make a thread, this could cause:
    (a) overheating and eventually jam the tap in the hole
    (b) the tap to cut the thread too quickly
    (c) the tap to be broken due to lack of 'feel'
    (d) the tap to cut a thread with several starting points.

19. The thread form used on low-carbon steel tubes is:
    (a) BSW
    (b) BSP
    (c) unified
    (d) BSF.

20. One of the main advantages of using a power-operated pipe threading machine, as opposed to hand-operated dies, is that it will produce:
    (a) accurate threads quickly and effortlessly
    (b) long continuous running threads
    (c) barrel nipples
    (d) tapered or parallel threads.

21. The most suitable power tool for removing the tongue from a floorboard, *in situ*, to allow it to be lifted without damage is a:
    (a) jigsaw
    (b) bandsaw
    (c) ripsaw
    (d) dimension saw.

22. If a wood screw is being inserted and it will no longer turn before it is fully home, it should be:
    (a) withdrawn and replaced by a shorter screw
    (b) driven home with a hammer on the screwdriver
    (c) fitted with a spacing washer over its head
    (d) withdrawn and a piece cut off the screw end.

23. The rule for recording the diameter of unequal tees is:
    (a) end, end, branch
    (b) in ascending order of diameters
    (c) end, branch, end
    (d) in descending order of diameters.

24. When using an electric power drill to cut through metal with a hole saw cutter, the saw should be:
    (a) lubricated during cutting
    (b) run dry through the metal
    (c) angled to cut through one side first
    (d) used in short bursts.

25. In order to keep twist drills in good condition, it is necessary to:
    (a) sharpen the flutes
    (b) oil the shank
    (c) maintain cutting angles
    (d) drill at slow speed.

26. When drilling a hole in a small metal bracket, the bracket should be held in:
    (a) a hand vice
    (b) a pipe-clamp
    (c) between two pieces of wood
    (d) a pair of Stillsons.

27. The length of a line on a drawing of a building measures 55 mm. If the line was drawn to a scale of 1:50, the actual length in the building would be:
    (a) 27.5 m
    (b) 2.75 m
    (c) 275 mm
    (d) 5.5 m.

28. Any employee who deliberately misuses or damages equipment on site may be contravening the:
    (a) Health and Safety at Work Act 1974
    (b) Site Equipment Inspection Regulations
    (c) Public Damages Act
    (d) Building Regulations.

29. The BS colour code on a power tool requires that the brown wire be connected to the:
    (a) earth pin
    (b) fused pin
    (c) neutral pin
    (d) central locating pin.

30. When cutting a circular hole through plaster board, the most suitable saw would be a:
    (a) pad saw
    (b) hacksaw
    (c) tenon saw
    (d) band saw.

Glossary

Industry terminology

BPEC (Training) Ltd.
The British Plumbing Employer's Council (Training) Ltd is the Industry Training Organization and Lead Body for Plumbing. BPEC's founding organizations are the NAPH & MSC and SNIPEF.

L.B. (Lead Body)
A body made up of representatives from employment, responsible for developing and maintaining appropriate occupational standards and vocational qualifications.

ITO
Industry Training Organization – responsible for identifying the training needs of the industry and taking positive steps to ensure that these needs are satisfied.

NAPH & MSC
National Association of Plumbing Heating and Mechanical Services Contractors. The major plumbing trade association in England and Wales.

SNIPEF
Scottish and Northern Ireland Plumbing Employers Federation. The major plumbing trade association in Scotland and Northern Ireland.

JIB for PMES
The Joint Industry Board for Plumbing Mechanical Engineering Services in England and Wales. The negotiating body for the plumbing mechanical engineering services industry in England and Wales. It has responsibility for grading purposes and operates the apprenticeship system for the plumbing industry.

C & G or CGLI
City and Guilds of London Institute. One of the constituent members of the MES-Plumbing awarding body.

MES-Plumbing Awarding Body
Constituent members-NAPH & MSC, JIB for PMES, and CGLI. The body responsible for the implementation of MES-Plumbing NVQs in England and Wales.

NCVQ terminology

NCVQ
National Council for Vocational Qualifications – Accreditation Body for NVQs.

SCOTVEC
Scottish Vocational Education Council – Accreditation Body for SVQs.

National Vocational Qualification (NVQ)
A qualification approved by the National Council for Vocational Qualifications, based upon national standards laid down by the Lead Body for implementation in England, Wales and Northern Ireland.

Scottish Vocational Qualifications (SVQ)
A qualification approved by SCOTVEC based upon national standards laid down by the Lead Body for implementation in Scotland.

Accreditation
The process by which the National Council for Vocational Qualifications approves a Lead Body's national standards and also an appropriate Awarding Body to offer, administer, and maintain the quality of the NVQs.

Accreditation of Prior Learning (APL)
The Assessment of an individual's past achievements against national standards.

Level
A sub-division of the NVQ framework used to define progressive degrees of competence.

Award
An award is made to an individual upon attainment of the NVQ.

Awarding Body
A body approved by NCVQ for the assessment, quality assurance and certification of NVQs (see MES Plumbing **Awarding Body).**

Competence
The ability to perform a range of work to standards laid down by industry.

Assessment
The process of collecting evidence and making judgements on whether national standards have been met.

Verification
The process of monitoring the quality assurance of the scheme and to ensure national standards are being met.

Standard (of performance)
The measure of performance required for the achievement of an element of competence as indicated by the related performance criteria.

S/NVQ terminology

Unit (of competence)
NVQs are made up of a number of units – each unit covers an area of the competence required. A unit is the smallest item worthy of accreditation.

Element (of competence)
Sub-division of unit of competence; it is a description of something which a person in a given occupational area should be able to do.

Performance Criteria
Statements against which an assessor judges the evidence that an individual can perform the activity specified in an element.

Range Statement
The range of contexts in which an individual will be required to demonstrate competence e.g. plumbing systems, system components and so on.

Portfolio
An individual's evidence of competence is gathered together and forms the portfolio.

Log Book
Candidate's self assessment document and part of the candidate's evidence of work activities.

Technical glossary

Accessory
Any device connected and used with other appliances/apparatus

Acid
A corrosive substance

Adhere
Stick (hold) together

Adhesion
The force of attraction between molecules of different substances

Alloy
A mixture of metals, or metal and non-metal substances

Ambient
Surrounding

Ambient temperature
The temperature of the surrounding element, i.e. air or water

Ammeter
An instrument used for measuring direct electric current

Anneal
To soften a metal by the application of heat

Anode
The electrode to which negative ions move, the positive electrode

Architect
One who designs and supervises the construction of buildings. His or her main duties are preparing designs, plans and specifications; inspecting sites; obtaining tenders for work and the legal negotiations needed before building commences

Atmospheric pressure
Pressure due to the atmosphere surrounding the earth

Backflow (cold water)
Flow in a direction contrary to the natural or intended direction of flow

Backnut
A locking nut provided on the screwed shank of a tap, valve or pipe fitting for securing it to some other object. A threaded nut, dished on one face to retain a grommet, used to form a watertight joint on a long threaded connector

Ball-peen hammer
A hammer with a hemispherical peen (also pein or pane)

Bar
A unit of pressure, equivalent to the weight of a column of mercury of unit area and 760 mm in height. 1 bar = 1000 millibars

Barff Process
An anticorrosion treatment of iron or steel by the action of steam on the red-hot metal; the layer of black oxide formed gives protection

Barometer
A device for measuring atmospheric pressure

Base exchange
A water softening process in which water is passed through a bed of mineral reagent called zeolite, which absorbs those salts in the water which make it hard

Bell-type joint
This is used on copper tube; one end of the pipe is opened to form a bell shaped socket which is then filled with bronze rod

Bends
(A) *Set*
A single bend
(B) *Offset*
A double bend
(C) *Passover/Crank*
A pipe formed
to pass over a pipe fixed at right-angles to it

Bibtap
A water tap which has a horizontal inlet connection which is externally threaded

Bonding
(A) This term used in soldering or welding refers to the adhesion of the solder to the parent metal
(B) Where the electrical system is earthed through the cold water supply pipe, the term bonding refers to the earth connection

Borax
A white crystalline solid used as a flux

Bore
The internal diameter of a pipe or fitting

Boss
An attached fitting on a vessel or pipe which facilitates the connection of a pipe or pipe fitting

Bossing
The art of shaping malleable materials such as lead and aluminium with hand tools usually made from boxwood or plastic

Bower-barffing
A process for rust proofing mild steel or cast iron in which the metal is raised to red heat and treated with live steam

Boxwood
A hardwood used for making hand tools, kept in good condition by a light application of linseed oil

Bradawl
A short awl with a narrow chisel point, used for making holes for screws or nails

Bronze
An alloy of copper and tin

Burring reamer
A tool used to remove the burr left by a pipe cutter inside the cut end of a pipe

Bush
A pipe fitting used for reducing the size of a threaded or spigot connection

Butt
To meet without overlapping

Cable
One or more conductors provided with insulation. The insulated conductor(s) may be provided with an overall covering to give mechanical protection

Calcium carbonate
The chemical name for chalk, limestone and marble

Calorifier
A cylindrical vessel in which water is heated indirectly, by means of hot water or steam contained in pipe coils, a radiator or a cylinder within a calorifier

Candela
A unit of luminous intensity based on electric lamps

Cap
A cover usually with an internal thread or socket joint for sealing the end of a pipe

Capacity
(A) *Actual*
is the volume of water that a vessel contains when filled up to its water line
(B) *Nominal*
is the theoretical capacity of a vessel calculated using overall dimensions

Capillary joint
A fine clearance spigot and socket joint into which molten solder is caused to flow by capillary action

Catalyst
A substance which increases the speed of a chemical reaction

Cathodic protection
A sacrificial metal (anode), usually a block of magnesium, is fixed in the system

Cat ladder
A ladder or board with cross cleats fixed to it, laid over a roof slope to protect it and give access for inspection or repairs (also called a duck board)

Caulking
The driving of cold lead into a recess or spigot/socket joint to form a tight mass – usually done with a blunt ended chisel

Cement
A powder used in conjunction with sand to form a mortar used in jointing. It is produced by a breaking down process of a special rock

Chain wrench
A steel pipe grip which holds the pipe by a chain linked to a bar which is grooved at the end touching the pipe

Chalk line
A length of line well rubbed with chalk, held tight and plucked against a wall, floor or other surface to mark a straight line on it

Chamfer
When the square end of the pipe is cut (worked) to a specific angle, i.e. 45°

Chase wedge
A wooden wedge-shaped tool, used for setting in a fold on sheet metal work

Chloramine process
This involves adding ammonia to water to remove the taste of chlorine

Chlorination
A method of treating water with chloride to sterilize it by destroying harmful bacteria

Circuit
An assembly of pipes and fittings, forming part of a hot water system through which water circulates

Circuit-breaker
A mechanical device designed to open or close an electrical circuit

Circulation
(A) *Primary*
is the circulation between the boiler and the hot storage vessel

(B) *Secondary*
is the circulation of the hot water to supply the appliances, and is taken from the vent pipe, returning into the top third of the cylinder
(C) *Gravity*
could also be called natural circulation because it is brought about naturally by the difference in weight between two columns of water (hot water is lighter than cold water and is therefore displaced, i.e. rises)
(D) *Forced*
is the movement of water brought about by the introduction of an impellor (pump)

Cistern
An open topped container for water in which the water is subject to atmospheric pressure only. The water usually enters the cistern via a ball valve

Clout nail
A galvanized nail usually between 12 mm and 50 mm long with a large round flat head

Cohesion
The force of attraction between molecules of the same substance

Collar
A pipe fitting in the form of a sleeve for joining the spigot ends of two pipes in the same alignment, also called a socket

Combustion
The burning of a substance or fuel brought about by rapid oxidation

Compression
This term refers to the compressive stress applied to metal when jointing, or the throat of the pipe when bending

Compression joint
A fitting used to joint copper, stainless steel and polythene tubes

Conductor
The conducting part of a cable or functioning metalwork which carries current

Connector
A means of connecting together pipes and cables

Contraction
The reverse of expansion, i.e. the decrease in size of a solid or liquid substance

Consumer Unit
A combined fuseboard and main switch controlling and protecting a consumer's final sub-circuits

Corrosion
This is the term given to the destruction of a metal,

i.e. the rusting of metal by oxidation. Water containing free oxygen being conveyed in unprotected steel pipes will cause corrosion

Cradle
A support shaped to fit the underside of a pipe, cylinder or appliance

Crown
The highest point of the outside surface of the pipe

Cupro-solvency
The ability of some waters to dissolve copper

Cylinders
(A) *Ordinary*
Cylindrical closed containers in which hot water is stored under pressure from the feed cistern
(B) *Indirect*
Sometimes called calorifiers, they are used where domestic hot water and heating are fed from the same boiler or where the water is of a temporary hard nature. They come as cylinders within a cylinder or with annular rings designed to keep the primary and secondary waters separate (two cisterns are required)
(C) *Patent indirect*
These do not require two cisterns, the filling, venting and expansion being taken care of in the unique patent cylinder

Density
The density of a substance is defined as its mass per unit volume. Relative density of a substance is the ratio of the mass of any volume of it to the mass of an equal volume of water

De-oxidation
The process of separating oxygen from a substance. This process is also called reduction and is a necessary part of the treatment of many metallic oxides and ores

Development
A geometrical method by which the whole of the surface area of a solid may be set out in one plane, as on sheet metal or drawing paper.

Dew point
Dew point is defined as the temperature at which the water vapour present in the air is just sufficient to saturate it (thus forming condensation when this air is in contact with colder surfaces)

De-zincification
The term used when the zinc used in the manufacture of brass (copper-zinc) is particially destroyed (becomes a porous mass)

Die
An internally threaded metal block for cutting male threads on pipes or tubes. The die block is held within a stock

Dresser
A hand tool made from boxwood or plastics material, used for flattening or dressing sheet materials such as a lead, copper or aluminium

Duct
A closed passage way formed in the structure or underground to receive pipes and cables

Ductility
A property which allows a metal to be elongated or drawn out without breaking or fracturing

Earth
Refers to the facility of a system being connected to a general mass of earth, i.e. by a wire and rod or through a metal pipe laid in the ground

Elasticity
The term referring to the elongation of a substance and its ability to return to its normal position when the load has been removed. It is a relationship of stress to strain within the elastic range of the material

Elbow
A sharp corner of change of direction in a pipe, usually a manufactured fitting.

Electric immersion heater
This is manufactured as either a single or dual element heater to be fitted in the hot storage vessel; it can be used as the sole means of heating or as a booster to the existing method

Electrolysis
This is a detrimental action between dissimilar metal. Increased action is brought about if there is an electrical contact, i.e. earth. One metal acts as a cathode, the other as an anode

Element
A material composed entirely of atoms of one kind. An element cannot be split into anything simpler than itself

Enamel
Vitreous enamel is a glass like surface attached by firing to cast iron or pressed steel articles such as baths or sink unit tops.

Epoxide resin
A synthetic resin used for glueing metal or concrete

Erosion
The wearing away of a surface

Eutectic
A term used in metallurgy in connection with the

solidifying or setting of alloys. When alloyed in varying proportions, one particular combination of metals will give the lowest solidifying point. This is known as the eutectic point

Evaporation
The loss of moisture in vapour form from a liquid

Expansion
An increase in the size of a material or substance usually brought about by an increase in temperature

Expansion joint
A joint fitted in pipework to allow for the linear expansion of the pipe material when the water temperature is raised

Ferrous
This is an iron-based material

Flammable
Combustible, burns with a flame

Flash point
The lowest temperature at which a substance momentarily ignites when a flame is put to it

Flexible joint
A joint designed to allow small angular deflection without loss of water tightness

Flow pipe
A pipe which conveys hot water from a boiler to a tank, cylinder or heating system

Flux
A substance used in soldering and/or welding to prevent oxidation

Footprints
An adjustable wrench with serrated jaws

Force cup
A tool used for unblocking wastes or drains. It consists of a rubber cup fixed on the end of a wooden handle

Furred
A term to describe pipes, boilers or components which have become encrusted with hard water lime or other salts deposited from the water heated in them

Fuse
Usually a small piece of wire in an electric circuit which melts when the current exceeds a certain value. The fuse is protection against short circuiting

Galvanize
A process used for protecting metals, usually steel. The process involves dipping the metal to be protected into molten zinc

Hard water
(A) Temporary hard water is water that can be softened by boiling. The hardness is due to carbonates of lime and magnesium
(B) Permanent hard water is water that cannot be softened by boiling. The hardness is due to sulphates of lime and magnesium

Head of water
This is the height to which the water will rise in a pipe under atmospheric pressure, i.e. in a domestic water system it is the water level in the cistern

Heel of bend
This is the back of the bend which is under tension during the bending operation

Hydraulic gradient
The 'loss of head' in liquid flowing in a pipe or channel, expressed per unit length of the pipe or channel

Hydraulic pressure
Fluid pressure

Insulation
The opposite of conduction. Insulators are bad conductors of electricity or heat (e.g. rubber, PVC, glass, wood, cork)

Invar
A nickel/steel alloy. Its coefficient of expansion is very low and for this reason it is used in bimetallic types of thermostat and steel measuring tapes

Isometric
A drawing method based on the principle that all vertical lines are drawn vertical while all horizontal lines are drawn at an angle of 30°. With this method several surfaces of the object can be exposed to view

Joint box
A box forming part of an electrical installation in which the cables are joined

Jig
An accessory usually purposely made to assist in the carrying out of an activity

Key
(A) A roughening or indentation made on a surface to provide better adherence of another surface, filler or jointing medium
(B) A tool or device provided to enable a person to operate a valve, tap, cock or device or to lift an access cover

Killed spirits
A term applied to zinc chloride which is used as a flux for soldering zinc, copper and brass. The chloride of zinc is made by dissolving small pieces of zinc in hydrochloric acid

Kite mark
This is the British Standards Mark; it is placed on all items manufactured up to an approved standard (ensures good quality)

Lagging
Material used for thermal or acoustic insulation

Latent heat
The amount of heat required to change the state of a substance from a solid to a liquid or from a liquid to a gas. The heat applied does not bring about a temperature rise

Leadwelding
A process of fusing together pieces of lead sheet or pipe. The basic process involves forming a small molten pool of lead, and adding further lead from a rod in order to reinforce the joint

Lime
(A) Carbonates of lime cause temporary hard water. When water containing these carbonates of lime is heated to a high temperature (approximately 70°C or above) the lime is deposited as a scale or fur in the boiler or flow pipe
(B) Sulphates of lime cause permanent hard water. These sulphates of lime are not removed when the water is heated, the water therefore remains hard after boiling

Longscrew
A piece of low carbon steel tube threaded externally at each end, one end having the thread sufficiently long to accommodate a backnut and the full length of a socket. It is used to join two pieces of steel tube, neither of which can be rotated. (It is also called a connector)

Magnet
Mass of iron or other metal which attracts or repels other similar masses and which exerts a force on a current-carrying conductor placed near it

Make good
To repair as new

Mallet
A tool like a hammer with a wooden, hide, rubber or plastic head

Mandrel
A cylindrical piece of hardwood which is pushed through a lead pipe to remove distortion

Manipulative joint
A compression joint in which the ends of the copper tubes are opened out

Masking
A form of tape, applied as a protection to sanitary ware

Mastic
A plastic permanently water-proof material, which hardens on its surface so that it can be painted. Used for sealing gaps in expansion joints, gutters and flashings

Mechanical advantage
The mechanical advantage of a machine is defined as the ratio of the load to the effort used

Meniscus
The curved surface of a liquid when it touches a solid object rising above the liquid level

Metal coating
A thin film of copper, nickel, cadmium, chromium, aluminium or zinc applied to corrodible metal surfaces

Module
A unit of length by which the planning of structures can to some extent be standardized

Mortar
A mixture of Portland cement, sand and water

Multimeter
An instrument used for measuring electrical current, voltage, etc.

Nail
A fixing device. Clout nails are large headed. Nails of brass, aluminium alloy or copper are used to provide fixings in certain types of roofing

Nail punch
A short blunt steel rod which tapers at one end. It is struck by a hammer to drive a nail head below its surrounding timber surface

Neoprene
The trade name for an American synthetic rubber which has excellent properties of non-inflammability

Nipple
A short section of pipe threaded at each end

Non-manipulative joint
A compression joint in which the ends of the copper tube are cut square and the internal and external burrs removed. Jointing is usually achieved with the aid of a cone, ring or olive which is compressed into the tube wall by the action of the joint nut being screwed on to the joint body

Notch
A groove in a timber to receive another timber or pipe

Offset
A double bend in a pipeline, formed so that the pipe continues in its original direction

Ordinary Portland cement
A hydraulic cement made by heating to clinker in a kiln, a slurry of clay and limestone

Orifice
A small opening intended for the passage of a fluid

Oxidation
This is an action brought about by the element oxygen, it is generally of a destructive nature, i.e. iron oxide (rusting)

Oxygen
A gas ever present in the atmosphere; it is a supporter of combustion

Parallel thread
A thread screwed to a uniform diameter. Used on mechanical connections such as bolts, but not generally on low carbon steel pipe fittings except running nipples and connectors. Compression fittings, taps and ball valves all make use of parallel threads

Patina
A thin, protective film of sulphate which forms on metals exposed to air, particularly the green coating on copper or its alloys

Perspex
A transparent acrylic resin

Pictorial Views
(A) *Isometric projection*
In this projection all horizontal lines are drawn at an angle of 30° to the horizontal, all vertical lines remain vertical
(B) *Axonometric projection*
In this projection all vertical lines are drawn vertical while all horizontal lines are drawn at an angle of 45°
(C) *Planometric projection*
In this the horizontal lines are drawn horizontal while all vertical lines are drawn at an angle of 60° to the horizontal

Pilot hole
A guiding hole, drilled in a material to form a route for a larger drill or bit

Pipe cutter
A tool for cutting copper, iron or steel pipes. Cutting is achieved by hard steel discs or wheels which bite into the pipe walls as the tool is revolved around the pipe

Pipe ring
A ring-shaped clamp or bracket, made in halves for screwing or bolting together, which forms part of an assembly for supporting a pipe

Pipe wrench
A heavy wrench with serrated jaws for gripping, screwing or unscrewing low carbon steel pipes and fittings.

Pitcher tee
A tee on which the branch is swept into the main pipe with a gently curved turn.

Plastics
A name commonly used to describe a group of materials including polyvinyl chloride, polystyrene, polythene, perspex etc. Plastics are either thermo-setting (those which harden once and for all time when heated), or thermoplastics (those which soften whenever they are heated).

Plastic memory
Plastic pipes when heated and bent, and most plastic mouldings, have a residual strain in them. When this strain is released, i.e. by heating, the pipe will try to revert to its original position. This is plastic memory

Pliers
A holding or gripping tool, pivoted like a pair of scissors. Some types have blades for cutting thin wire built into the jaws

Plug
(A) A fitting used to seal off a pipe or section of pipeline, usually fitting into the bore of the pipe
(B) An electrical device intended for connection to a flexible cord or flexible cable

Polystyrene
A material used in its expanded form as an insulator for pipes and cisterns.

Polytetrafluroethylene (PTFE)
A plastic material which is used as a thin tape or paste as a jointing medium in pipe threads

Polythene
A chemically inert synthetic rubber used for making pipes and cisterns for cold water services

Polyurethane
A plastic which in foamed form is used as an insulating material in cavity walls

Polyvinyl chloride (PVC)
A vinyl resin, which is impervious to water, oils and petrol and is particularly incombustible. Used for making gutters, soil and waste pipes, storage cisterns, drainage components

Portable electric tool
A hand-held tool, driven by an electric motor, e.g. electric drill

Pressed steel
A sheet steel which is hot pressed into plumbing

components such as baths, sink units and flushing cisterns. The steel is protected by a layer of vitreous enamel

Pressure
Defined as the force acting normally per unit area (here the word normally means vertically)

Pressure (bar)
The reading of the air pressure is recorded as so many bars (one bar is equivalent to one atmosphere)

Propane
A colourless gas which burns in air to carbon dioxide and water

PVC
see Polyvinyl chloride

Radius
A straight line running from the centre of a circle to any point on the circumference. Its length is half that of the diameter

Reducer
A fitting which enables a pipe diameter or socket connection to be reduced in bore

Saddle clip A fixing which passes round the front of a pipe and is screwed to the surface behind the pipe via two lugs which are part of the saddle.

Sal-ammoniac
(NH_4Cl, ammonium chloride). A flux used in soldering

Scale
see Lime

Scribe
To cut a line on the surface of a material with a sharp pointed tool

Sealing compound
A material used to fill and seal the surface of an expansion joint or sleeve. It can be applied like a mastic from a pressure cartridge or gun

Seam
A joint, fold or welt formed in sheet metal weatherings. A seamed edge is often formed at the front of an apron flashing to stiffen the edge, provide a more attractive finish, resist the possibility of capillary attraction between the roof and slates or surface and the flashing, or to form a safety edge so that the material is easier to handle and fix

Seaming pliers
A pair of pliers with jaws specially shaped and extended for forming seams or welts

Self-aligning pipe
A pipe which by means of the shape of the socket and spigot is naturally held in a straight line

Shave hook
A hand tool used for shaving or cleaning the surface of lead pipes or sheet before soldering or welding

Sheet
A description of aluminium, copper, lead or zinc which is thicker than foil, thinner than 6.35 mm and more than 450 mm wide. Foil is thinner than the size quoted. Strip is narrower than the width quoted

Sherardizing
The coating of small iron or steel components with zinc by heating them with zinc dust in a revolving drum at about 350 °C

Sleeve
A pipe built into a wall or floor to allow a smaller diameter service to pass through, leaving it free to expand or contract, without damaging the fabric or structure of the building

Socket
The enlarged end of a pipe into which a similar pipe (spigot) is fixed, or, a fitting threaded internally, used for jointing threaded ends of pipe or tube

Socket outlet
A device connected to the electrical installation to enable a flexible cord or cable to be connected by means of a plug

Solder
An alloy used for joining other metals

Solvent
A liquid capable of dissolving solids

Solvent cement
(weld) A liquid used in the jointing of plastic; it has the property of eating into the plastic material so producing a homogeneous bond

Space nipple
A short section of threaded pipe with a space between the threads. Nipples with a formed grip surface are called hexagon nipples

Spigot
The plain end of a pipe, inserted into a socket to make a spigot and socket joint

Spring
A steel coil used for bending copper and lead pipes

Stainless steel
A steel containing chromium and nickel. It is highly

corrosion-resistant and is used for waste and sanitary appliances and small diameter plumbing pipework

Stratification
The term given to the layers of hot water in the hot water vessel

Step turner
A hardwood tool used for forming the turned step (usually 25 mm wide through 90°) on sheet metal stepped flashing.

Storage cistern
An open-topped vessel used for storing a quantity of cold water to supply cold water draw-off points at a lower level. The cistern should have a close fitting lid or cover to keep its contents clean and uncontaminated

Straight edge
A long piece of seasoned timber or metal with parallel and straight edges often used in conjunction with a spirit level

Surface Tension
The elastic skin effect present in liquids; forces between the molecules cause a state of tension in the surface of the liquid

Sweat
To unite or bond metal surfaces together by allowing molten solder to flow between them and adhere to their surfaces

Sweep tee
A pitcher tee, usually for copper or low carbon steel pipes in which the branch connection gently curves into the main run

Switch
A means of connecting or disconnecting an electrical supply

Tang
The pointed end of a steel tool such as a file, rasp or wood chisel, which is driven into the wooden handle

Tank
A closed straight sided storage vessel generally used for storing hot water or oil

Tan pin
A conical shaped boxwood tool used for opening out the end of a lead pipe. Steel tan pins are available for copper pipes

Tap
A screwed plug, accurately threaded, made of hard steel and used for cutting internal threads

Taper thread
A standard screwed thread used on pipes and fittings to ensure a watertight or gas tight joint

Tee
A fitting, which is a short section of pipe with three openings, one of which is a branch which is usually set at a right angle and located midway between the other two openings

Temper
To toughen steels and non-ferrous metals by the application of controlled heat and cooling

Template
A full size pattern of metal or wood used for forming shapes or testing the accuracy of a manufactured component

Tension
This is the stretching of the material

Thermal movement
Movement caused by expansion or contraction due to temperature change

Thermoplastic
Description of a synthetic resin or other material which softens on heating and hardens again on cooling

Throat of a bend
The surface of the pipe on the inside of the bend

Tinman's solder
A fine solder containing more tin than wiping solder (grade D), so that its melting point is lower

Tinning
Coating copper, brass, lead or other metals with a film of tin or tin alloy (solder)

Tin snips
Strong scissors used for cutting sheet metals

Toe board
A scaffold board set on its edge at the side of a scaffold to prevent materials or tools being kicked or knocked off the working platform

Toggle bolt
A fixing device which enables a sound fixing to be made to thin board such as hardboard or plasterboard

Tommy bar
A loose bar or rod inserted into a hole in a box spanner or capstan to provide the leverage for turning it

Twist drill
A hardened steel bit with helical cutting edges, used in electric or hand drills for cutting circular holes in metal or wood

Union
A screwed pipe fitting, usually of brass or low carbon steel. It enables pipes or appliances to be quickly connected or disconnected

uPVC
This abbreviation means 'unplasticized polyvinyl chloride' and is a plastic material used in the manufacture of pipes and fittings

'U' value
A thermal transmittance value, determined by experiment for $1\,m^2$ of a certain floor, wall, roof in a particular situation

Verdigris
Green basic acetate of copper formed as a protective patina over copper exposed to the air

Vermiculite
A mica which is used as a light insulating aggregate

Vice
A screwed metal or timber clamp, usually fixed to a workbench or tripod and used for holding materials while they are being worked

Viscosity
This is the measure of the ease of flow of a liquid

Vitreous china
A ceramic material used for the manufacture of sanitary appliances

Vitreous enamel
A hard, smooth, glass-like surface attached to cast iron or pressed steel

Vitrified clay
A vitreous form of clay used for the manufacture of drainage pipes and components

Volt
The unit of electrical pressure, related to the units of flow (amperes) and power (watts), watts = volts × amperes. Electromotive force

Voltage
The term used to designate an electrical installation, i.e. normal domestic consumers' supply has a voltage of 240

Washer
A flat ring made of rubber, leather, plastics or fibrous composition used to form or make a seal between two surfaces. Alternatively, a flat ring made of metal

Waste water
All dirty water discharged from a waste appliance (bath, wash basin, sink, shower) but excluding soil or rainwater discharge

Water
(A) *Soft water*
is a water that lathers readily. This is because it contains only a small amount of lime
(B) *Hard water*
is a water with which it is difficult to obtain a lather. This is because it contains a large amount of lime
(C) *Temporary hard water*
is a water that contains carbonates of lime together with carbon dioxide gas which dissolves the lime. This type of hardness can be softened by boiling
(D) *Permanently hard water*
is a water that contains sulphates of lime which are dissolved in the water without the assistance of gases. This type of hardness cannot be softened by boiling

Water level
An instrument for setting out or transferring levels on a building site. It consists of a rubber tube connecting two vertical glass tubes containing water. The level of water in one tube is the same as that in the other if there are no kinks or air locks in the rubber tube

Water line
A line marked inside a cistern to indicate the highest level of water at which the supply valve should be adjusted to shut off the supply

Water softener
A chemical plant for treating water. It removes from the water the calcium and manganese salts which cause hardness. The most used types are base exchange softeners, and the soda-lime process

Watt
A unit of power

Wing nut
A thumb screw nut, which has wings, enabling it to be turned by hand without the use of a spanner

Wrench
A form of gripping tool or spanner, usually adjustable

Zeolites
Minerals which are used in the base exchange process of water softening

Index